BUREAU FOR PARANORMAL • RESEARCH AND DEFENSE •

PLAGUE OF FROGS

Created by MIKE MIGNOLA

JOHANN KRAUS

A medium whose physical form was destroyed while his ectoplasmic projection was out-of-body. That essence now resides in a containment suit. A psychic empath, Johann can create temporary forms for the dead to speak to the living.

LIZ SHERMAN

A fire-starter since the age of 11, when she accidentally burned her entire family to death. She has been a ward of the B.P.R.D. since then, learning to control her pyrokinetic abilities and cope with the trauma those abilities have wrought.

ABE SAPIEN

An amphibious man discovered in a long-forgotten subbasement beneath a Washington, D.C. hospital sealed inside a primitive stasis chamber. All indications suggest a previous life, dating back to the Civil War—an unfolding mystery for Abe.

ROGER

A homunculus made from human blood and herbs. Discovered in Romania, Roger was first brought to life by Liz's pyrokinetic touch. Whether or not he is actually alive may be up for debate, but his child-like love of that life is not.

DR. KATE CORRIGAN

A former professor at New York University, an authority on folklore and occult history. Dr. Corrigan has been a B.P.R.D. consultant for over 10 years, now serving as special liaison to the enhanced talents task force

MIKE MIGNOLA'S

B.P.R.D.™

PLAGUE OF FROGS

Story by
MIKE MIGNOLA

Art by
GUY DAVIS

Colors by
DAVE STEWART

Letters by
CLEM ROBINS

Editor
SCOTT ALLIE

Assistant Editor
MATT DRYER

Collection Designer
LANI SCHREIBSTEIN

Publisher
MIKE RICHARDSON

DARK HORSE BOOKS™

NEIL HANKERSON ♦ *executive vice president*

TOM WEDDLE ♦ *vice president of finance*

RANDY STRADLEY ♦ *vice president of publishing*

CHRIS WARNER ♦ *senior books editor*

ANITA NELSON ♦ *vice president of sales & marketing*

MICHAEL MARTENS ♦ *vice president of business development*

DAVID SCROGGY ♦ *vice president of product development*

LIA RIBACCHI ♦ *art director*

DALE LAFOUNTAIN ♦ *vice president of information technology*

DARLENE VOGEL ♦ *director of purchasing*

KEN LIZZI ♦ *general counsel*

Published by Dark Horse Books
A division of Dark Horse Comics, Inc.
10956 SE Main Street
Milwaukie, OR 97222

First edition January 2005
ISBN: 1-59307-288-0

1 3 5 7 9 10 8 6 4 2

Printed in China

B.P.R.D.: Plague of Frogs. January, 2005. Published by Dark Horse Comics, Inc., 10956 SE Main Street, Milwaukie, Oregon 97222. B.P.R.D.: Plague of Frogs Copyright © 2004 Mike Mignola. Abe Sapien™, Liz Sherman™, Hellboy™, and all other prominently featured characters are trademarks of Mike Mignola. Dark Horse Comics® is a trademark of Dark Horse Comics, Inc., registered in various categories and countries. All rights reserved. No portion of this publication may be reproduced or transmitted, in any form or by any means, without the express written permission of Dark Horse Comics, Inc. Names, characters, places, and incidents featured in this publication either are the product of the author's imagination or are used fictitiously. Any resemblance to actual persons (living or dead), events, institutions, or locales, without satiric intent, is coincidental.

This book collects the *B.P.R.D. Plague of Frogs* issues 1-5, published by Dark Horse Comics.

Chapter One

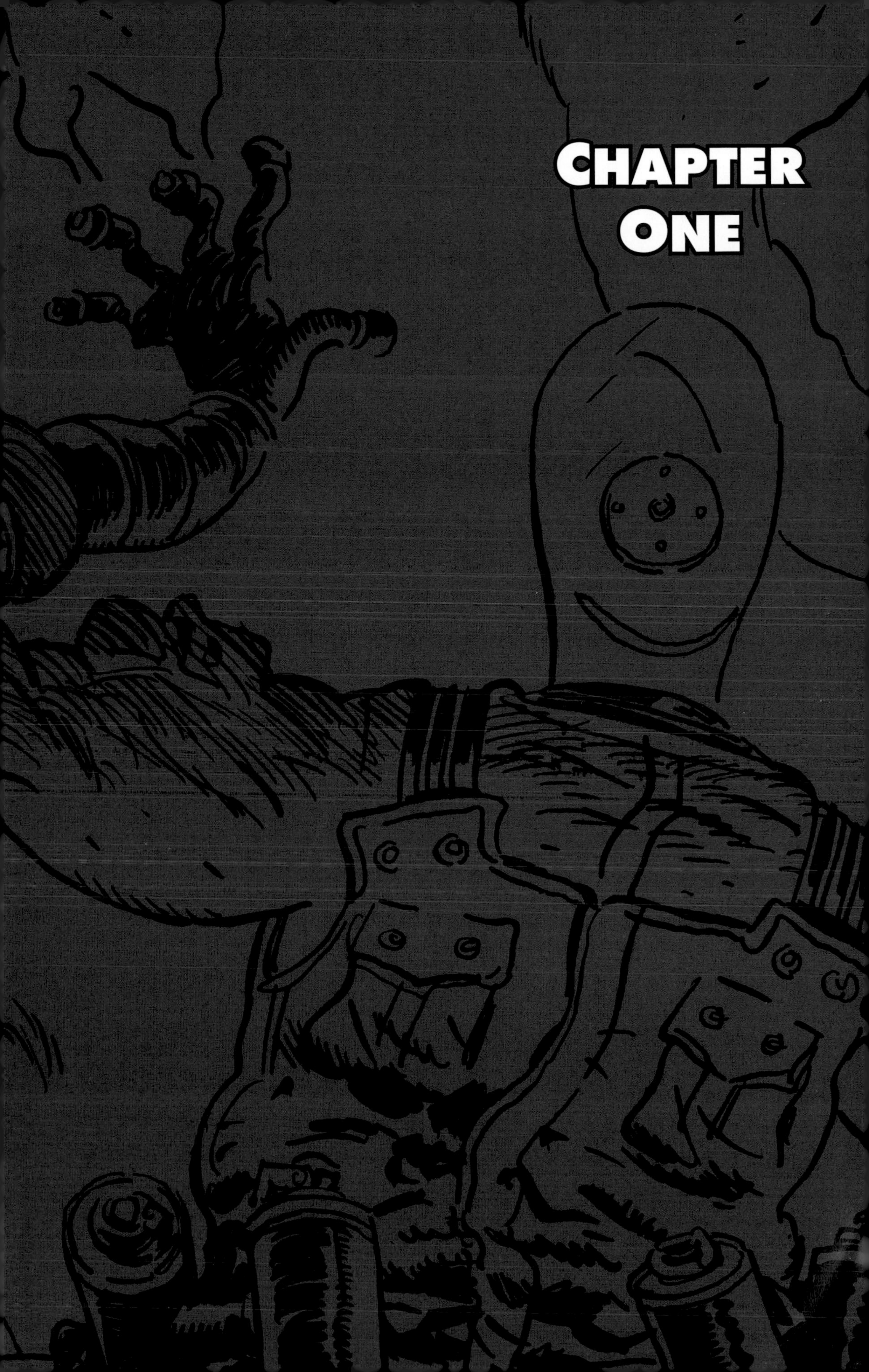

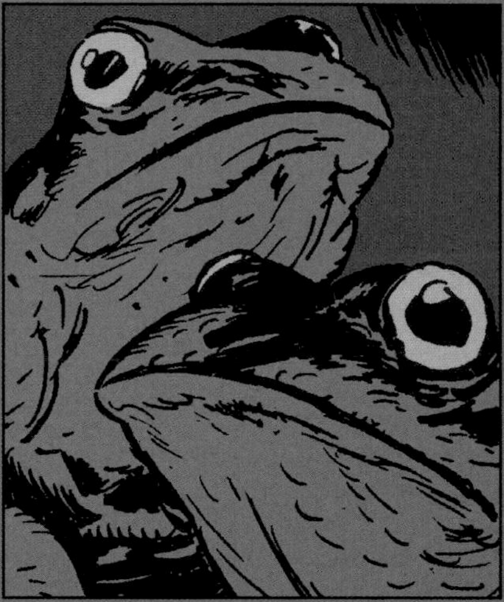

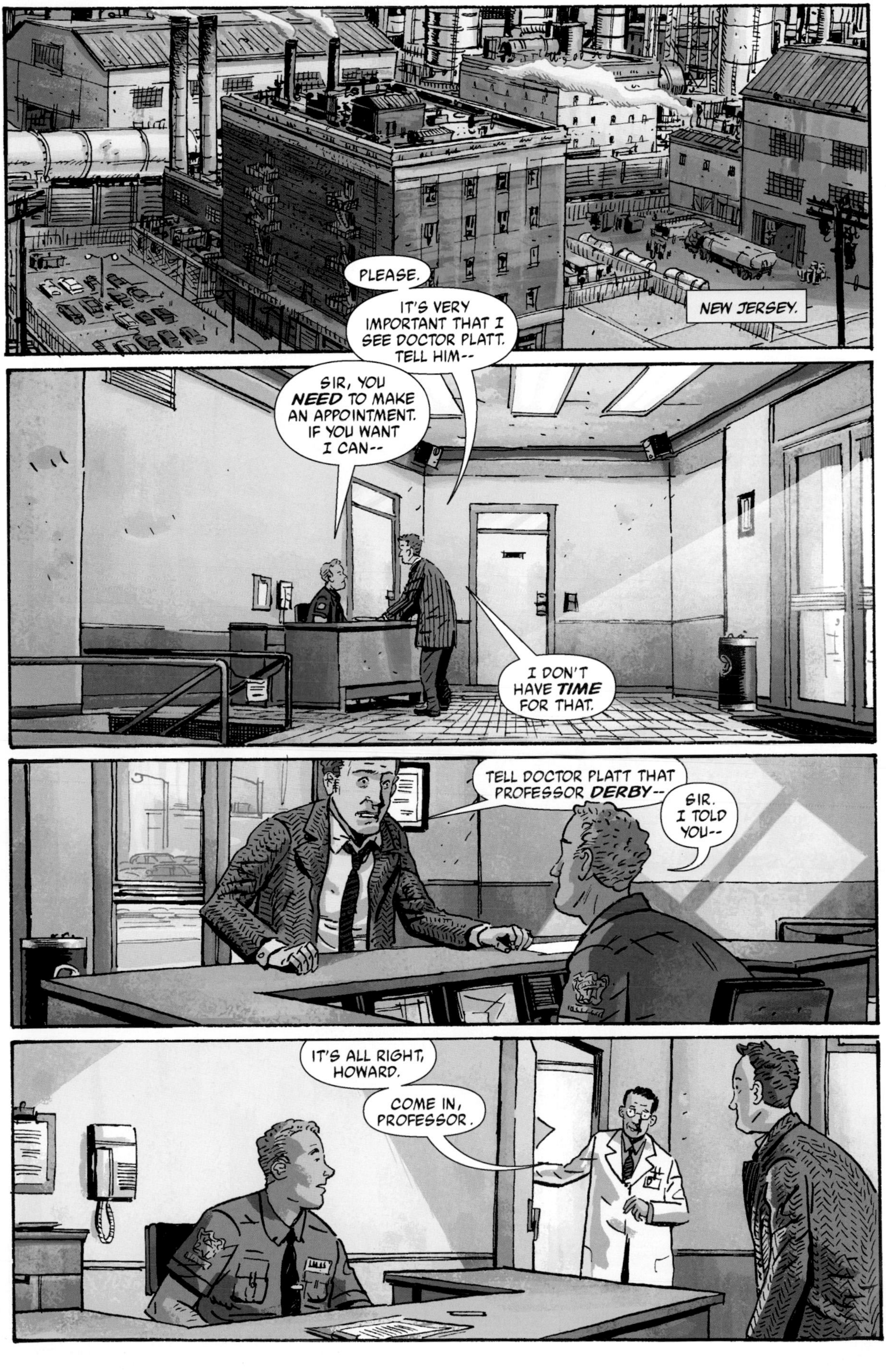
NEW JERSEY.
PLEASE.
IT'S VERY IMPORTANT THAT I SEE DOCTOR PLATT. TELL HIM--
SIR, YOU NEED TO MAKE AN APPOINTMENT. IF YOU WANT I CAN--
I DON'T HAVE TIME FOR THAT.
TELL DOCTOR PLATT THAT PROFESSOR DERBY--
SIR. I TOLD YOU--
IT'S ALL RIGHT, HOWARD.
COME IN, PROFESSOR.

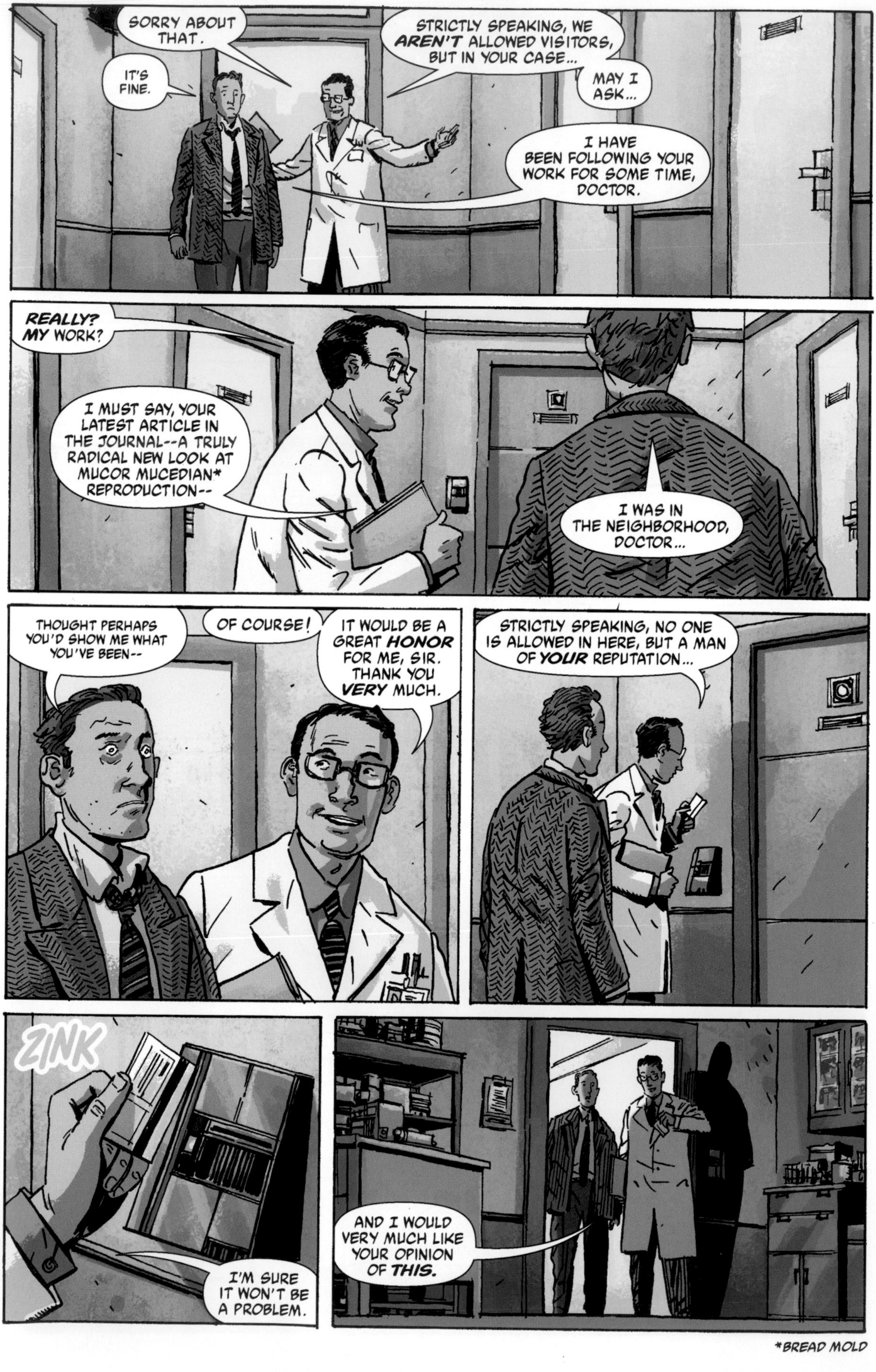
SORRY ABOUT THAT.
IT'S FINE.
STRICTLY SPEAKING, WE AREN'T ALLOWED VISITORS, BUT IN YOUR CASE...
MAY I ASK...
I HAVE BEEN FOLLOWING YOUR WORK FOR SOME TIME, DOCTOR.
REALLY? MY WORK?
I MUST SAY, YOUR LATEST ARTICLE IN THE JOURNAL--A TRULY RADICAL NEW LOOK AT MUCOR MUCEDIAN* REPRODUCTION--
I WAS IN THE NEIGHBORHOOD, DOCTOR...
THOUGHT PERHAPS YOU'D SHOW ME WHAT YOU'VE BEEN--
OF COURSE!
IT WOULD BE A GREAT HONOR FOR ME, SIR. THANK YOU VERY MUCH.
STRICTLY SPEAKING, NO ONE IS ALLOWED IN HERE, BUT A MAN OF YOUR REPUTATION...
ZINK
I'M SURE IT WON'T BE A PROBLEM.
AND I WOULD VERY MUCH LIKE YOUR OPINION OF THIS.

*BREAD MOLD

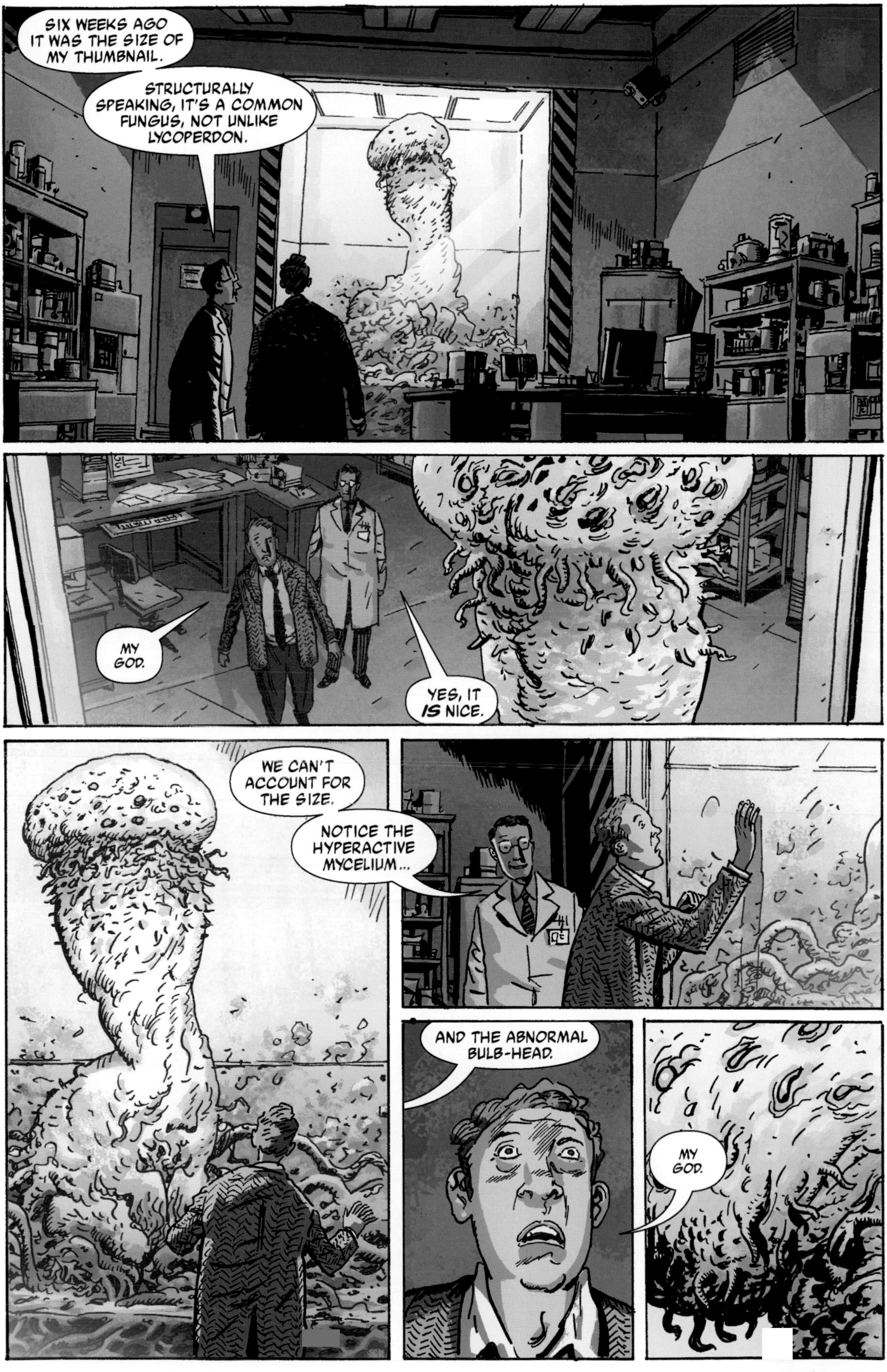
SIX WEEKS AGO IT WAS THE SIZE OF MY THUMBNAIL.
STRUCTURALLY SPEAKING, IT'S A COMMON FUNGUS, NOT UNLIKE LYCOPERDON.
MY GOD.
YES, IT *IS* NICE.
WE CAN'T ACCOUNT FOR THE SIZE.
NOTICE THE HYPERACTIVE MYCELIUM...
AND THE ABNORMAL BULB-HEAD.
MY GOD.

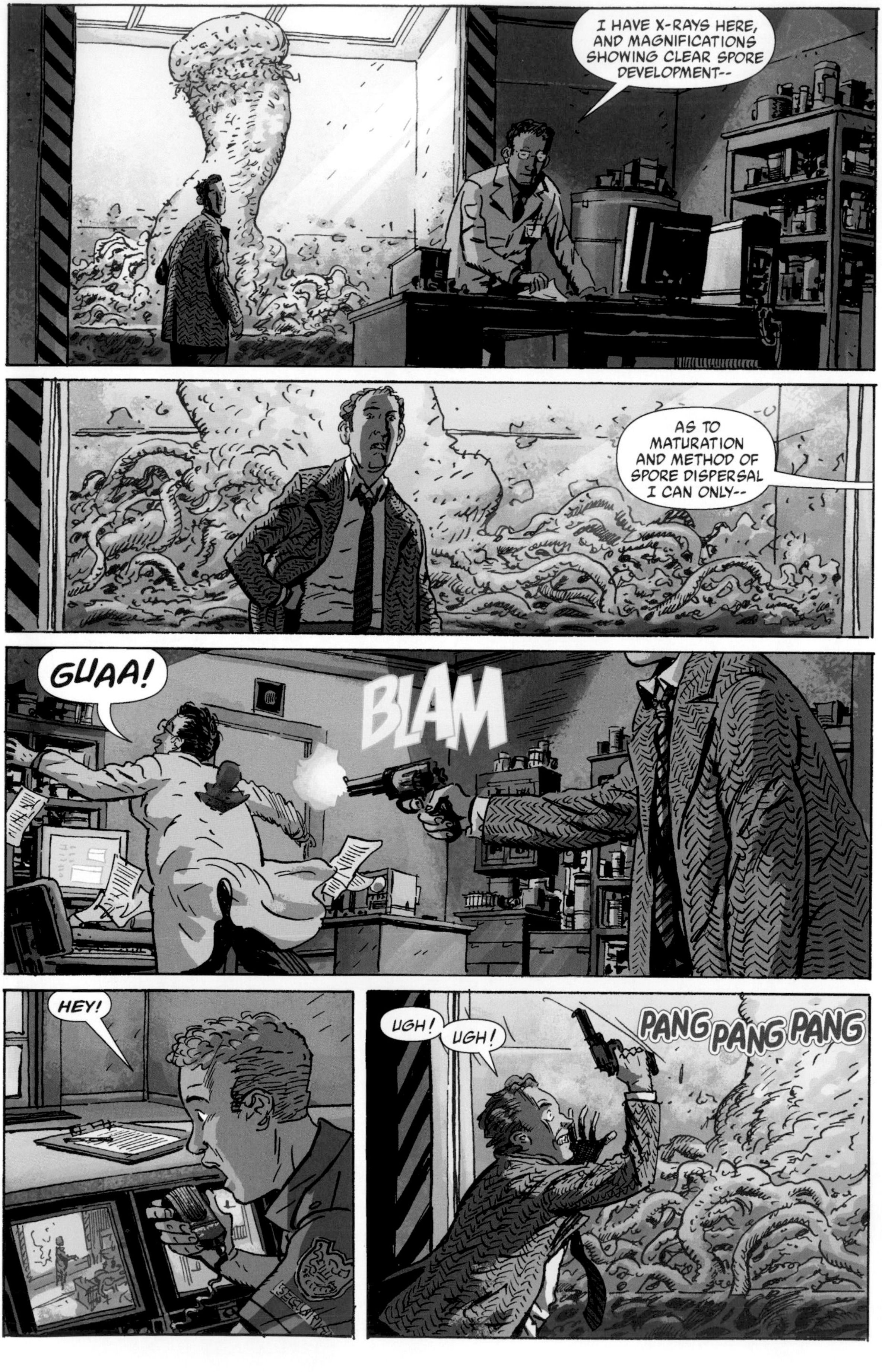

I HAVE X-RAYS HERE, AND MAGNIFICATIONS SHOWING CLEAR SPORE DEVELOPMENT--
AS TO MATURATION AND METHOD OF SPORE DISPERSAL I CAN ONLY--
GUAA!
BLAM
HEY!
UGH!
UGH!
PANG PANG PANG

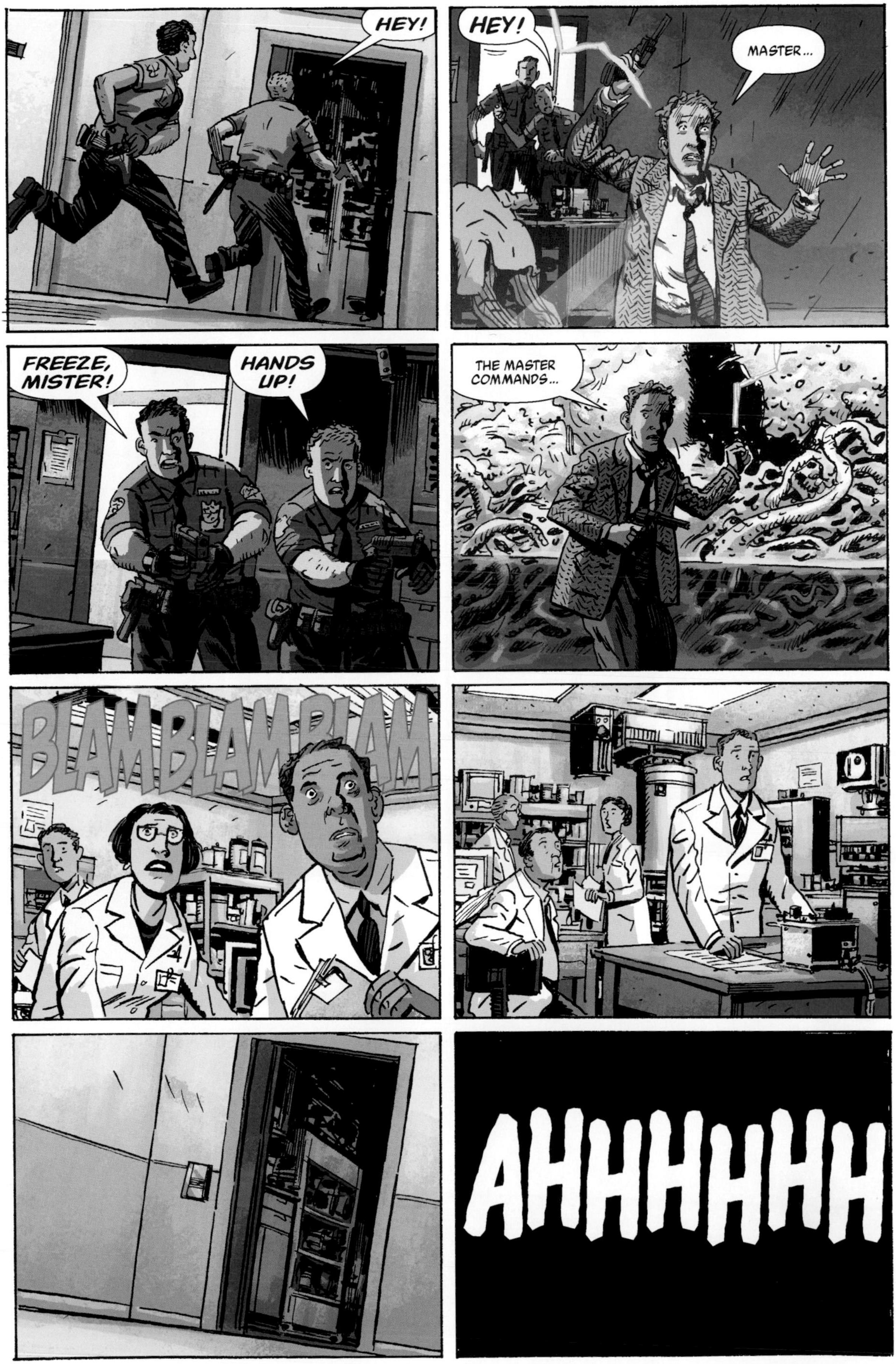
HEY!
HEY!
MASTER...
FREEZE, MISTER!
HANDS UP!
THE MASTER COMMANDS...
BLAMBLAMBLAM
AHHHHHH

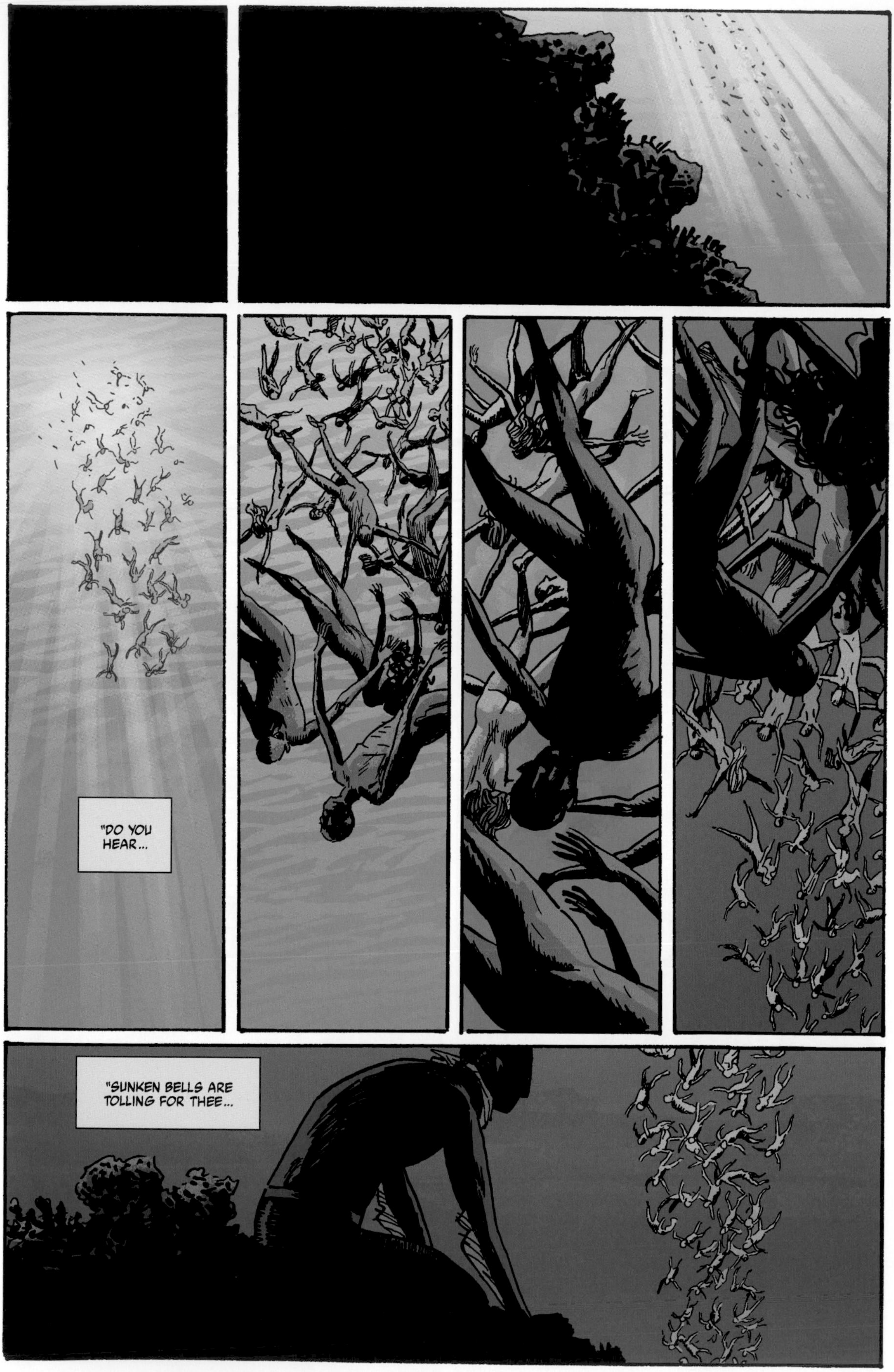
"DO YOU HEAR...
"SUNKEN BELLS ARE TOLLING FOR THEE...

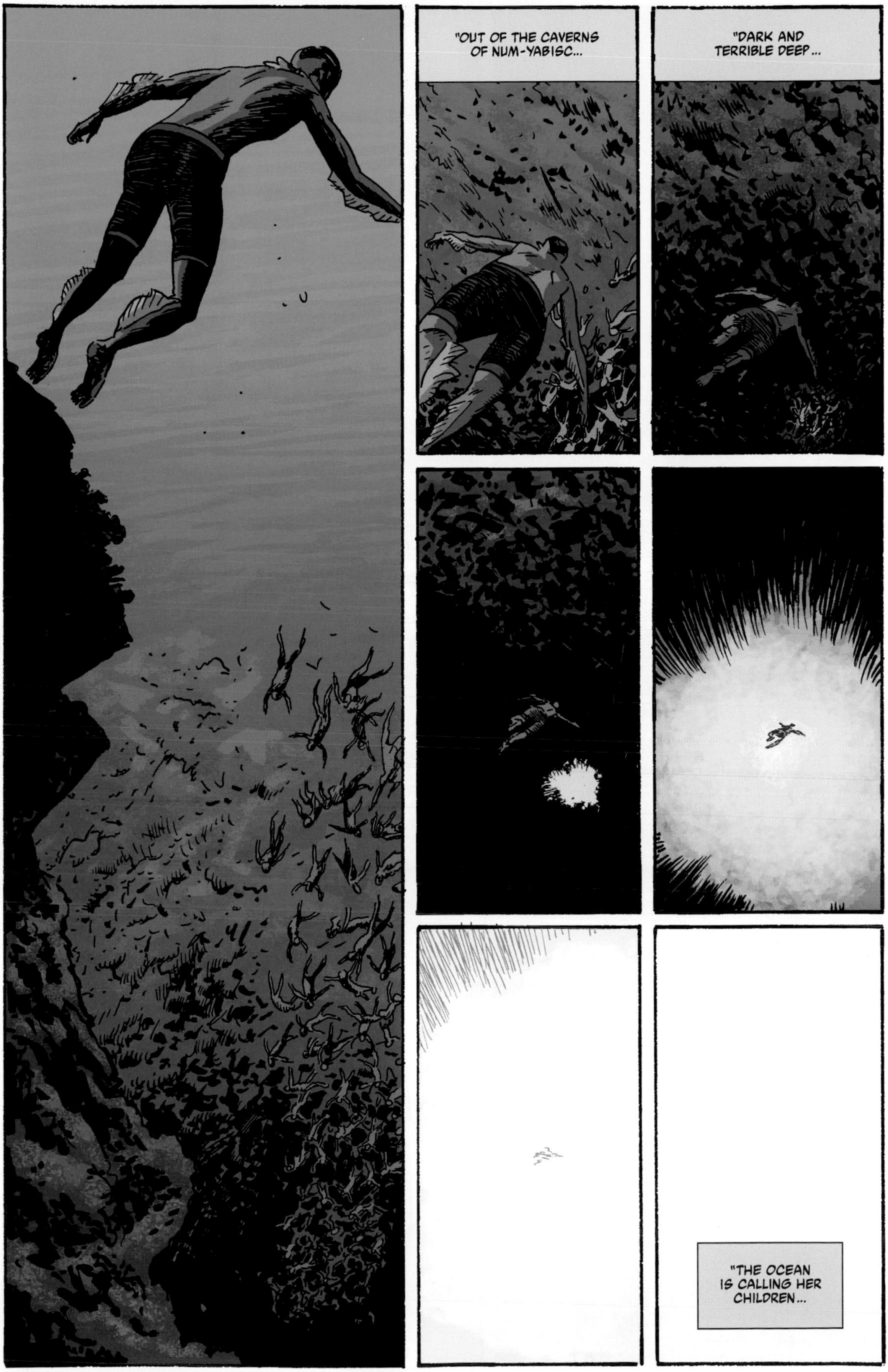
"OUT OF THE CAVERNS OF NUM-YABISC...
"DARK AND TERRIBLE DEEP...
"THE OCEAN IS CALLING HER CHILDREN...

"HOME."

!

B.P.R.D. HEADQUARTERS.

FAIRFIELD, CT.

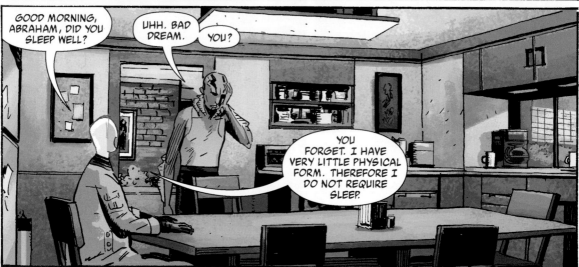

GOOD MORNING, ABRAHAM, DID YOU SLEEP WELL?

UHH. BAD DREAM. YOU?

YOU FORGET. I HAVE VERY LITTLE PHYSICAL FORM. THEREFORE I DO NOT REQUIRE SLEEP.

LIKE THE SCARECROW IN THE WIZARD OF OZ?

IN THE BOOK DOROTHY SLEEPS AND THE SCARECROW SITS UP ALL NIGHT WATCHING OVER HER.

CREEPY.

NO OFFENSE.

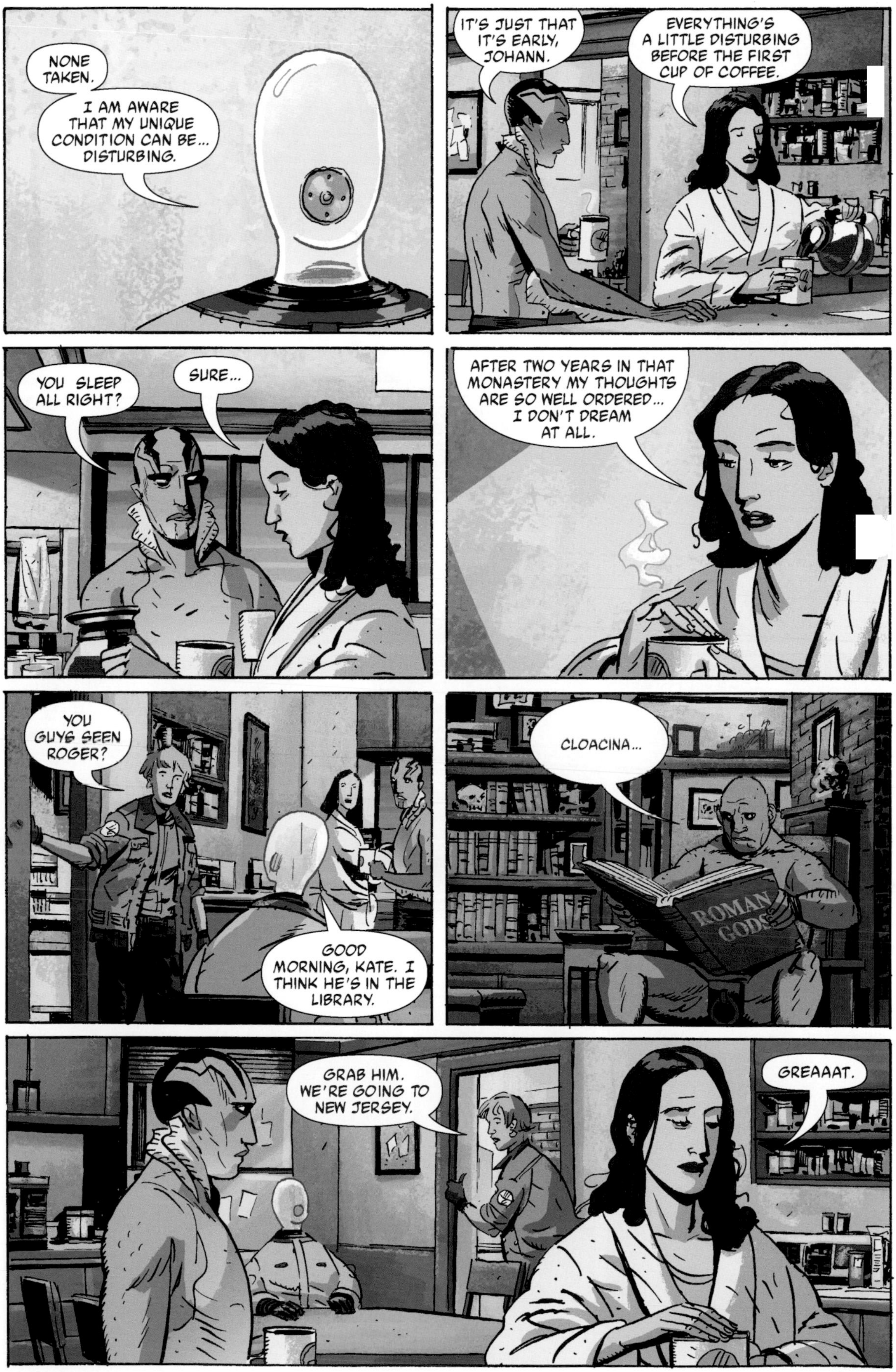
NONE TAKEN.
I AM AWARE THAT MY UNIQUE CONDITION CAN BE... DISTURBING.
IT'S JUST THAT IT'S EARLY, JOHANN.
EVERYTHING'S A LITTLE DISTURBING BEFORE THE FIRST CUP OF COFFEE.
YOU SLEEP ALL RIGHT?
SURE...
AFTER TWO YEARS IN THAT MONASTERY MY THOUGHTS ARE SO WELL ORDERED... I DON'T DREAM AT ALL.
YOU GUYS SEEN ROGER?
GOOD MORNING, KATE. I THINK HE'S IN THE LIBRARY.
CLOACINA...
ROMAN GODS
GRAB HIM. WE'RE GOING TO NEW JERSEY.
GREAAAT.

THE BUREAU'S BEEEN USING THIS PLACE SINCE THE '50S, MOSTLY TO WAREHOUSE STUFF THAT ISN'T *TECHNICALLY* SUPERNATURAL.

BUT STUFF THEY DON'T WANT THE PUBLIC TO KNOW ABOUT.

THAT'S RIGHT.

BUT THIS MORNING SOMEBODY GOT IN AND THERE WAS A SHOOTING.

SOUNDS LIKE A JOB FOR THE POLICE.

WUP WUPWUP

YEAH, WELL THEY KEEP SOME PRETTY WEIRD STUFF IN THERE.

UH HUHH...

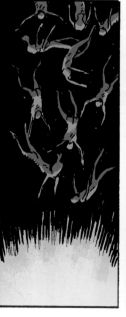

ABE. YOU OKAY?

SORRY...

ROUGH NIGHT?

BAD DREAM.

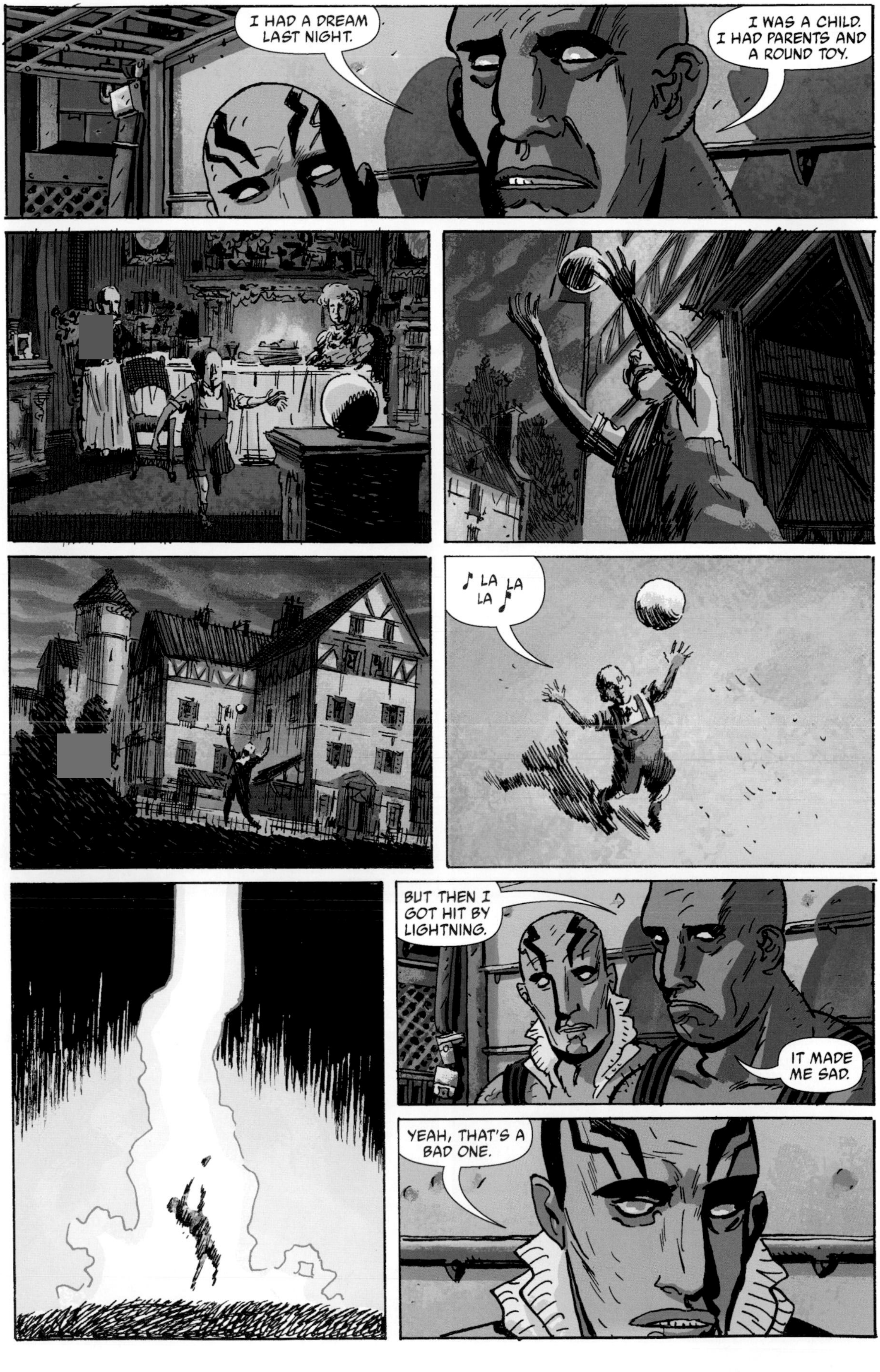
I HAD A DREAM LAST NIGHT.
I WAS A CHILD. I HAD PARENTS AND A ROUND TOY.
♪ LA LA LA ♪
BUT THEN I GOT HIT BY LIGHTNING.
IT MADE ME SAD.
YEAH, THAT'S A BAD ONE.

"BUT I THINK MINE WAS WORSE."

WHAT HAVE YOU GOT?

I'VE PATCHED TOGETHER WHAT I COULD GET OFF THE SECURITY CAMERAS.

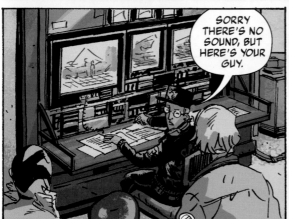

SORRY THERE'S NO SOUND, BUT HERE'S YOUR GUY.

PROFESSOR IRWIN DERBY...

"HE TALKS HIS WAY PAST SECURITY...

"...SHOOTS DOCTOR ARNOLD PLATT...

"...SECURITY SHOOTS HIM...

"...AND..."

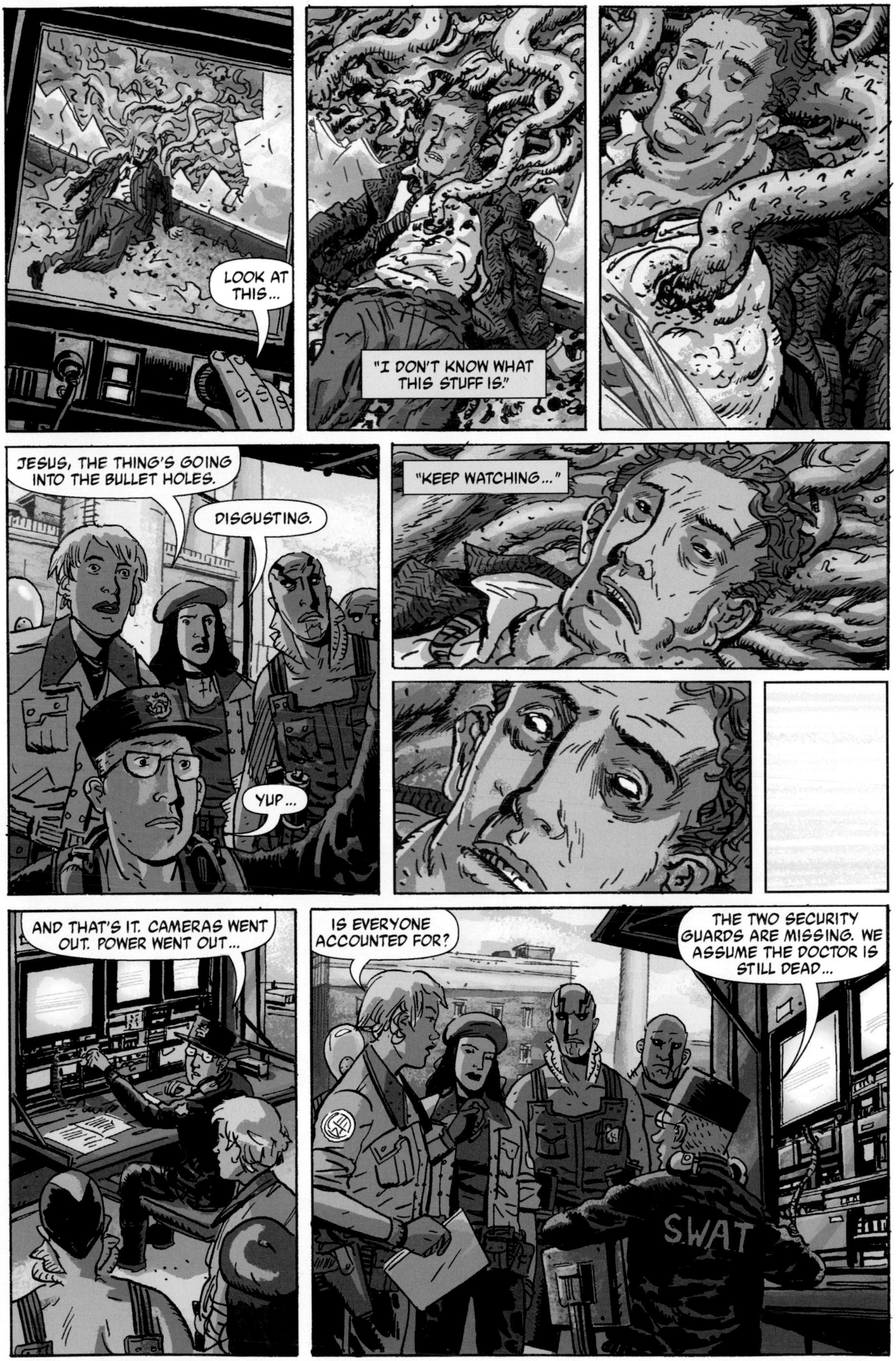
LOOK AT THIS...
"I DON'T KNOW WHAT THIS STUFF IS."
JESUS, THE THING'S GOING INTO THE BULLET HOLES.
DISGUSTING.
YUP...
"KEEP WATCHING..."
AND THAT'S IT. CAMERAS WENT OUT. POWER WENT OUT...
IS EVERYONE ACCOUNTED FOR?
THE TWO SECURITY GUARDS ARE MISSING. WE ASSUME THE DOCTOR IS STILL DEAD...
SWAT

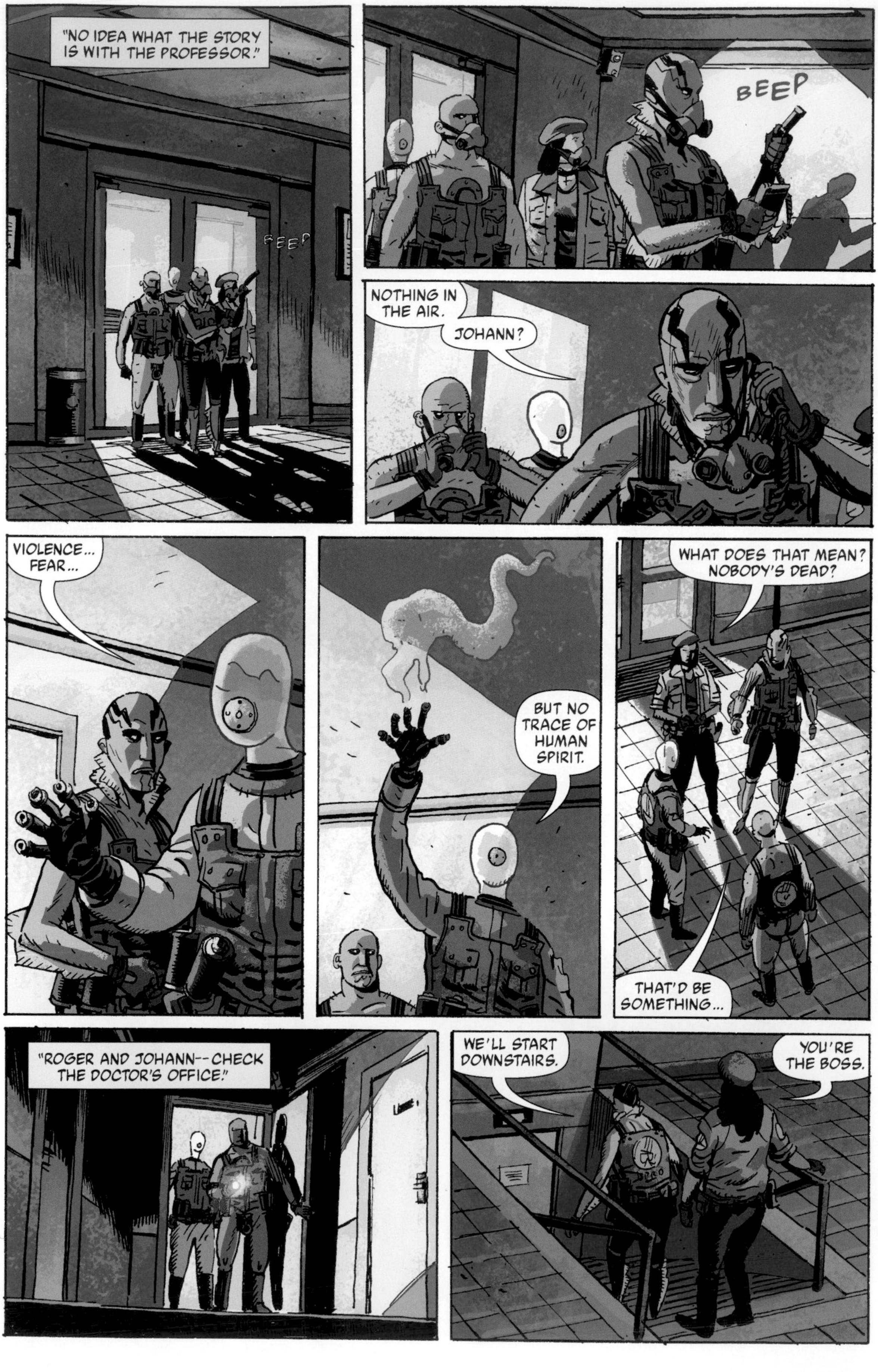
"NO IDEA WHAT THE STORY IS WITH THE PROFESSOR."
BEEP
BEEP
NOTHING IN THE AIR.
JOHANN?
VIOLENCE... FEAR...
BUT NO TRACE OF HUMAN SPIRIT.
WHAT DOES THAT MEAN? NOBODY'S DEAD?
THAT'D BE SOMETHING...
"ROGER AND JOHANN-- CHECK THE DOCTOR'S OFFICE."
WE'LL START DOWNSTAIRS.
YOU'RE THE BOSS.

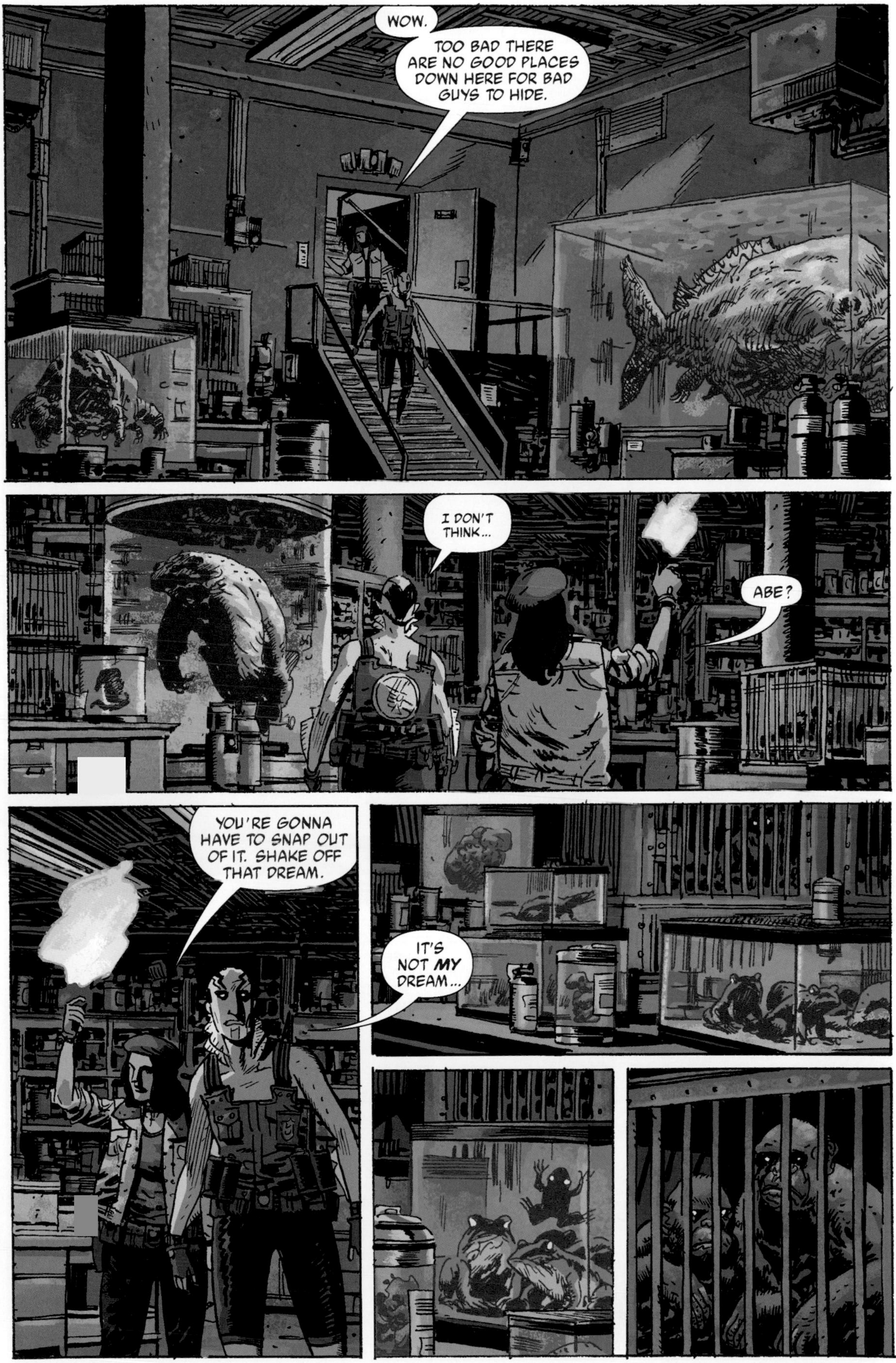
WOW.
TOO BAD THERE ARE NO GOOD PLACES DOWN HERE FOR BAD GUYS TO HIDE.
I DON'T THINK...
ABE?
YOU'RE GONNA HAVE TO SNAP OUT OF IT. SHAKE OFF THAT DREAM.
IT'S NOT MY DREAM...

YEAH?

IT'S ROGER. I'M WORRIED ABOUT HIM.

WHY?

BECAUSE HE WAS GROWN IN A JAR AND LEFT IN A ROMANIAN BASEMENT FOR FIVE HUNDRED YEARS...?

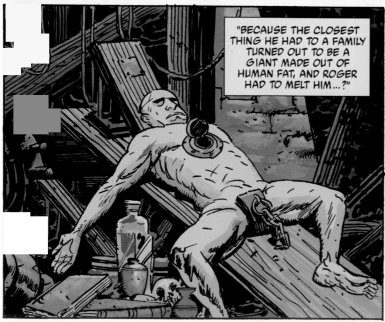

"BECAUSE THE CLOSEST THING HE HAD TO A FAMILY TURNED OUT TO BE A GIANT MADE OUT OF HUMAN FAT, AND ROGER HAD TO MELT HIM...?"

WE KNOW *HIS* STORY, ABE...*

*HELLBOY: WAKE THE DEVIL AND ALMOST COLOSSUS

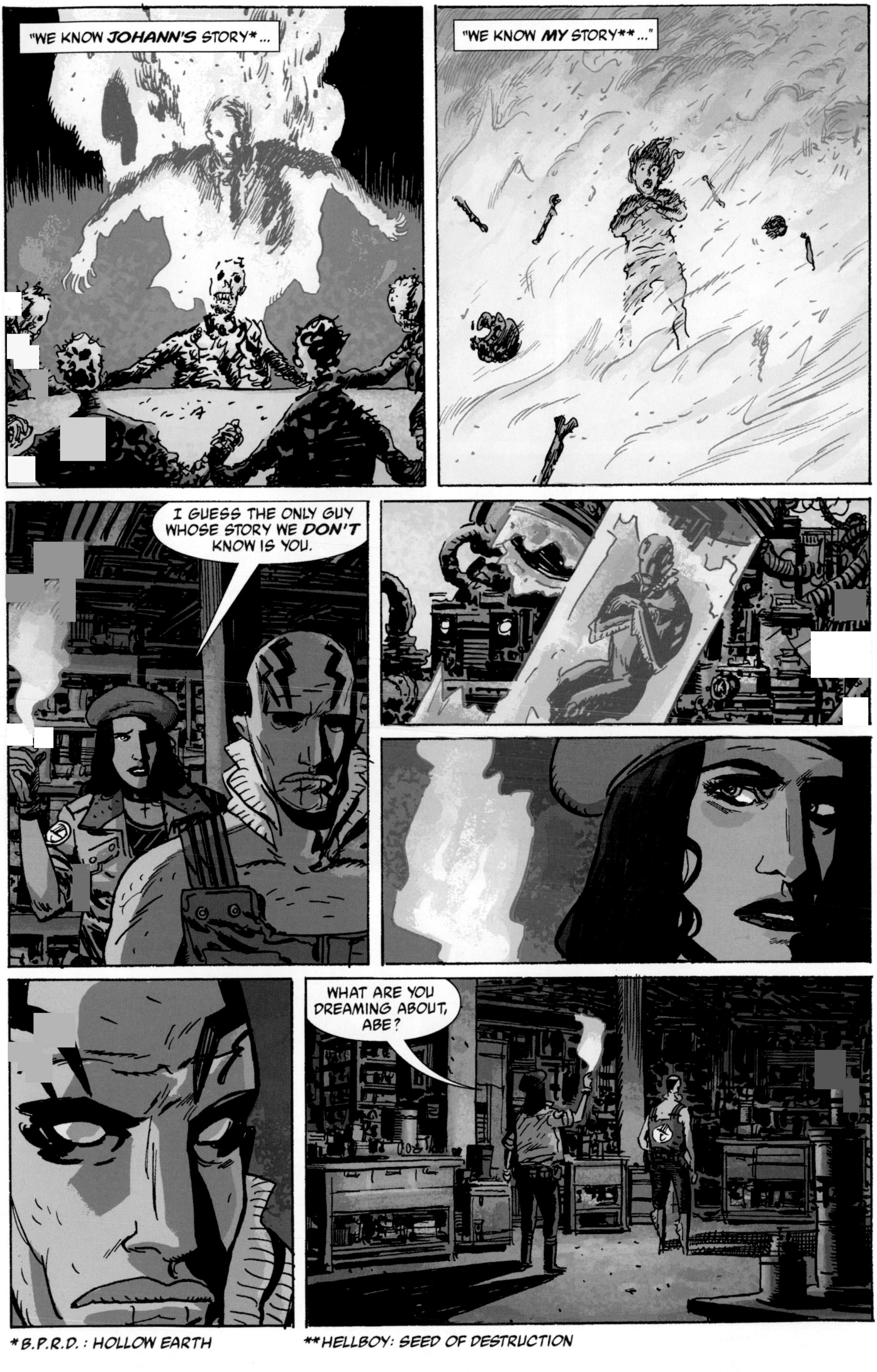
"WE KNOW JOHANN'S STORY*...
"WE KNOW MY STORY**..."
I GUESS THE ONLY GUY WHOSE STORY WE DON'T KNOW IS YOU.
WHAT ARE YOU DREAMING ABOUT, ABE?

*B.P.R.D.: HOLLOW EARTH

**HELLBOY: SEED OF DESTRUCTION

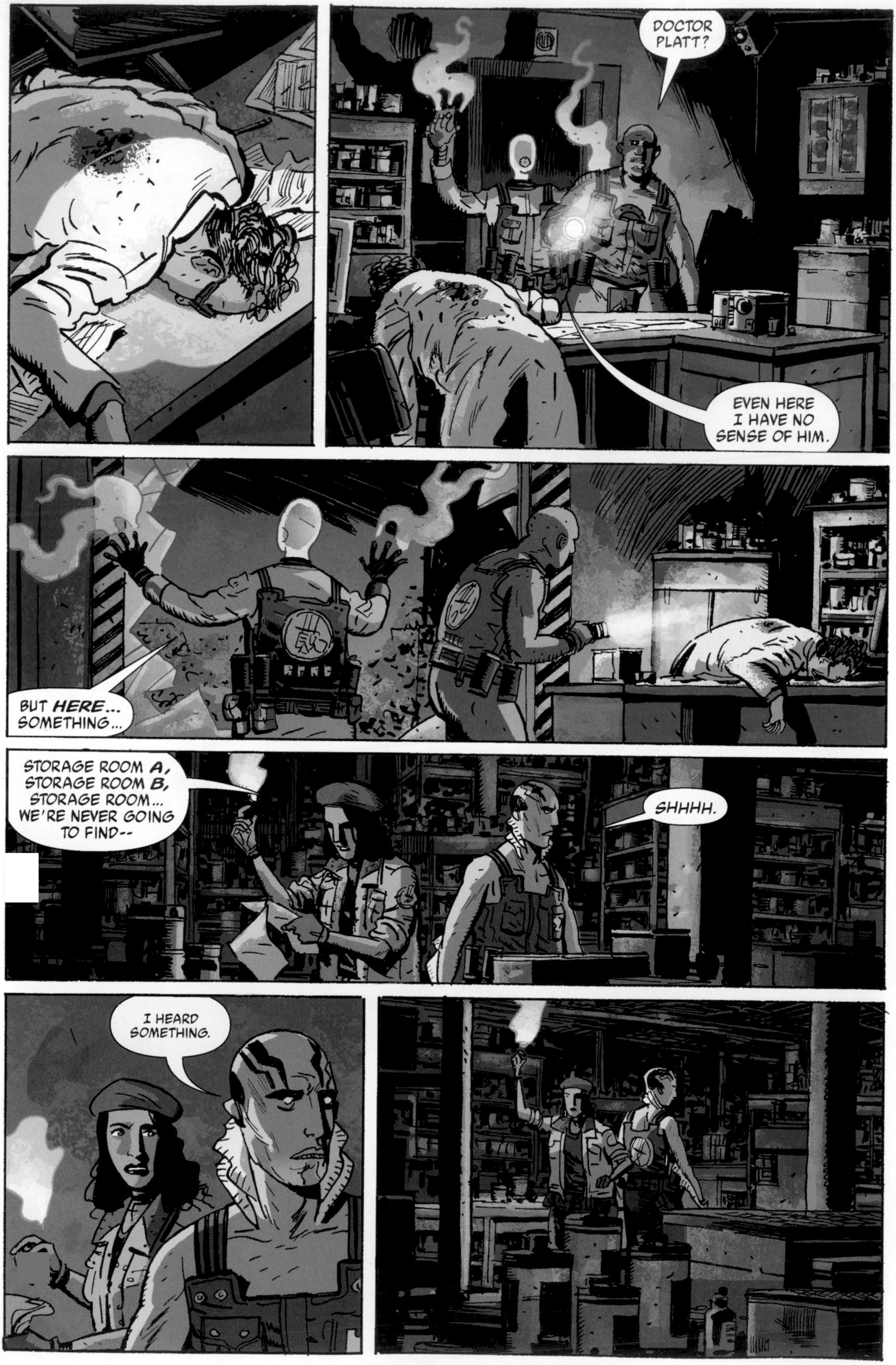
DOCTOR PLATT?
EVEN HERE I HAVE NO SENSE OF HIM.
BUT **HERE...** SOMETHING...
STORAGE ROOM **A**, STORAGE ROOM **B**, STORAGE ROOM... WE'RE NEVER GOING TO FIND--
SHHHH.
I HEARD SOMETHING.

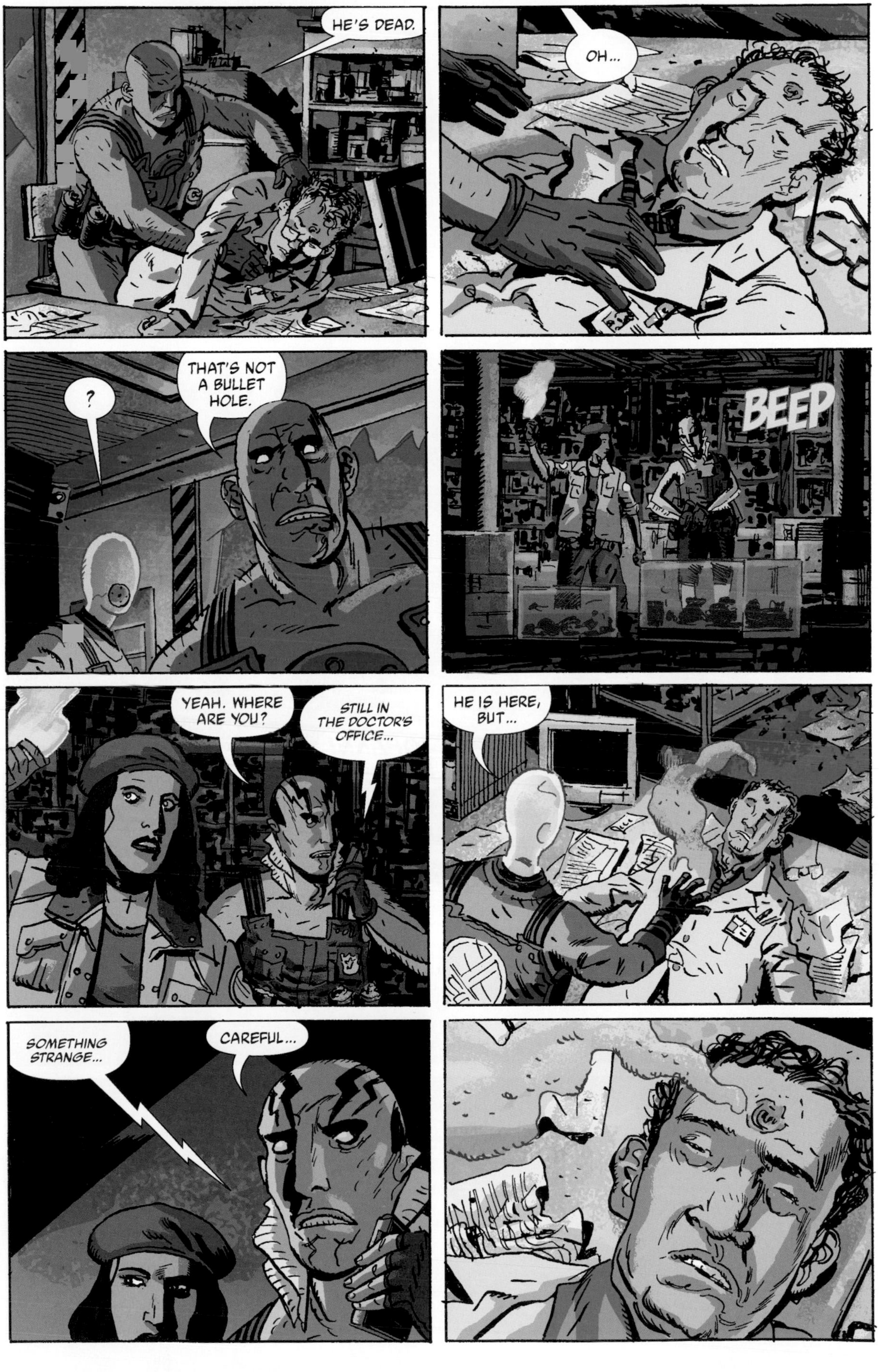
HE'S DEAD.
OH...
?
THAT'S NOT A BULLET HOLE.
BEEP
YEAH. WHERE ARE YOU?
STILL IN THE DOCTOR'S OFFICE...
HE IS HERE, BUT...
SOMETHING STRANGE...
CAREFUL...

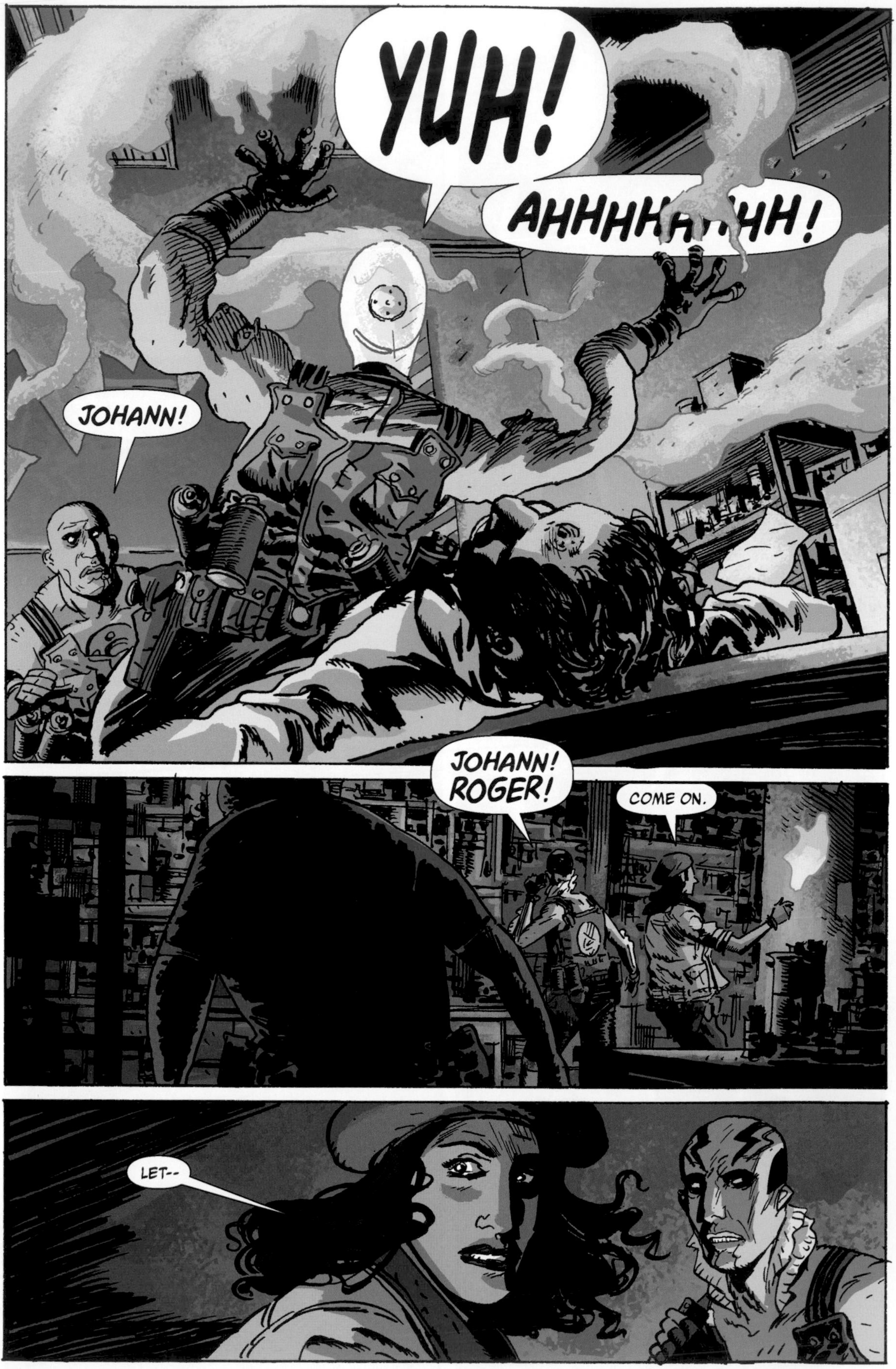
YUH!
AHHHHHHHH!
JOHANN!
JOHANN! ROGER!
COME ON.
LET--

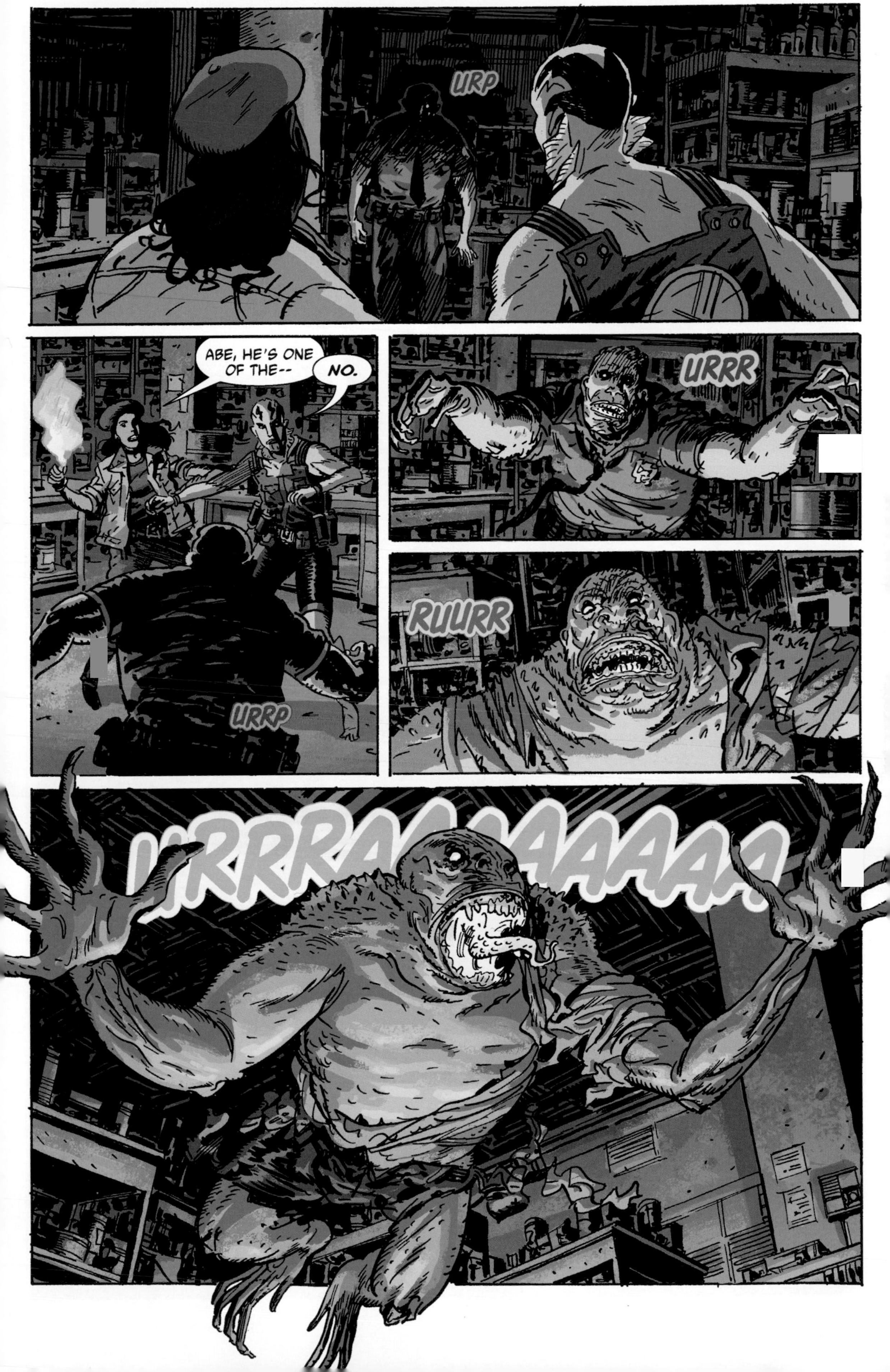
URP
ABE, HE'S ONE OF THE--
NO.
URRP
URRR
RUURR

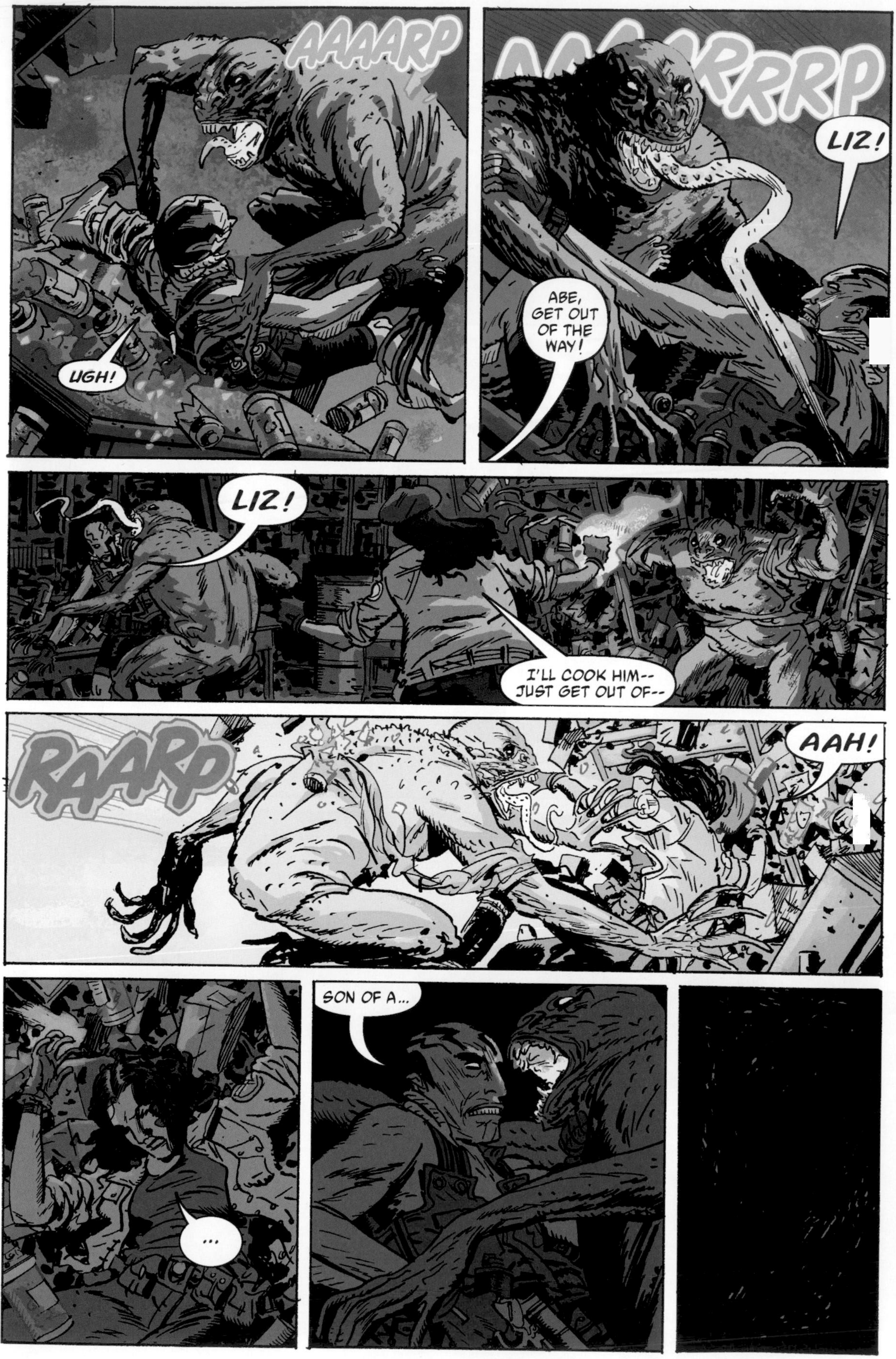
AAAARP
UGH!
AAAARRRRP
LIZ!
ABE, GET OUT OF THE WAY!
LIZ!
I'LL COOK HIM-- JUST GET OUT OF--
RAARP
AAH!
...
SON OF A...

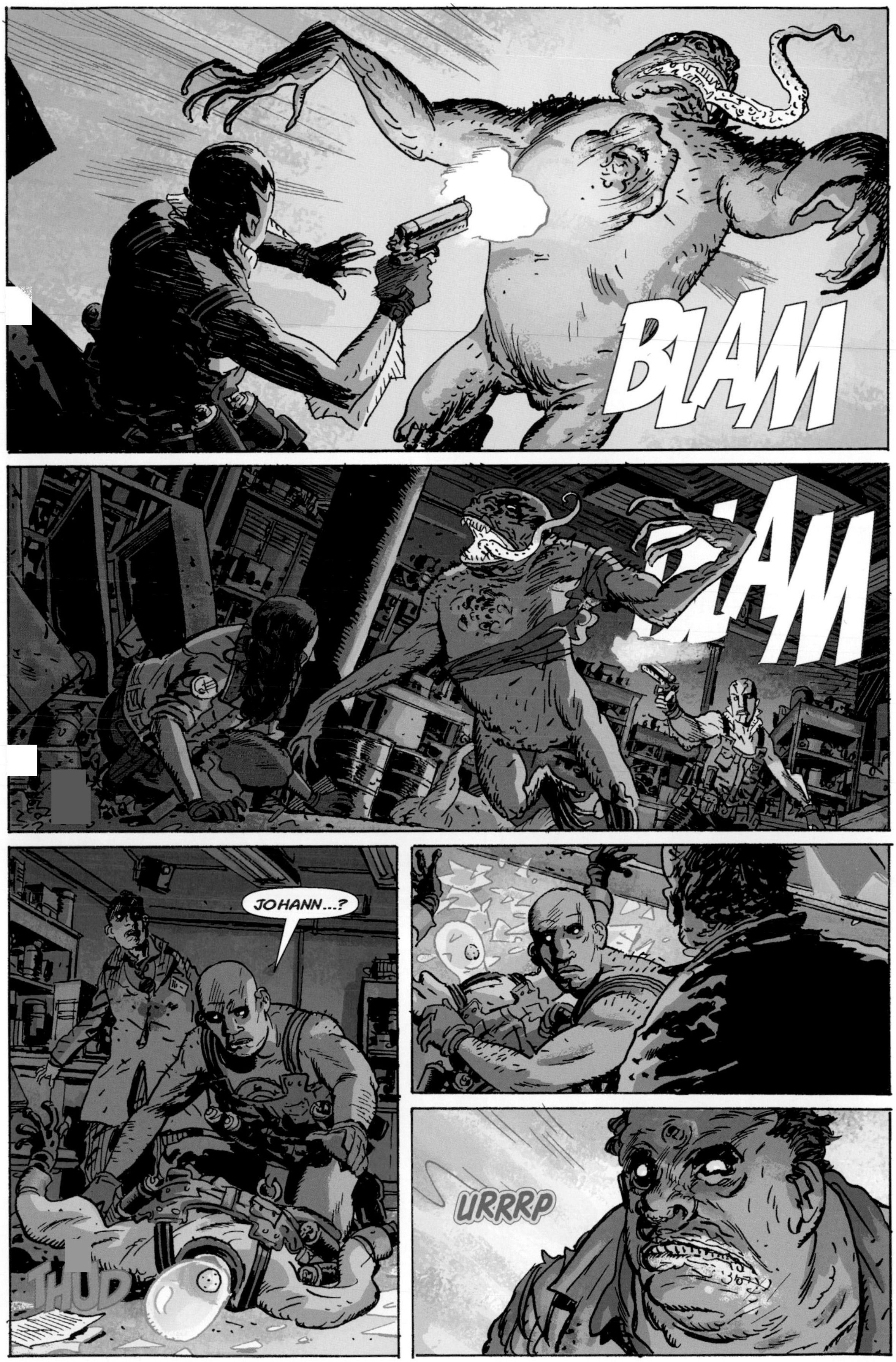
BLAM
BLAM
JOHANN...?
THUD
URRRP

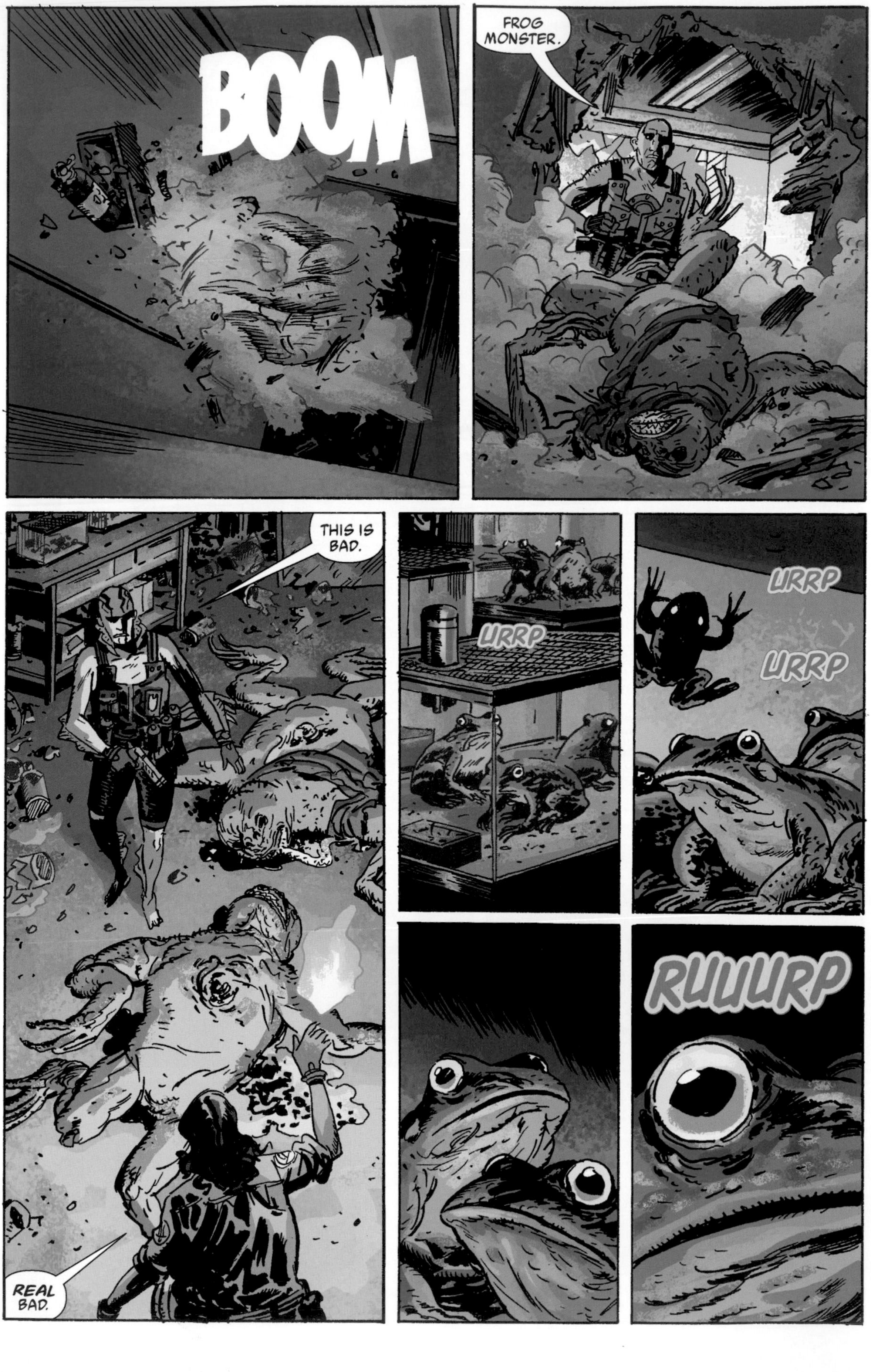
BOOM
FROG MONSTER.
THIS IS BAD.
REAL BAD.
URRP
URRP
URRP
RUUURP

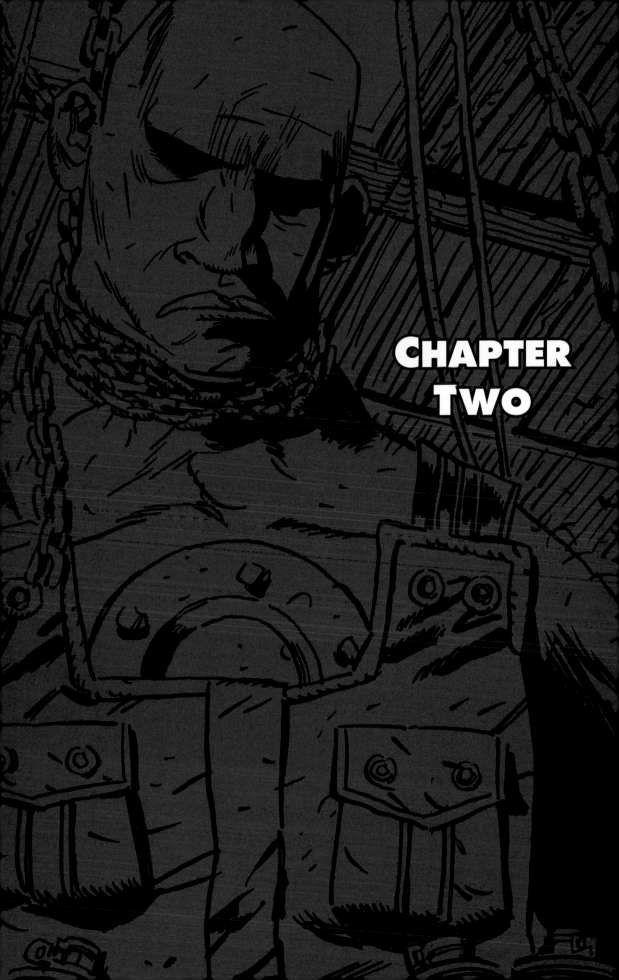

CHAPTER
TWO

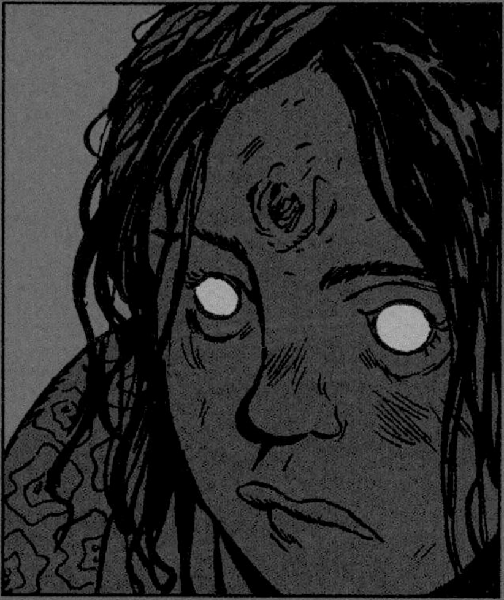

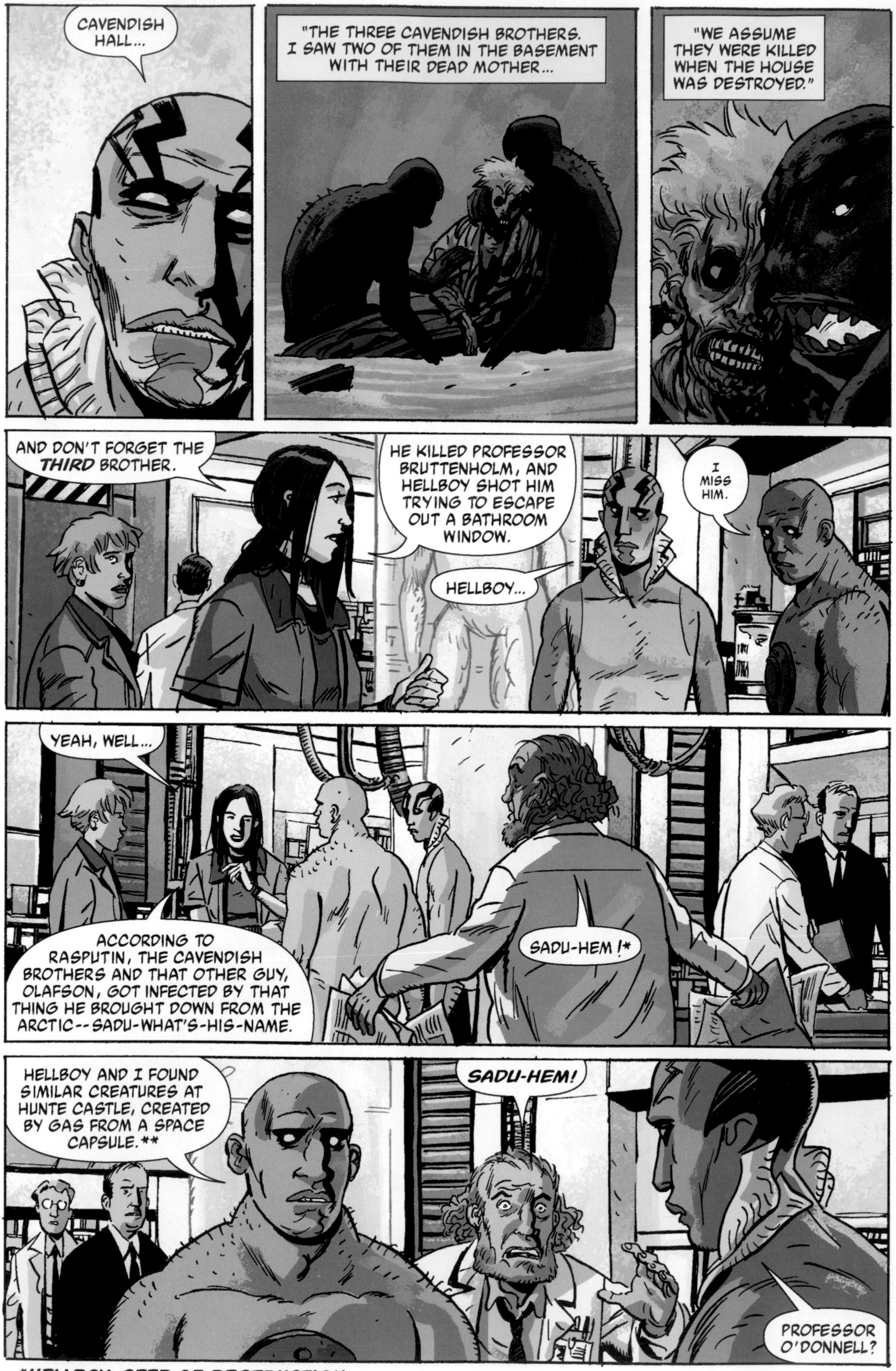
CAVENDISH HALL...
"THE THREE CAVENDISH BROTHERS. I SAW TWO OF THEM IN THE BASEMENT WITH THEIR DEAD MOTHER...
"WE ASSUME THEY WERE KILLED WHEN THE HOUSE WAS DESTROYED."
AND DON'T FORGET THE THIRD BROTHER.
HE KILLED PROFESSOR BRUTTENHOLM, AND HELLBOY SHOT HIM TRYING TO ESCAPE OUT A BATHROOM WINDOW.
HELLBOY...
I MISS HIM.
YEAH, WELL...
ACCORDING TO RASPUTIN, THE CAVENDISH BROTHERS AND THAT OTHER GUY, OLAFSON, GOT INFECTED BY THAT THING HE BROUGHT DOWN FROM THE ARCTIC-- SADU-WHAT'S-HIS-NAME.
SADU-HEM !*
HELLBOY AND I FOUND SIMILAR CREATURES AT HUNTE CASTLE, CREATED BY GAS FROM A SPACE CAPSULE.**
SADU-HEM!
PROFESSOR O'DONNELL?

***HELLBOY: SEED OF DESTRUCTION**
****HELLBOY: CONQUEROR WORM**

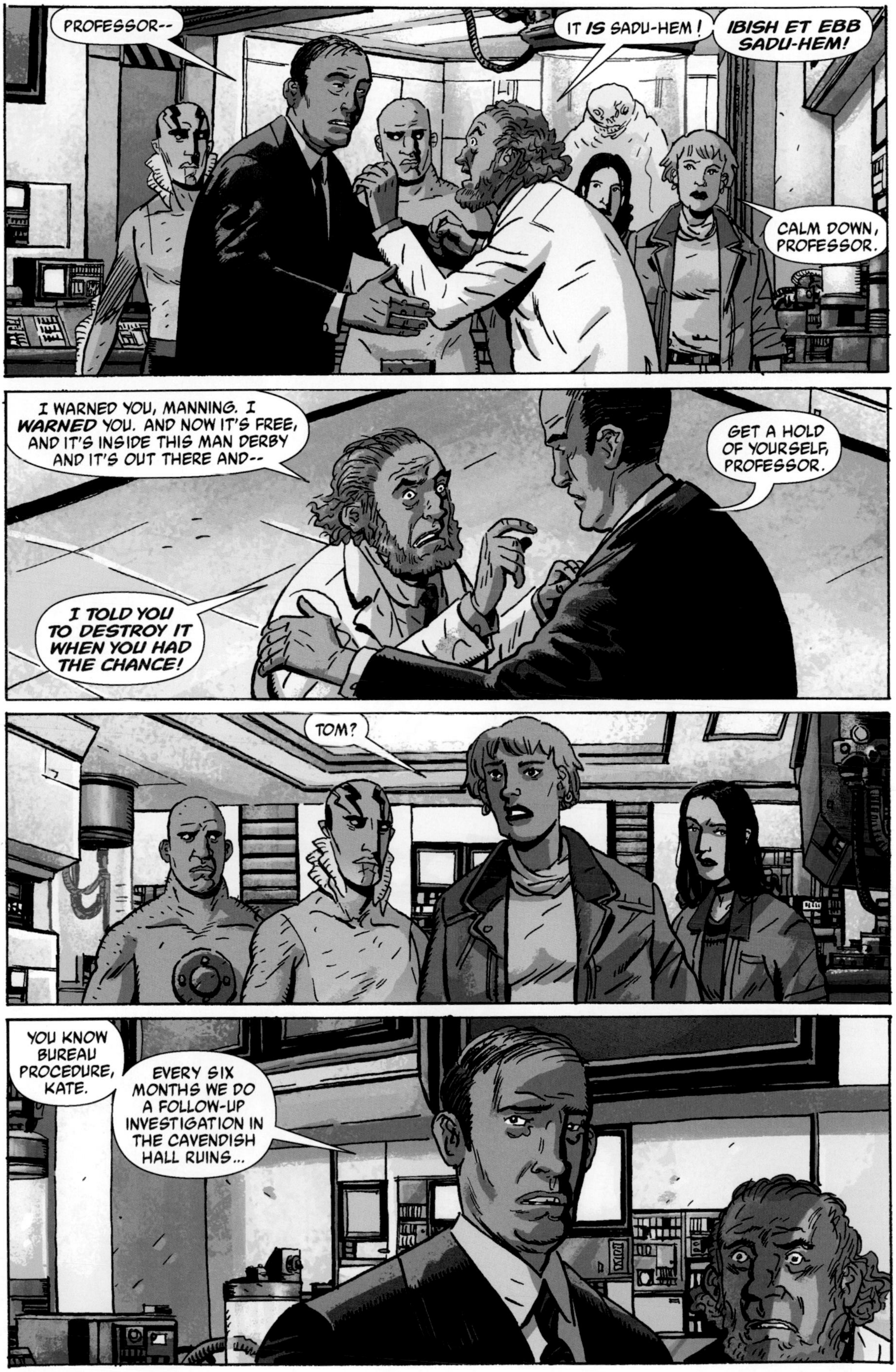
PROFESSOR--
IT IS SADU-HEM!
IBISH ET EBB SADU-HEM!
CALM DOWN, PROFESSOR.
I WARNED YOU, MANNING. I WARNED YOU. AND NOW IT'S FREE, AND IT'S INSIDE THIS MAN DERBY AND IT'S OUT THERE AND--
GET A HOLD OF YOURSELF, PROFESSOR.
I TOLD YOU TO DESTROY IT WHEN YOU HAD THE CHANCE!
TOM?
YOU KNOW BUREAU PROCEDURE, KATE.
EVERY SIX MONTHS WE DO A FOLLOW-UP INVESTIGATION IN THE CAVENDISH HALL RUINS...

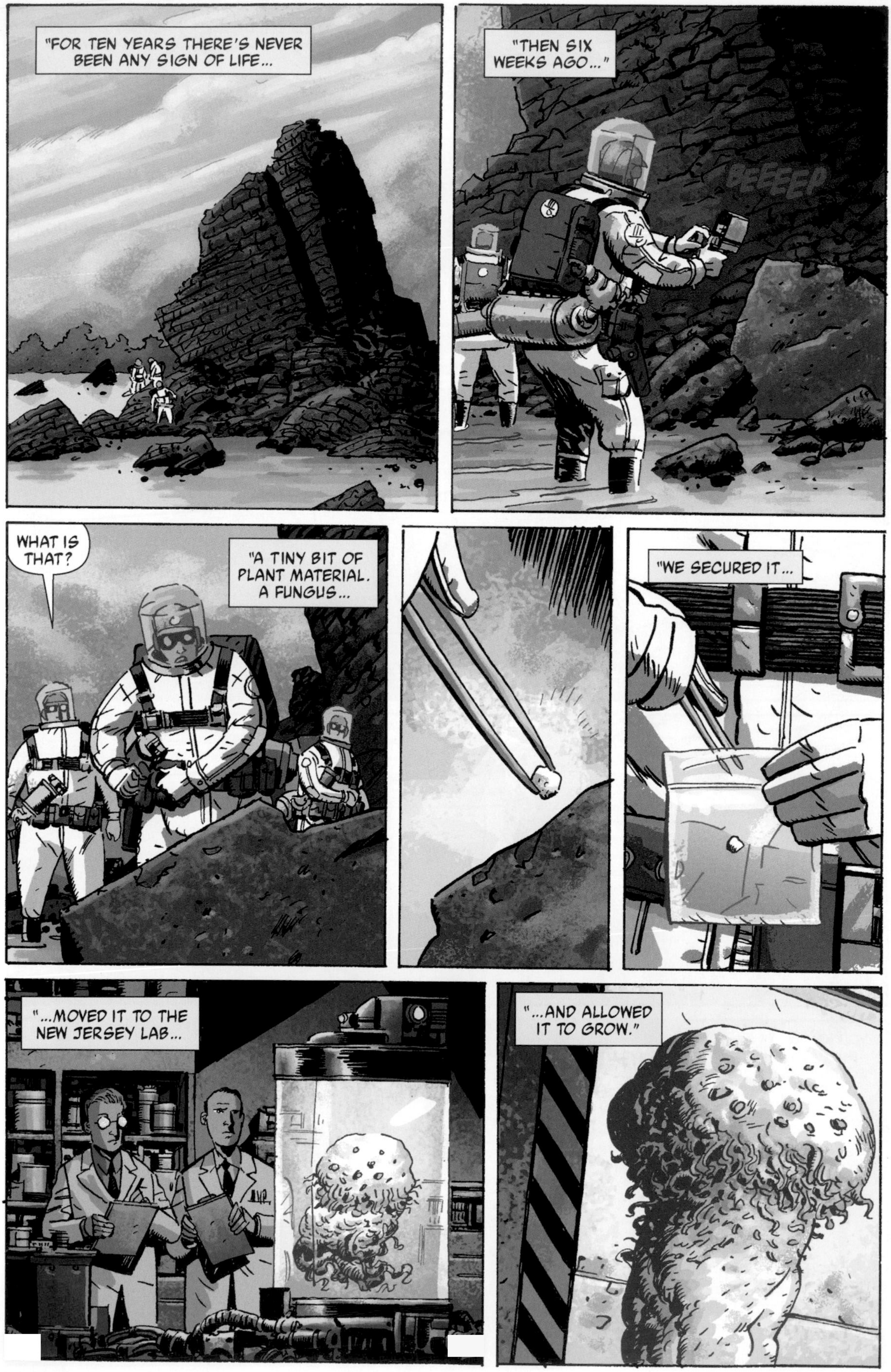
"FOR TEN YEARS THERE'S NEVER BEEN ANY SIGN OF LIFE...
"THEN SIX WEEKS AGO..."
BEEEEP
WHAT IS THAT?
"A TINY BIT OF PLANT MATERIAL. A FUNGUS...
"WE SECURED IT...
"...MOVED IT TO THE NEW JERSEY LAB...
"...AND ALLOWED IT TO GROW."

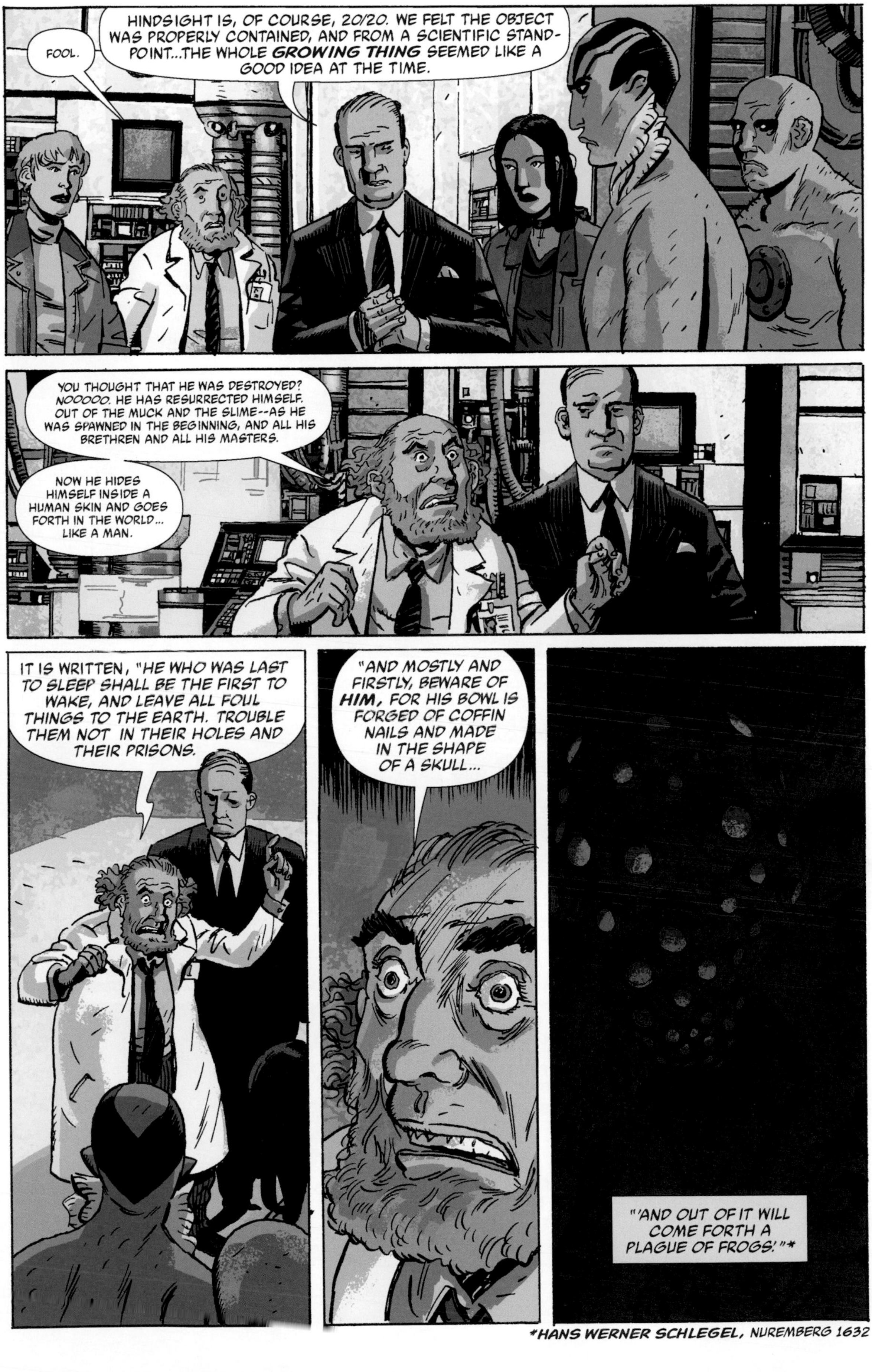
FOOL.
HINDSIGHT IS, OF COURSE, 20/20. WE FELT THE OBJECT WAS PROPERLY CONTAINED, AND FROM A SCIENTIFIC STANDPOINT...THE WHOLE GROWING THING SEEMED LIKE A GOOD IDEA AT THE TIME.
YOU THOUGHT THAT HE WAS DESTROYED? NOOOOO. HE HAS RESURRECTED HIMSELF. OUT OF THE MUCK AND THE SLIME--AS HE WAS SPAWNED IN THE BEGINNING, AND ALL HIS BRETHREN AND ALL HIS MASTERS.
NOW HE HIDES HIMSELF INSIDE A HUMAN SKIN AND GOES FORTH IN THE WORLD... LIKE A MAN.
IT IS WRITTEN, "HE WHO WAS LAST TO SLEEP SHALL BE THE FIRST TO WAKE, AND LEAVE ALL FOUL THINGS TO THE EARTH. TROUBLE THEM NOT IN THEIR HOLES AND THEIR PRISONS.
"AND MOSTLY AND FIRSTLY, BEWARE OF HIM, FOR HIS BOWL IS FORGED OF COFFIN NAILS AND MADE IN THE SHAPE OF A SKULL...
"'AND OUT OF IT WILL COME FORTH A PLAGUE OF FROGS!'"*

*HANS WERNER SCHLEGEL, NUREMBERG 1632

ALL RIGHT, PROFESSOR. ALL RIGHT...

LET'S SEE IF WE CAN FIND YOUR PILLS.

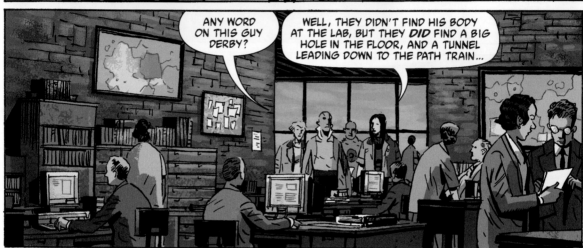

ANY WORD ON THIS GUY DERBY?

WELL, THEY DIDN'T FIND HIS BODY AT THE LAB, BUT THEY *DID* FIND A BIG HOLE IN THE FLOOR, AND A TUNNEL LEADING DOWN TO THE PATH TRAIN...

SO HE COULD BE ANY-WHERE.

WHAT DO WE KNOW ABOUT HIM?

NOT MUCH SO FAR. HE WAS A PROFESSOR AT CORNELL, BUT A COUPLE WEEKS AGO HE JUST UP AND QUIT.

JIM? ANY-THING?

THE GUY WAS BORING. PAID ALL HIS BILLS ON TIME, AND NOTHING WEIRD TILL ABOUT A MONTH AGO...

THEN HE STARTED WRITING BIG CHECKS TO SOMETHING CALLED *"THE NEW TEMPLE OF MYSTERIES."*

THE WHAT?

WHERE'S THAT?

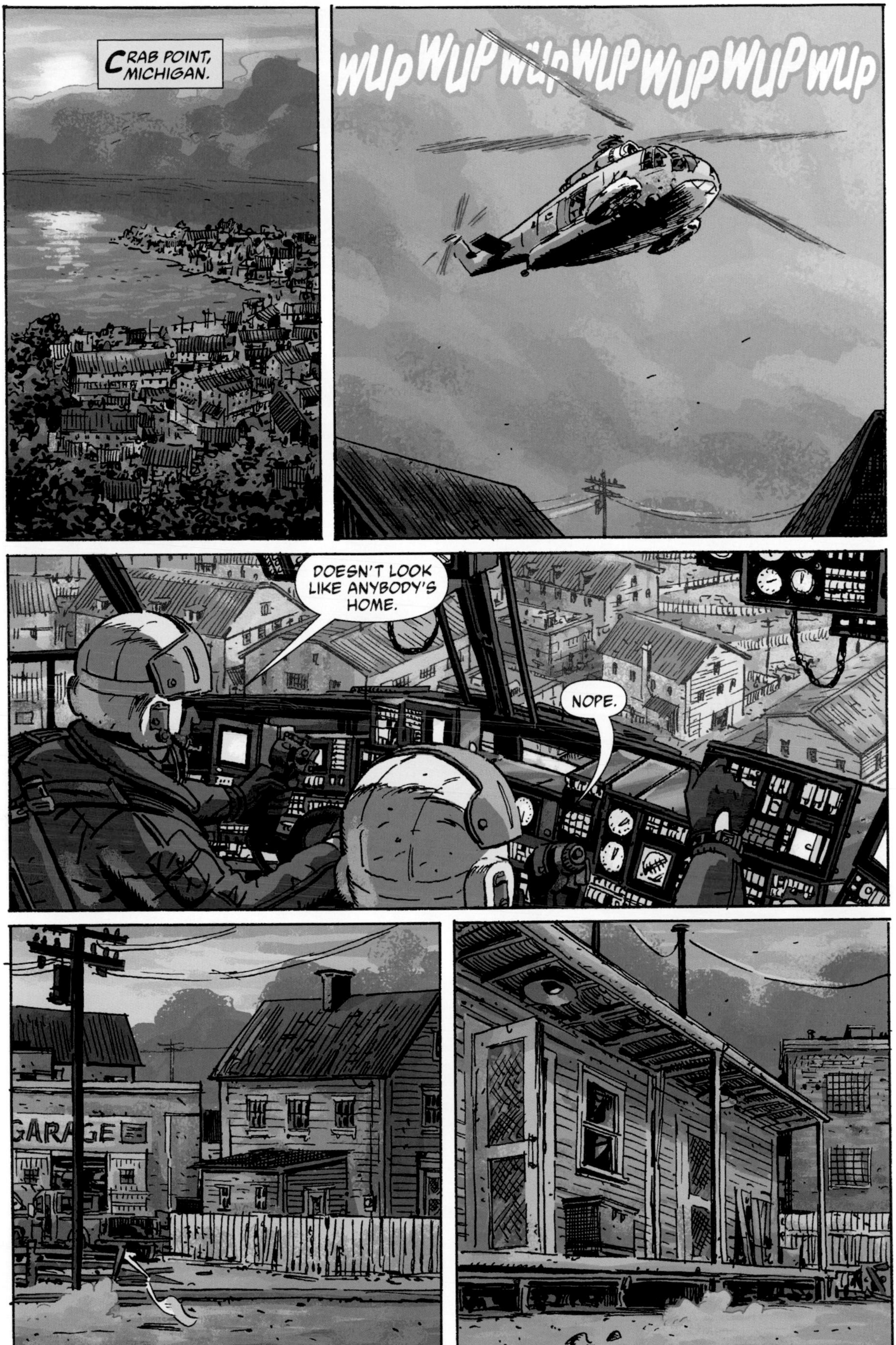

CRAB POINT, MICHIGAN.
WUP WUP WUP WUP WUP WUP WUP
DOESN'T LOOK LIKE ANYBODY'S HOME.
NOPE.
GARAGE

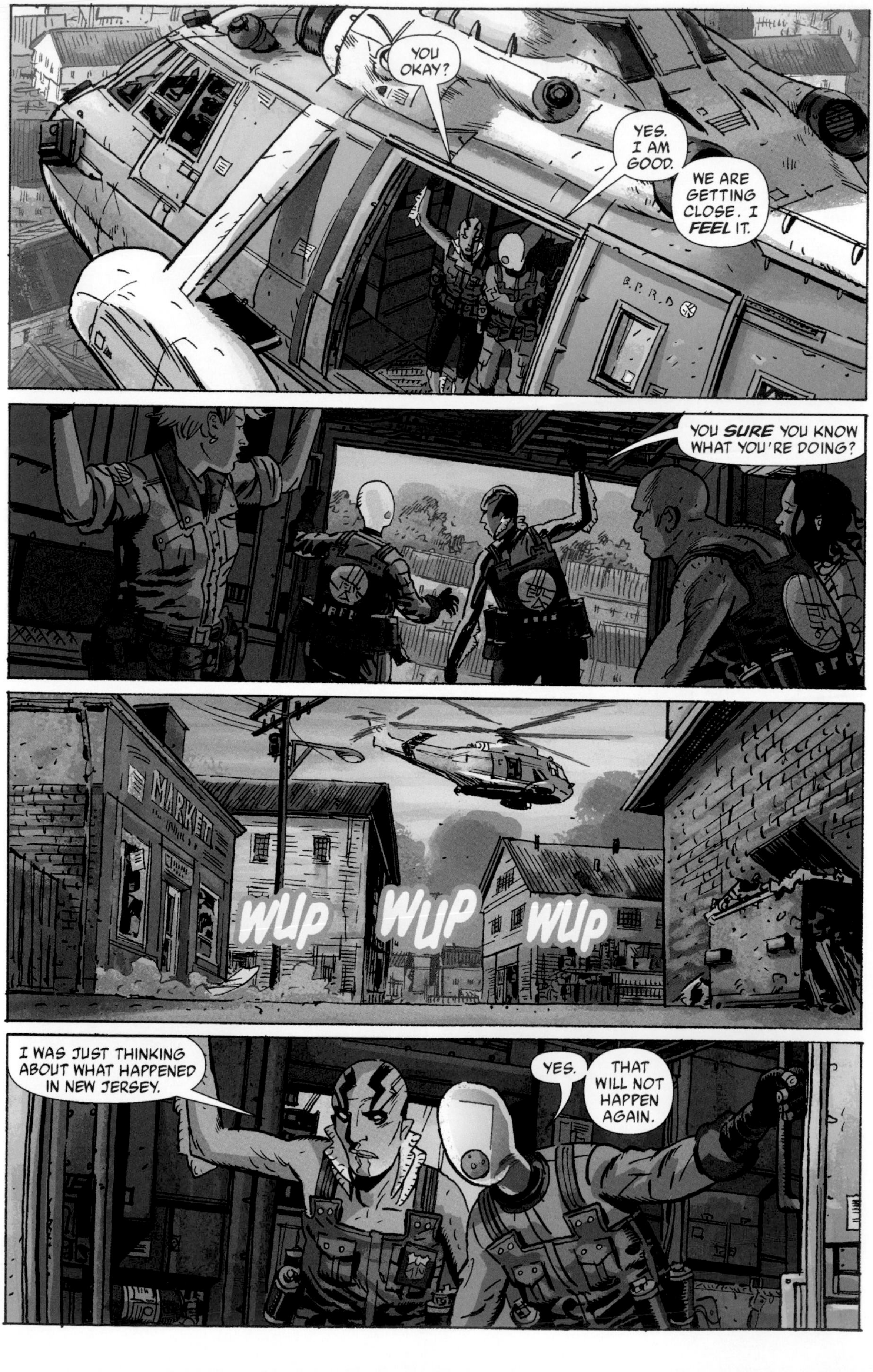
YOU OKAY?
YES. I AM GOOD.
WE ARE GETTING CLOSE. I FEEL IT.
B.P.R.D.
YOU SURE YOU KNOW WHAT YOU'RE DOING?
MARKET
WUP WUP WUP
I WAS JUST THINKING ABOUT WHAT HAPPENED IN NEW JERSEY.
YES.
THAT WILL NOT HAPPEN AGAIN.

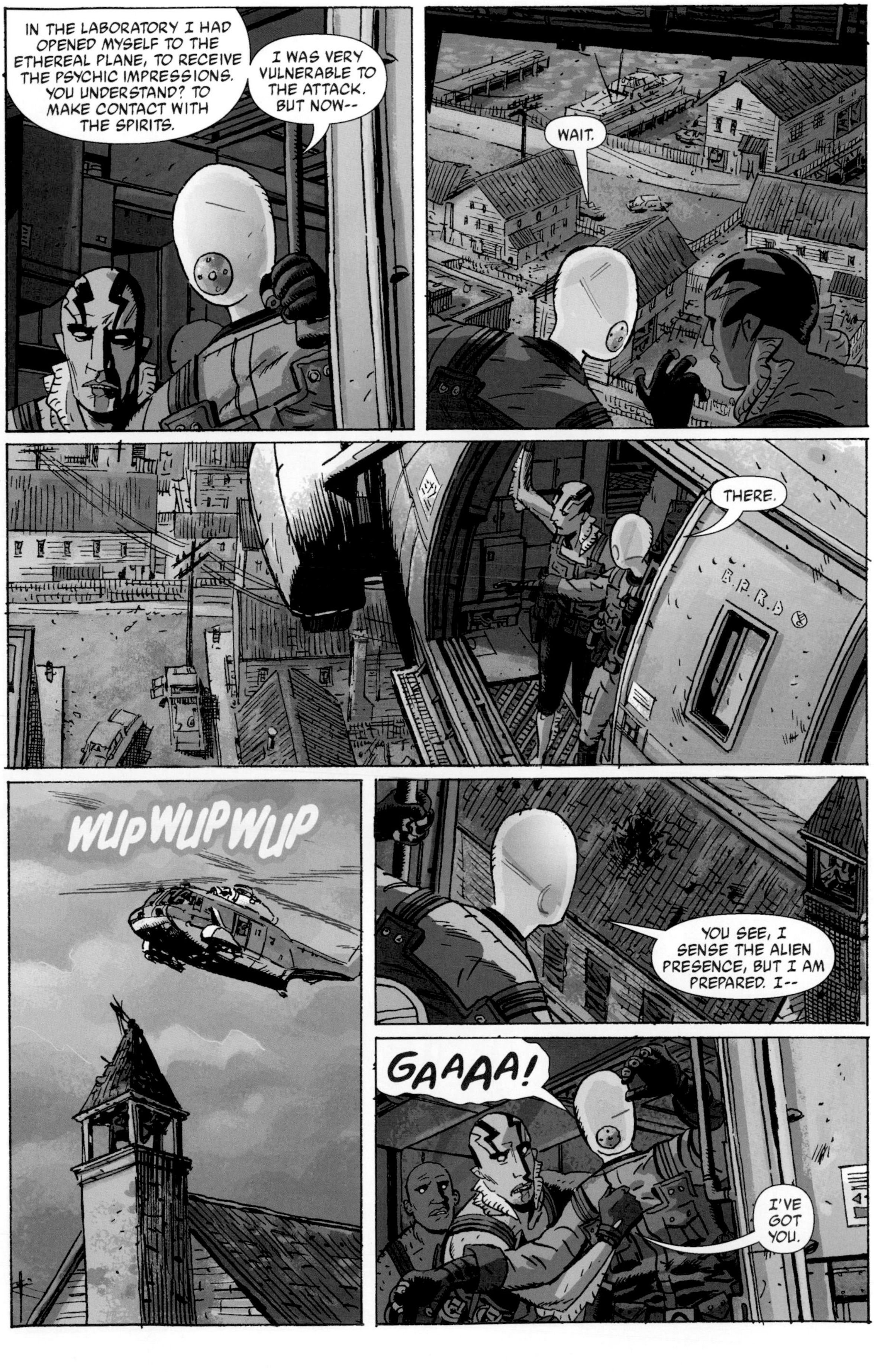
IN THE LABORATORY I HAD OPENED MYSELF TO THE ETHEREAL PLANE, TO RECEIVE THE PSYCHIC IMPRESSIONS. YOU UNDERSTAND? TO MAKE CONTACT WITH THE SPIRITS.
I WAS VERY VULNERABLE TO THE ATTACK. BUT NOW--
WAIT.
THERE.
B.P.R.D.
WUP WUP WUP
YOU SEE, I SENSE THE ALIEN PRESENCE, BUT I AM PREPARED. I--
GAAAA!
I'VE GOT YOU.

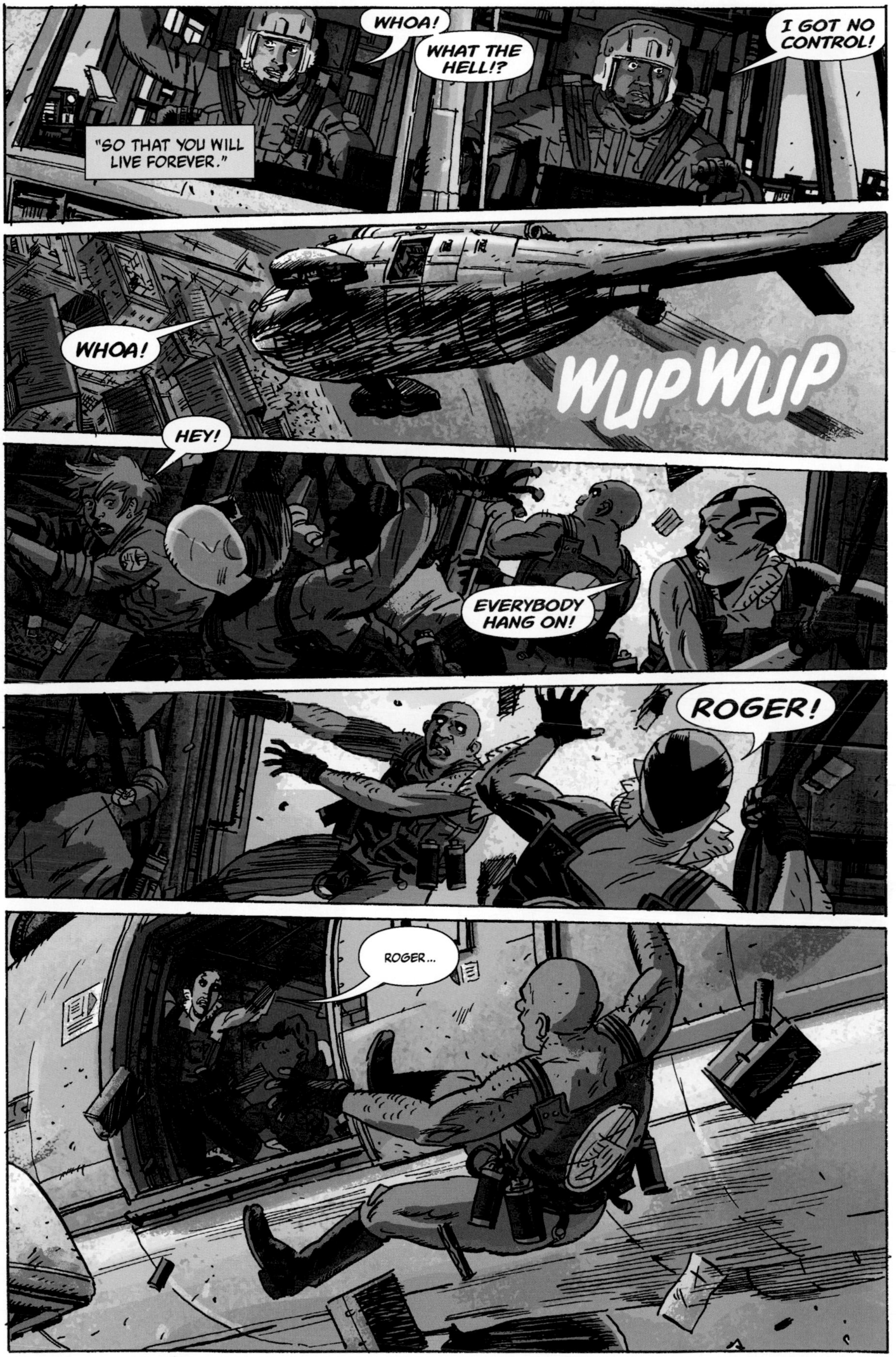
WHOA!
WHAT THE HELL!?
I GOT NO CONTROL!
"SO THAT YOU WILL LIVE FOREVER."
WHOA!
WUP WUP
HEY!
EVERYBODY HANG ON!
ROGER!
ROGER...

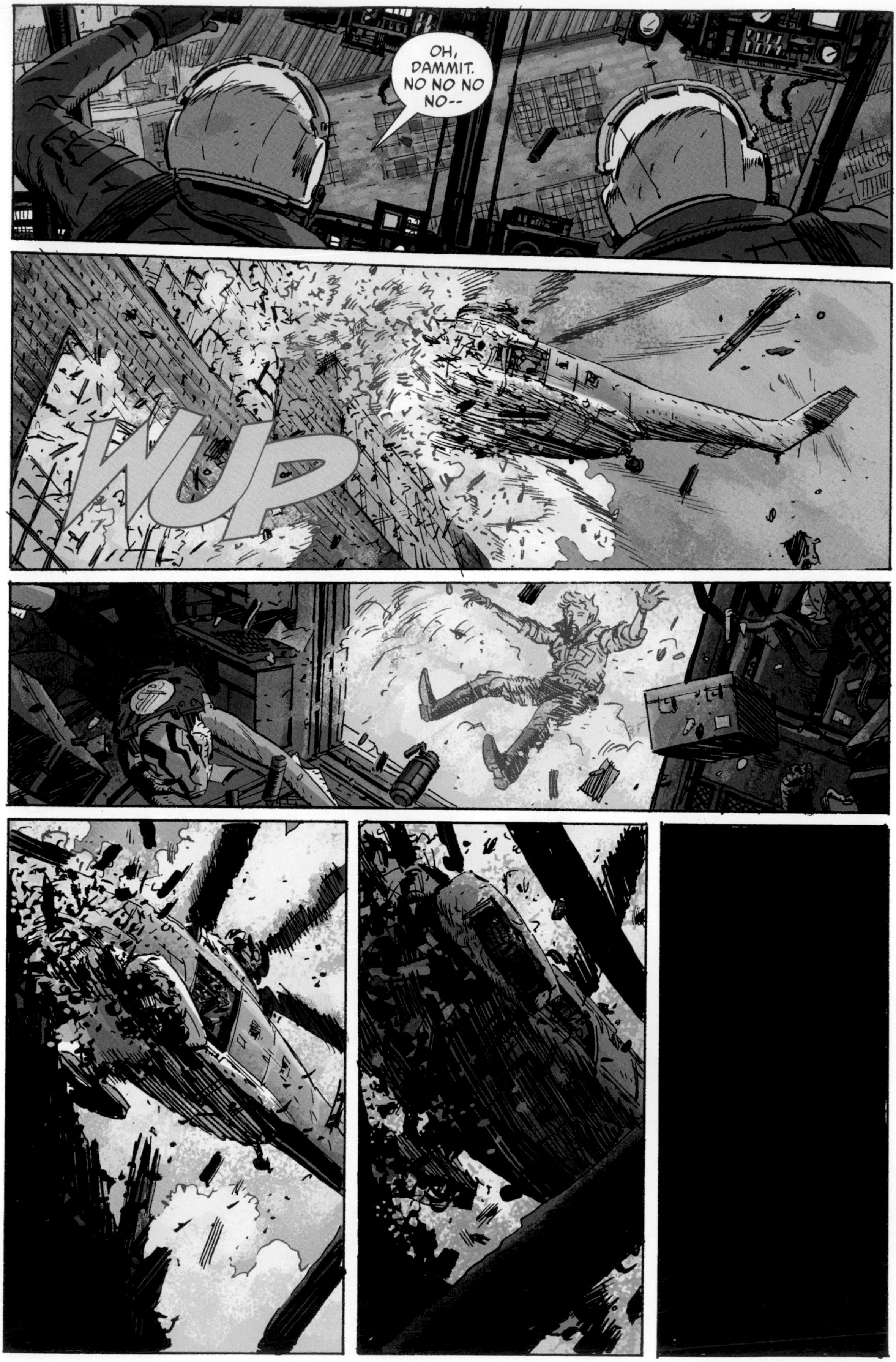
OH, DAMMIT. NO NO NO NO--
WUP

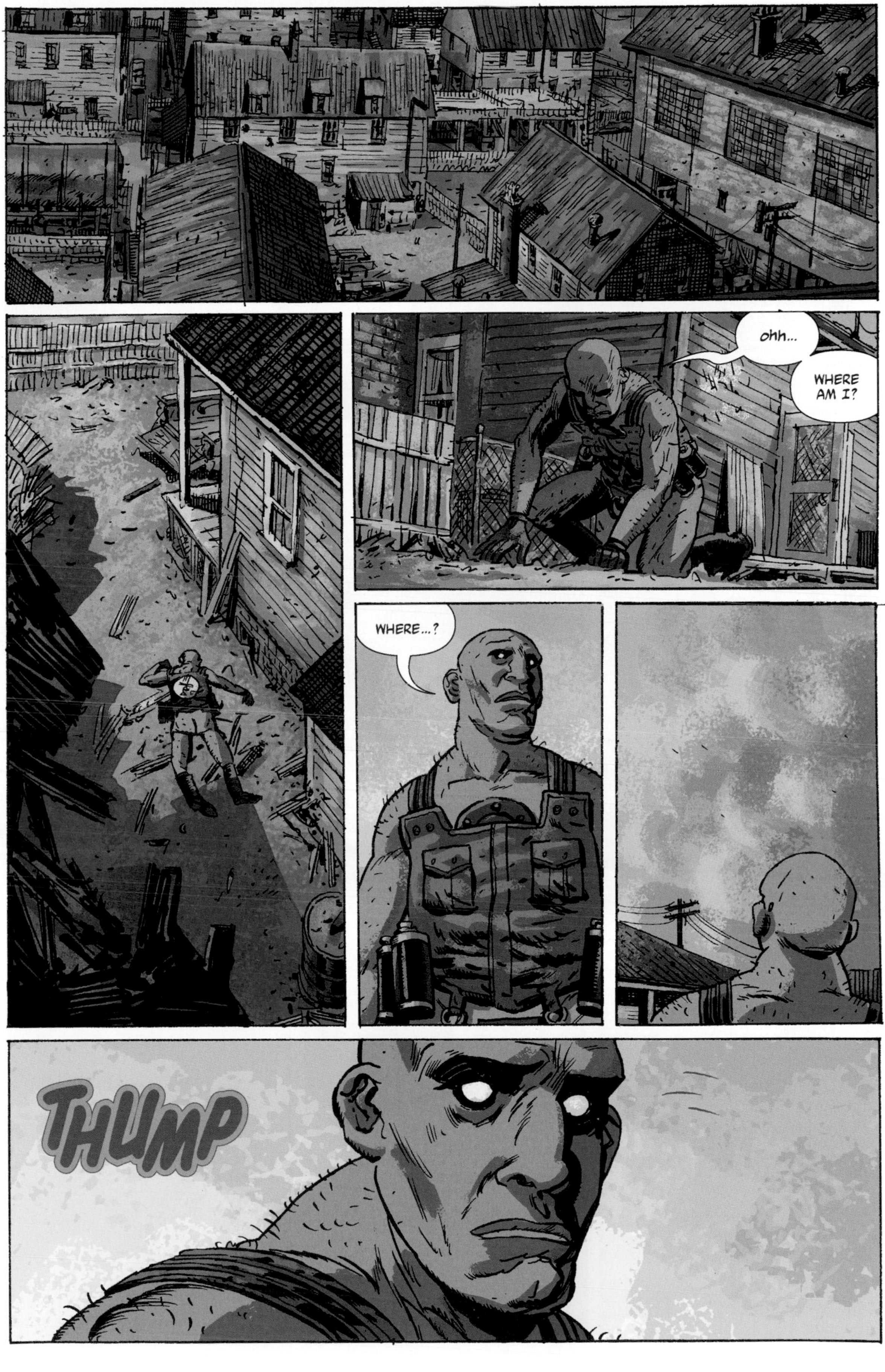
ohh...
WHERE AM I?
WHERE...?
THUMP

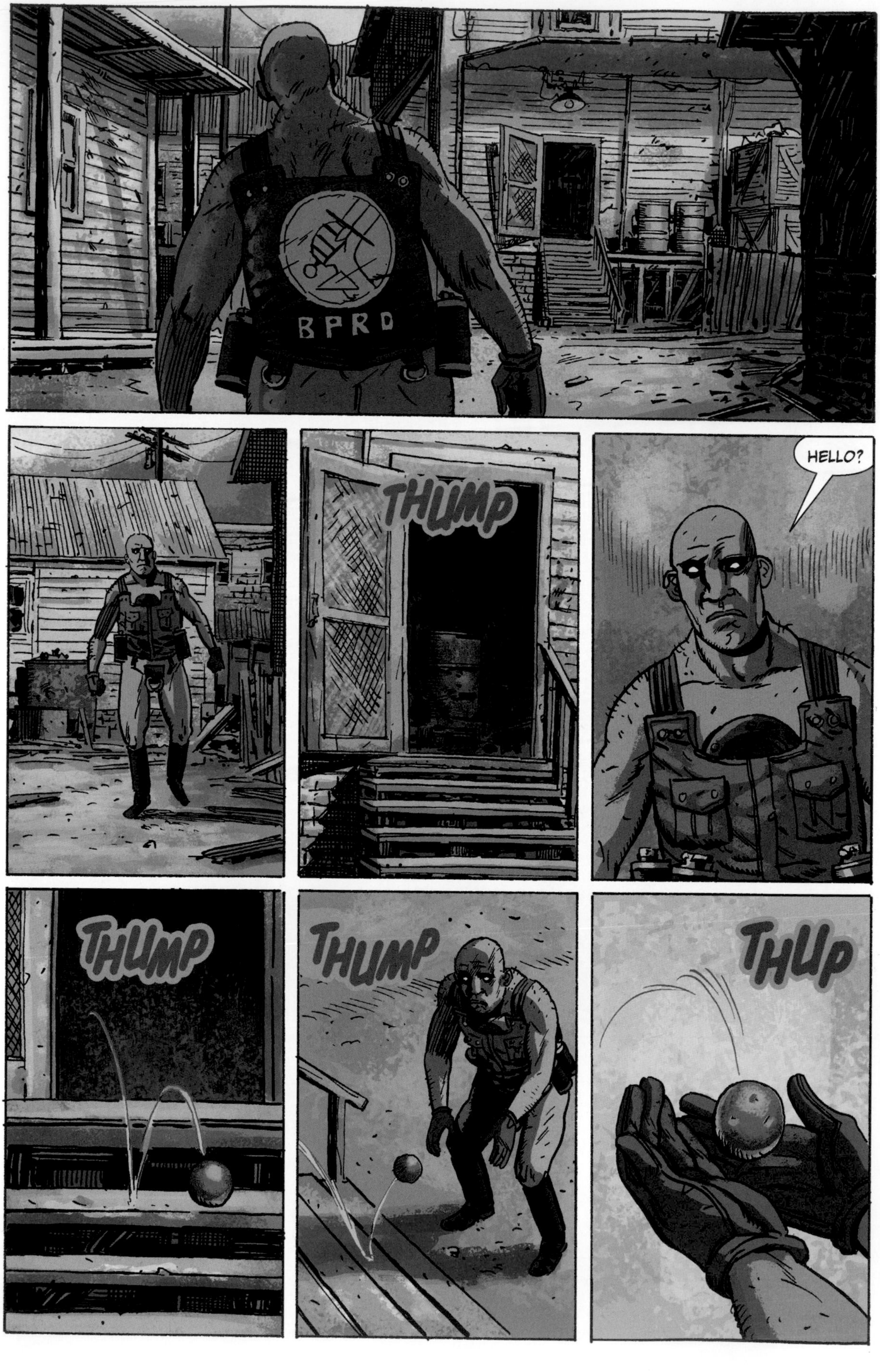
BPRD
THUMP
HELLO?
THUMP
THUMP
THUP

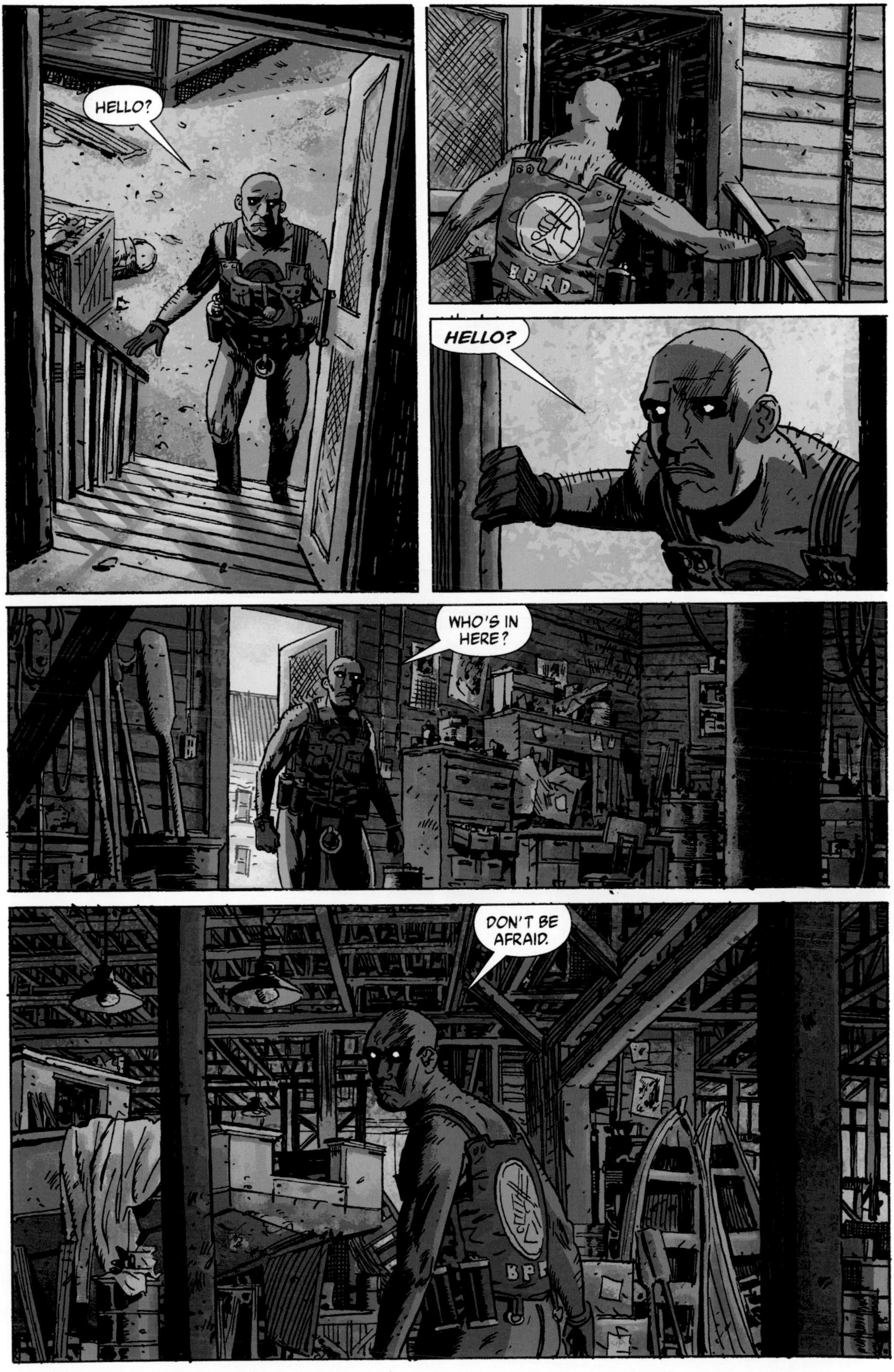
HELLO?
HELLO?
WHO'S IN HERE?
DON'T BE AFRAID.

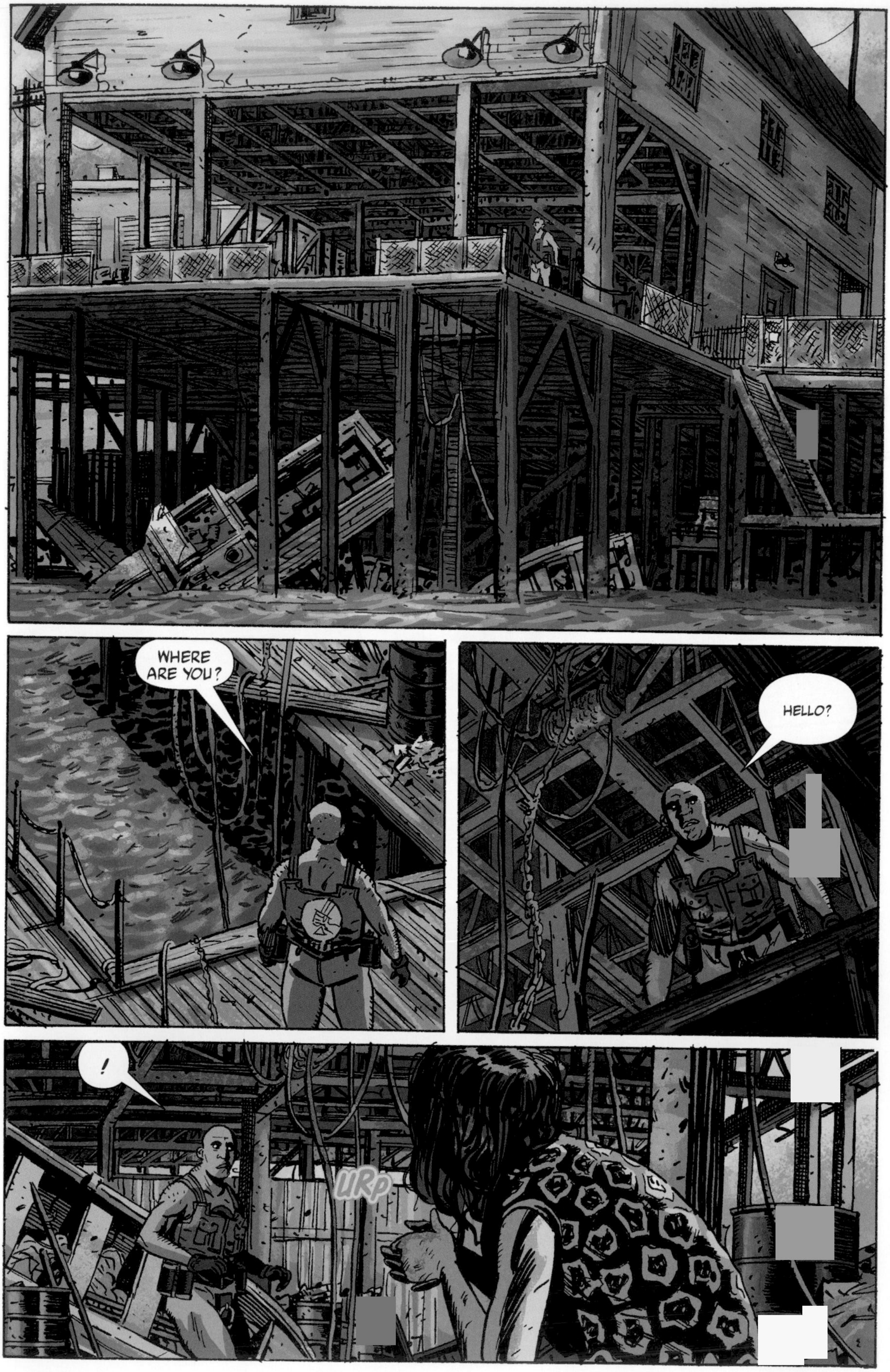
WHERE ARE YOU?
HELLO?
!
URP

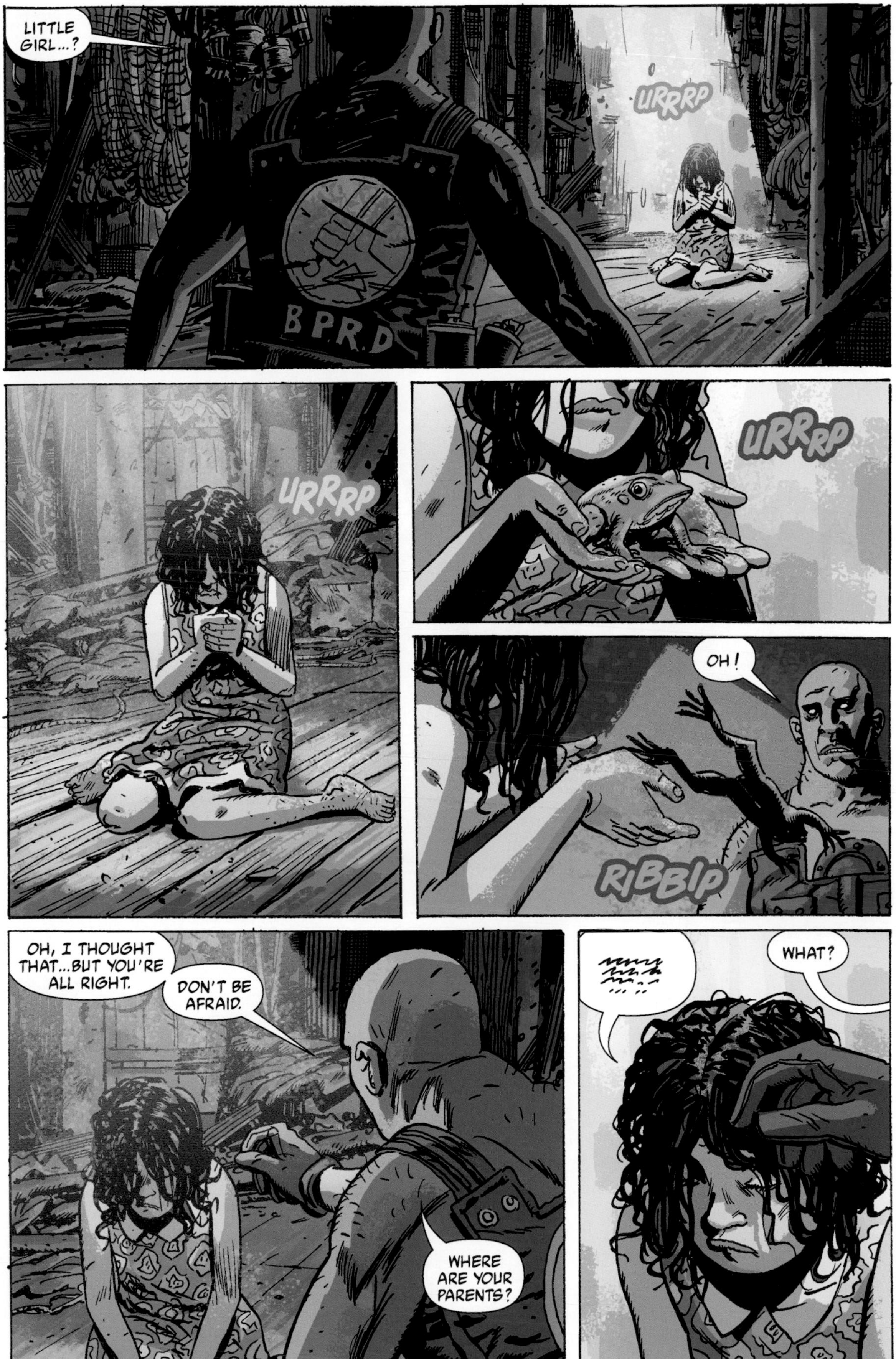

LITTLE GIRL...?
URRRP
URRRP
URRRP
OH!
RIBBIP
OH, I THOUGHT THAT...BUT YOU'RE ALL RIGHT.
DON'T BE AFRAID.
WHERE ARE YOUR PARENTS?
WHAT?

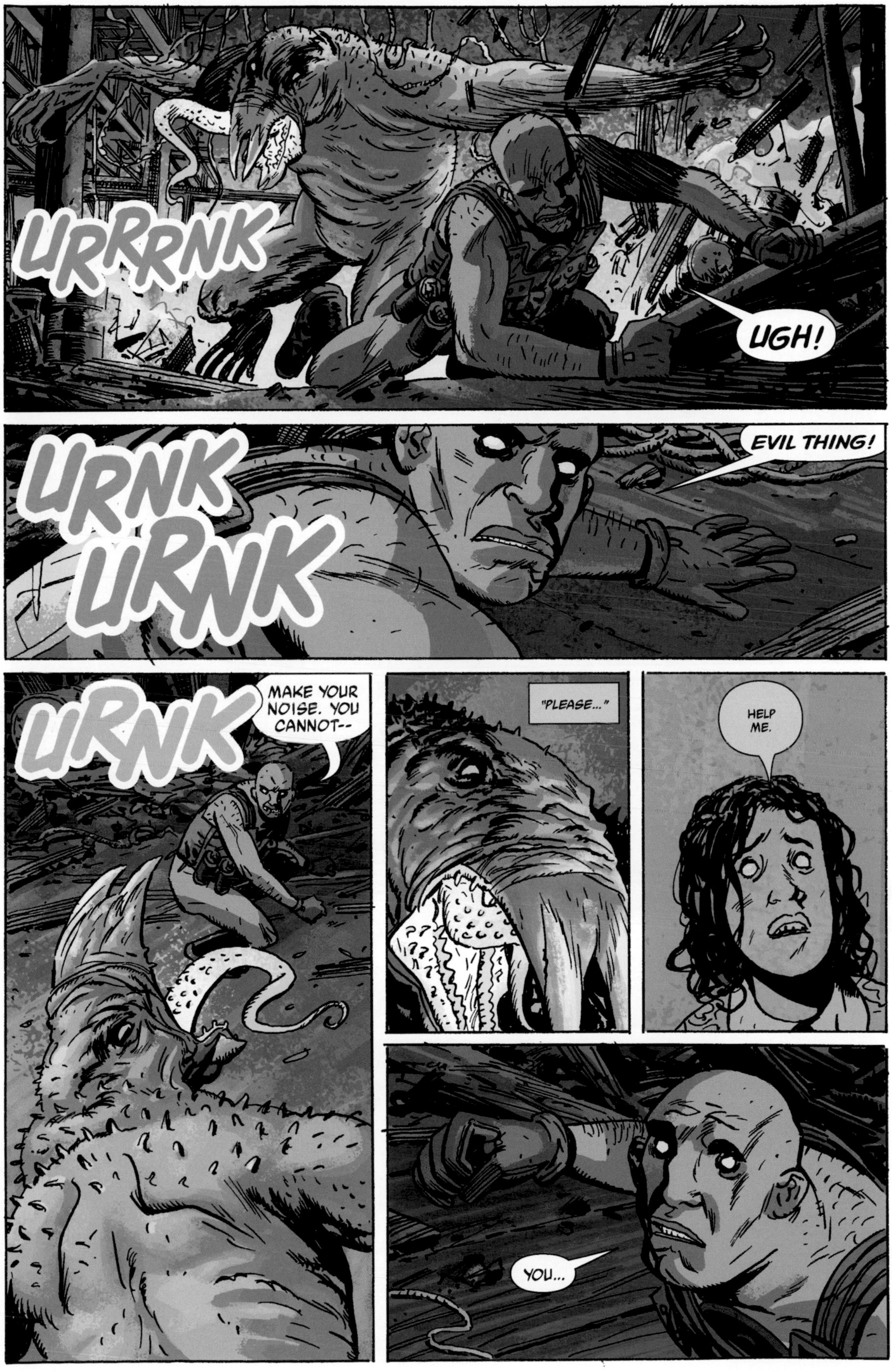
URRRNK
UGH!
URNK
URNK
EVIL THING!
URNK
MAKE YOUR NOISE. YOU CANNOT--
"PLEASE..."
HELP ME.
YOU...

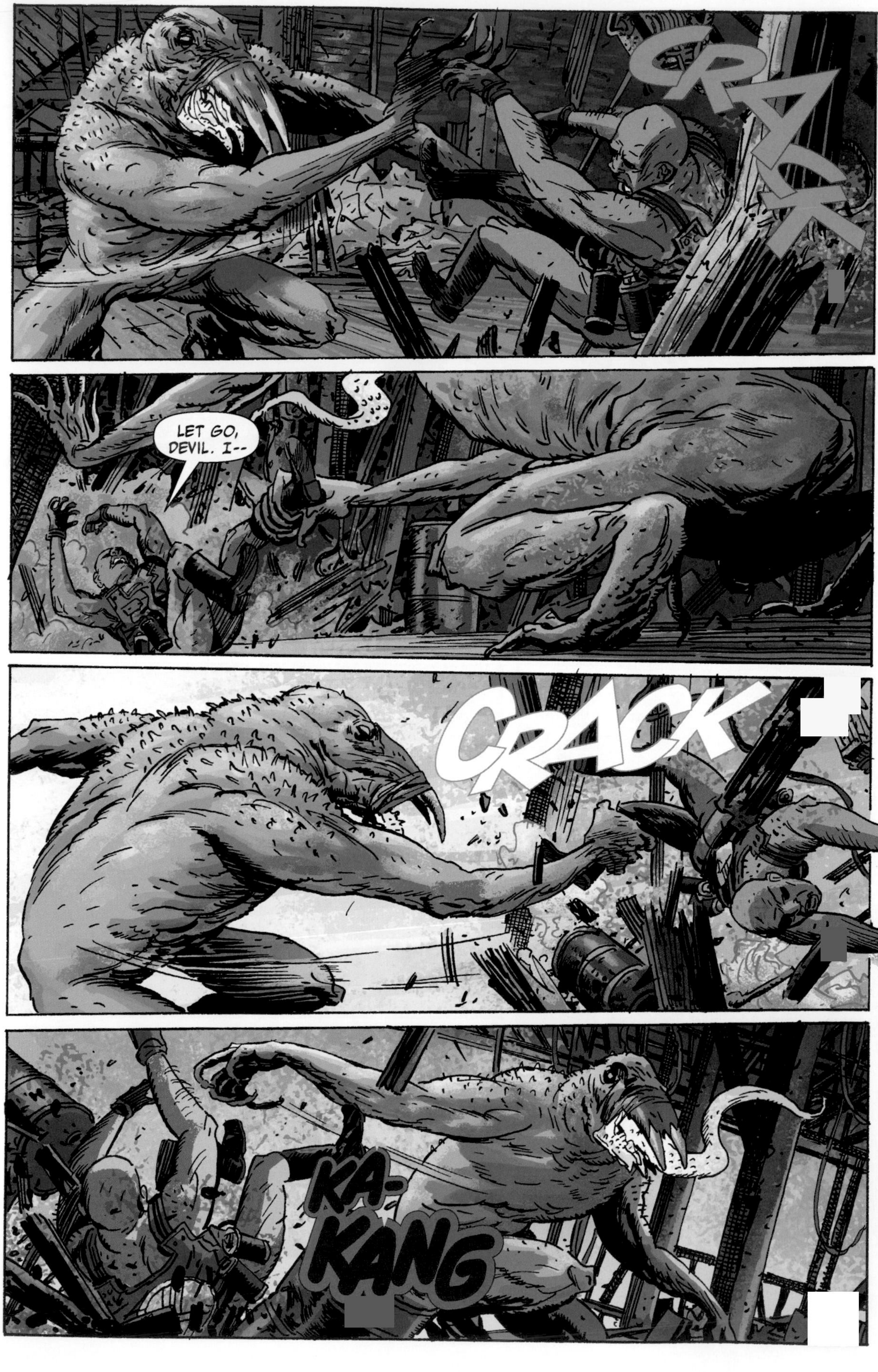
CRACK
LET GO, DEVIL. I--
CRACK
KA-KANG

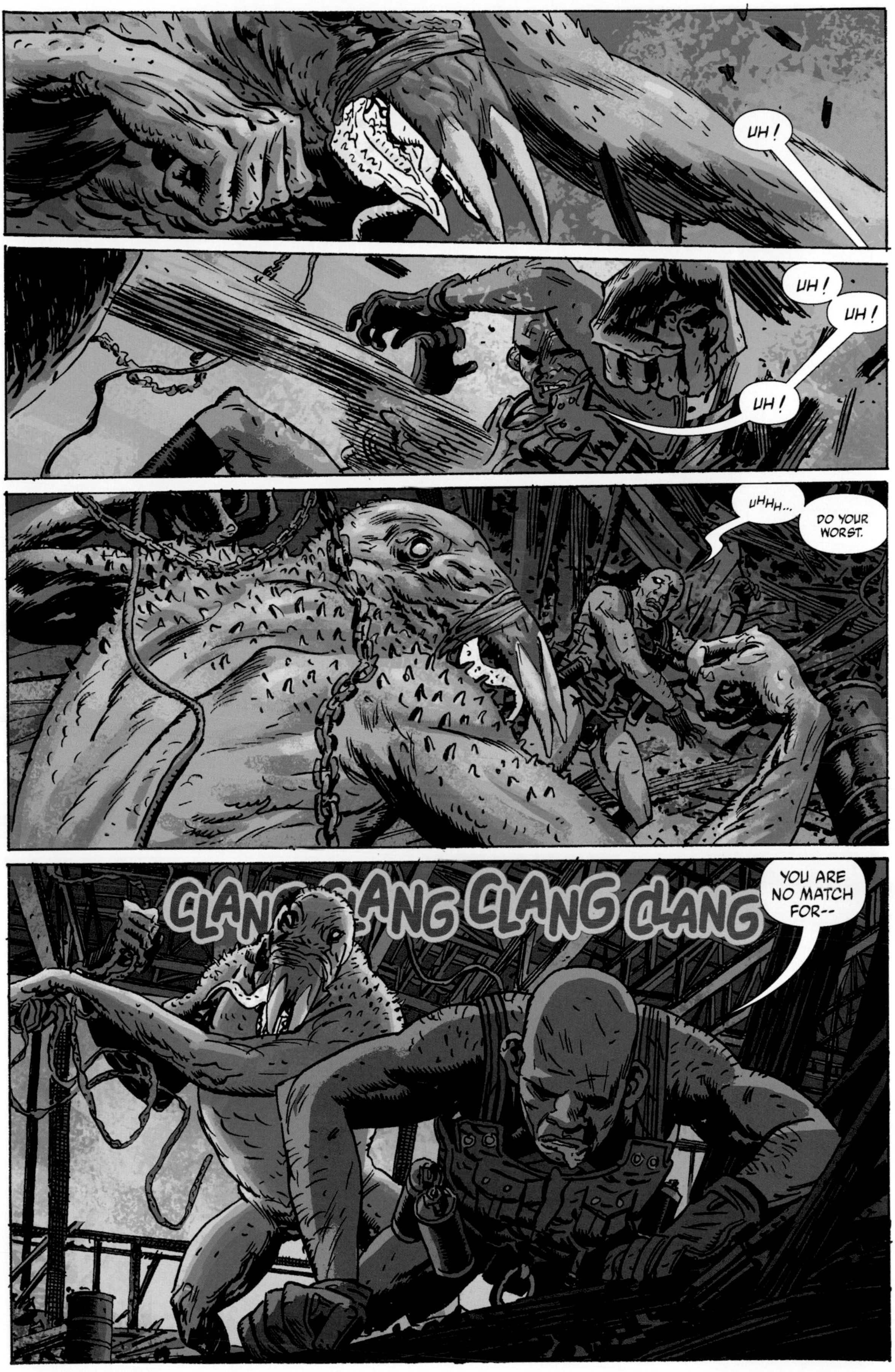
UH!
UH!
UH!
UH!
UHHH...
DO YOUR WORST.
CLANG CLANG CLANG CLANG
YOU ARE NO MATCH FOR--

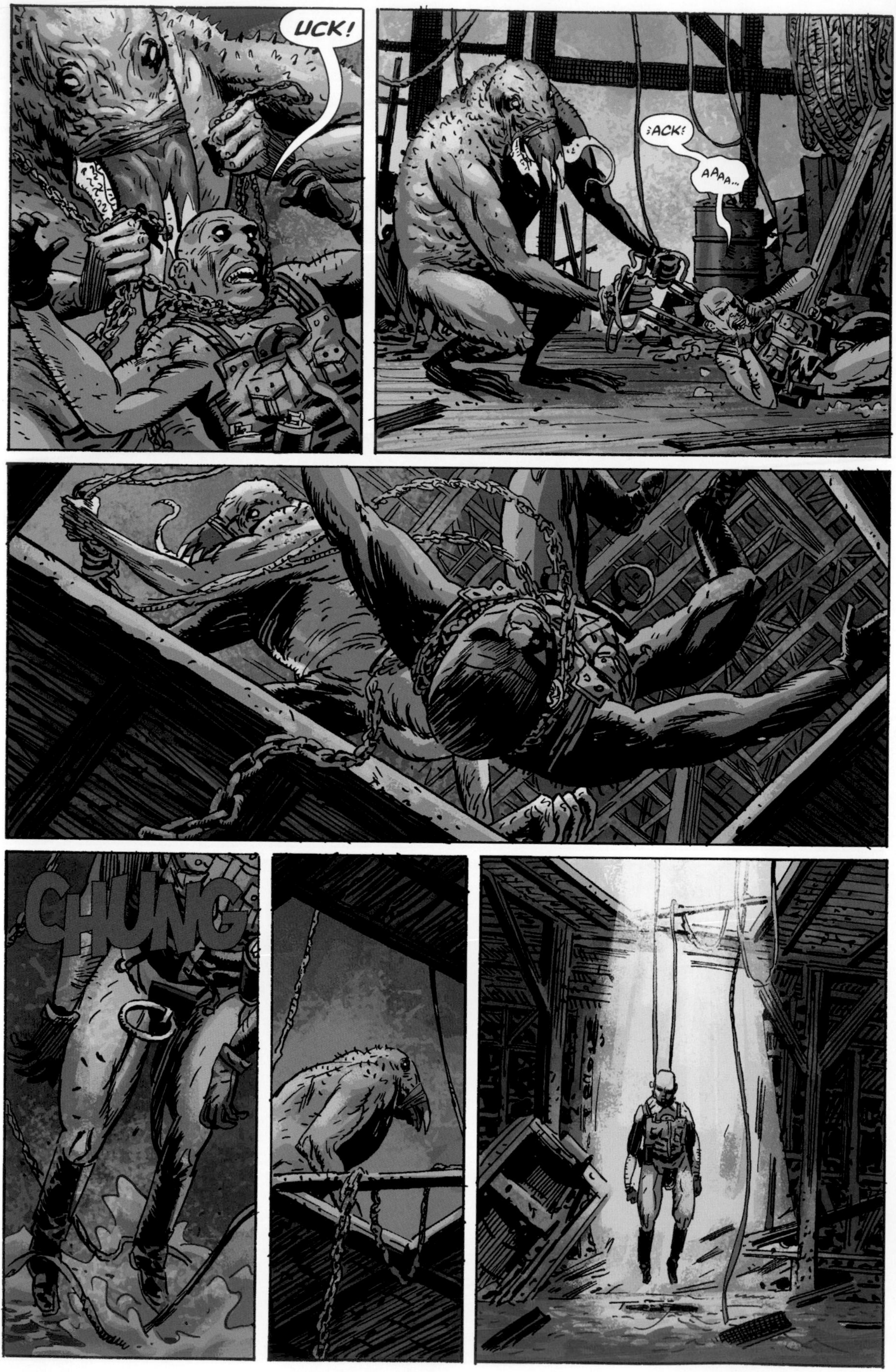
UCK!
ACK!
AAAA...
CHUNG

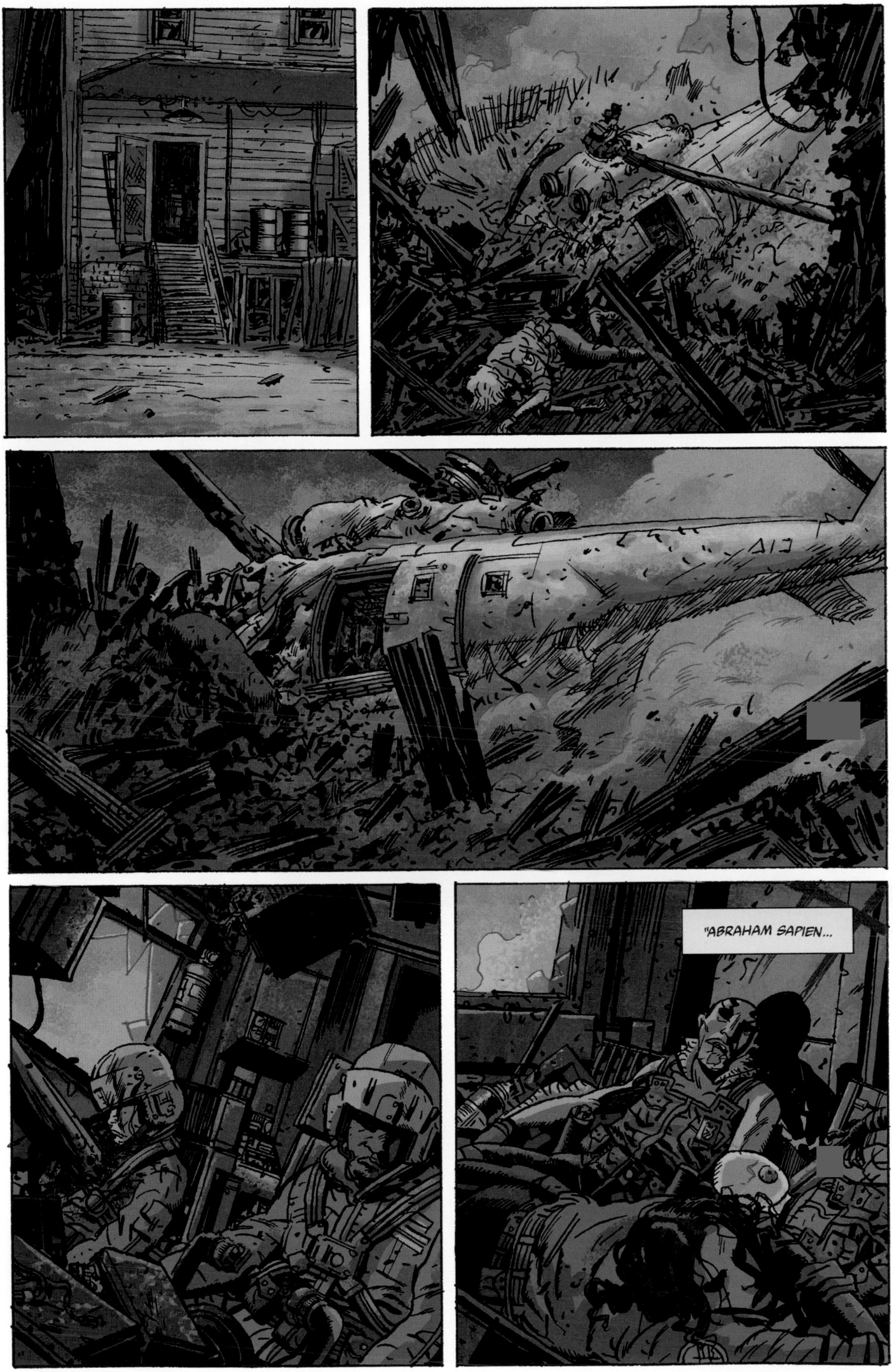
"ABRAHAM SAPIEN...

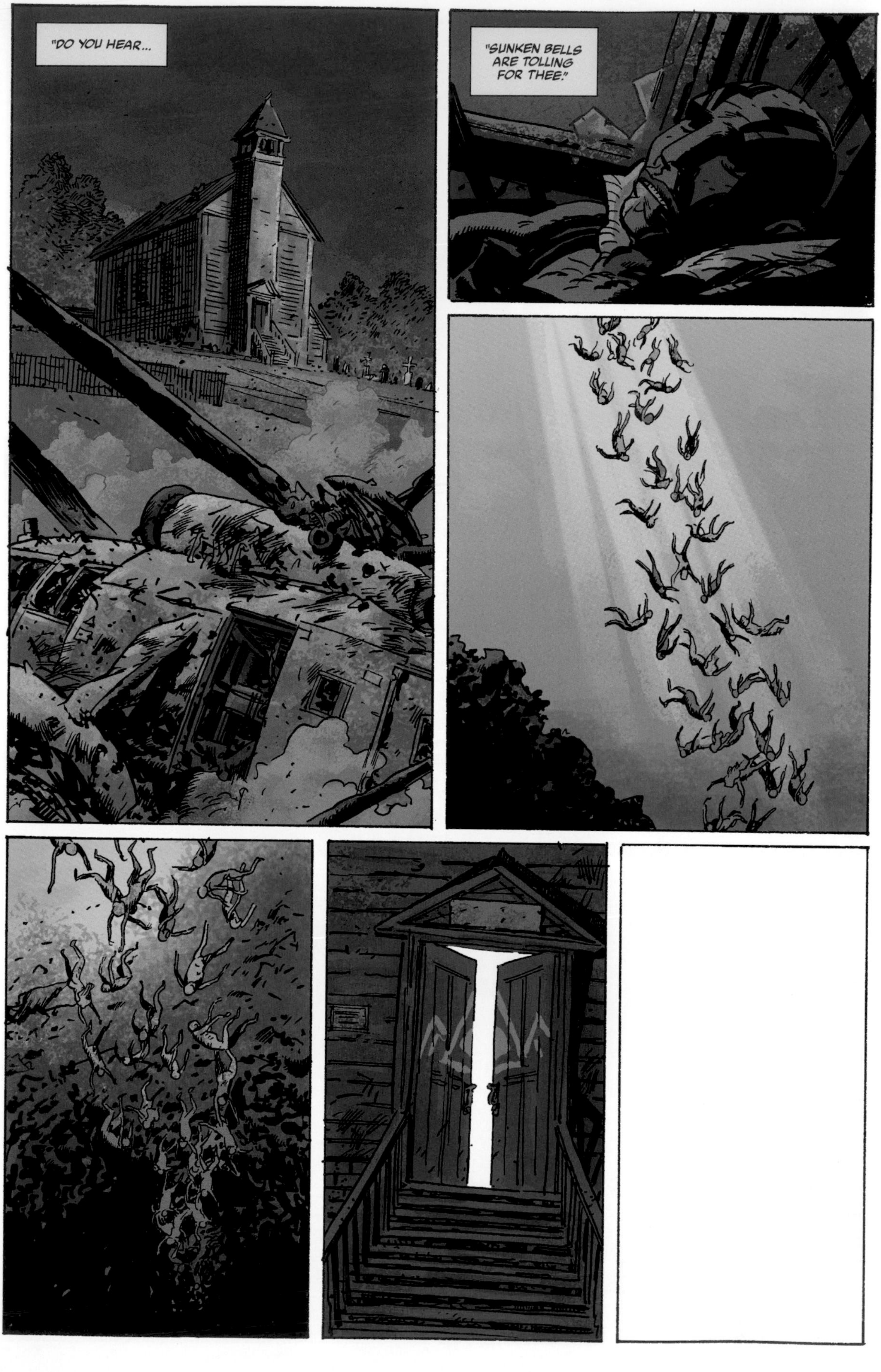
"DO YOU HEAR...
"SUNKEN BELLS ARE TOLLING FOR THEE."

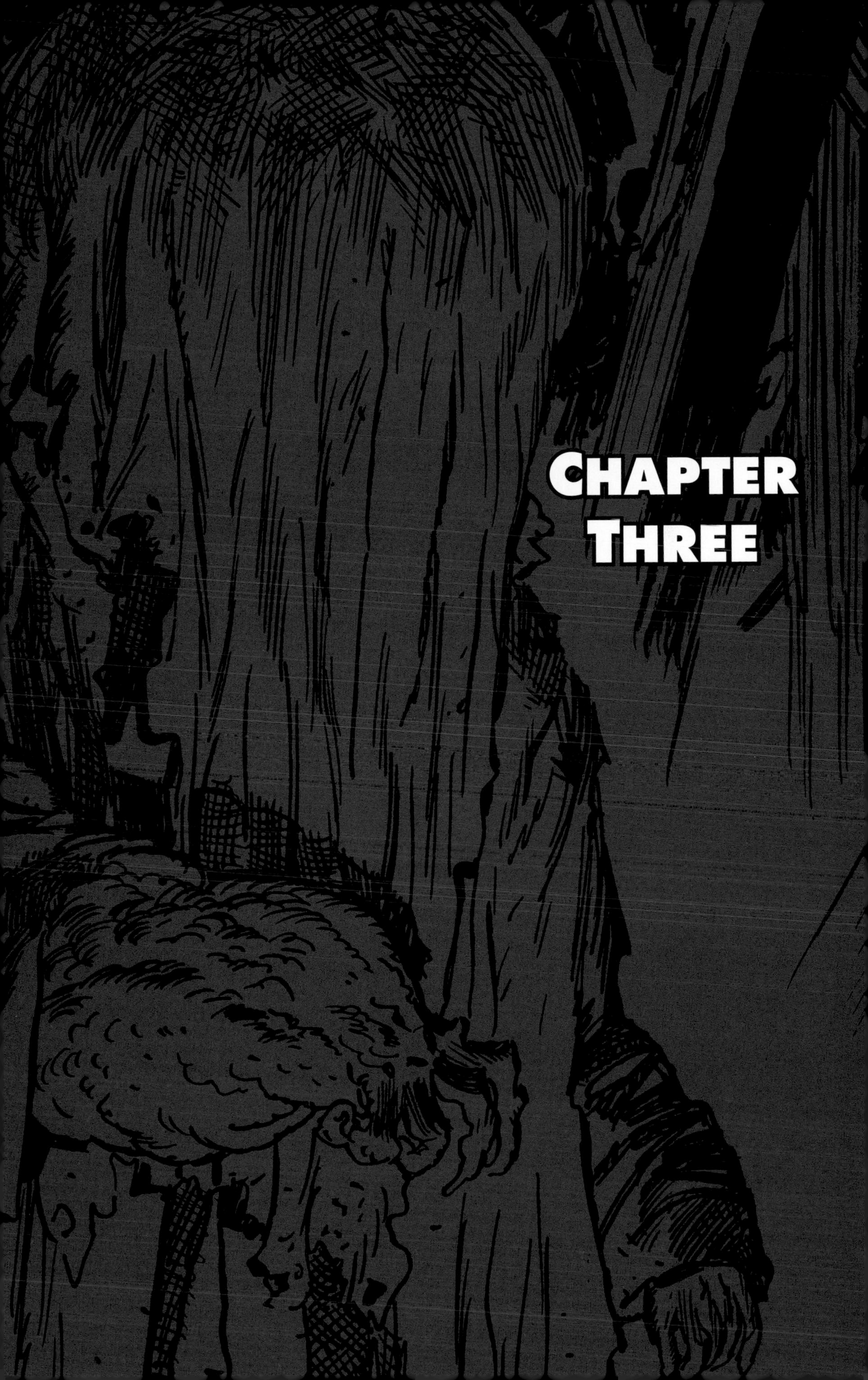
CHAPTER
THREE

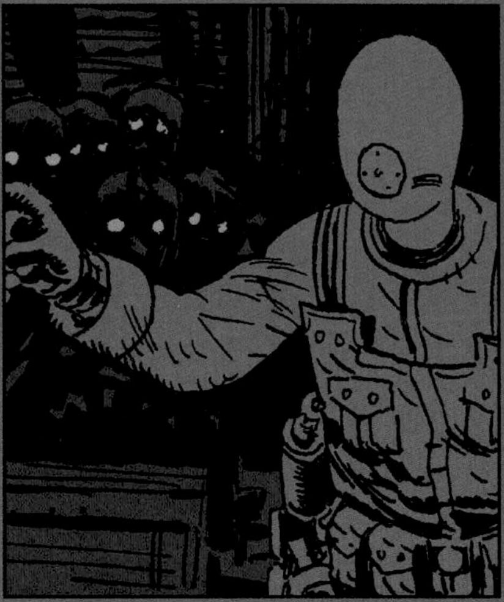

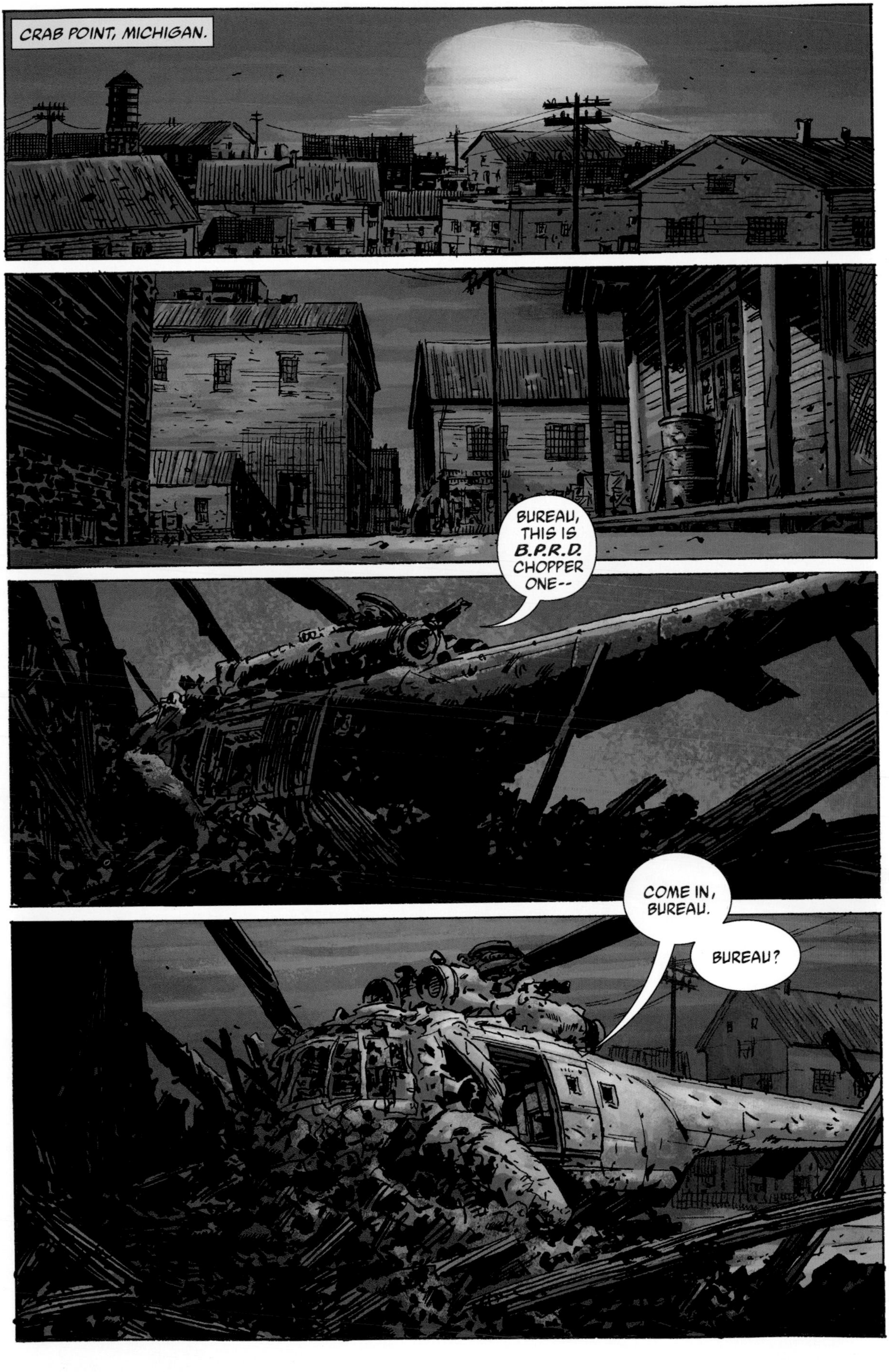
CRAB POINT, MICHIGAN.
BUREAU, THIS IS B.P.R.D. CHOPPER ONE--
COME IN, BUREAU.
BUREAU?

B.P.R.D. HEADQUARTERS.

FAIRFIELD, CONNECTICUT.

ANYTHING YET?

WE HAD A SIGNAL FOR A SECOND. IT *MIGHT* HAVE BEEN KATE. I COULDN'T MAKE OUT WHAT SHE WAS SAYING.

I THINK WE NEED TO SEND IN MORE AGENTS.

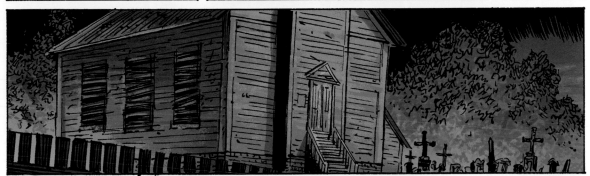

LET'S GIVE THEM ANOTHER HOUR, BUT CONTACT LOCAL AUTHORITY AND HAVE ALL ROADS IN AND OUT OF THAT PLACE SHUT DOWN. AND HAVE OUR PEOPLE STANDING BY.

YES, SIR.

THE NEW TEMPLE OF MYSTERIES
ESTABLISHED 1934

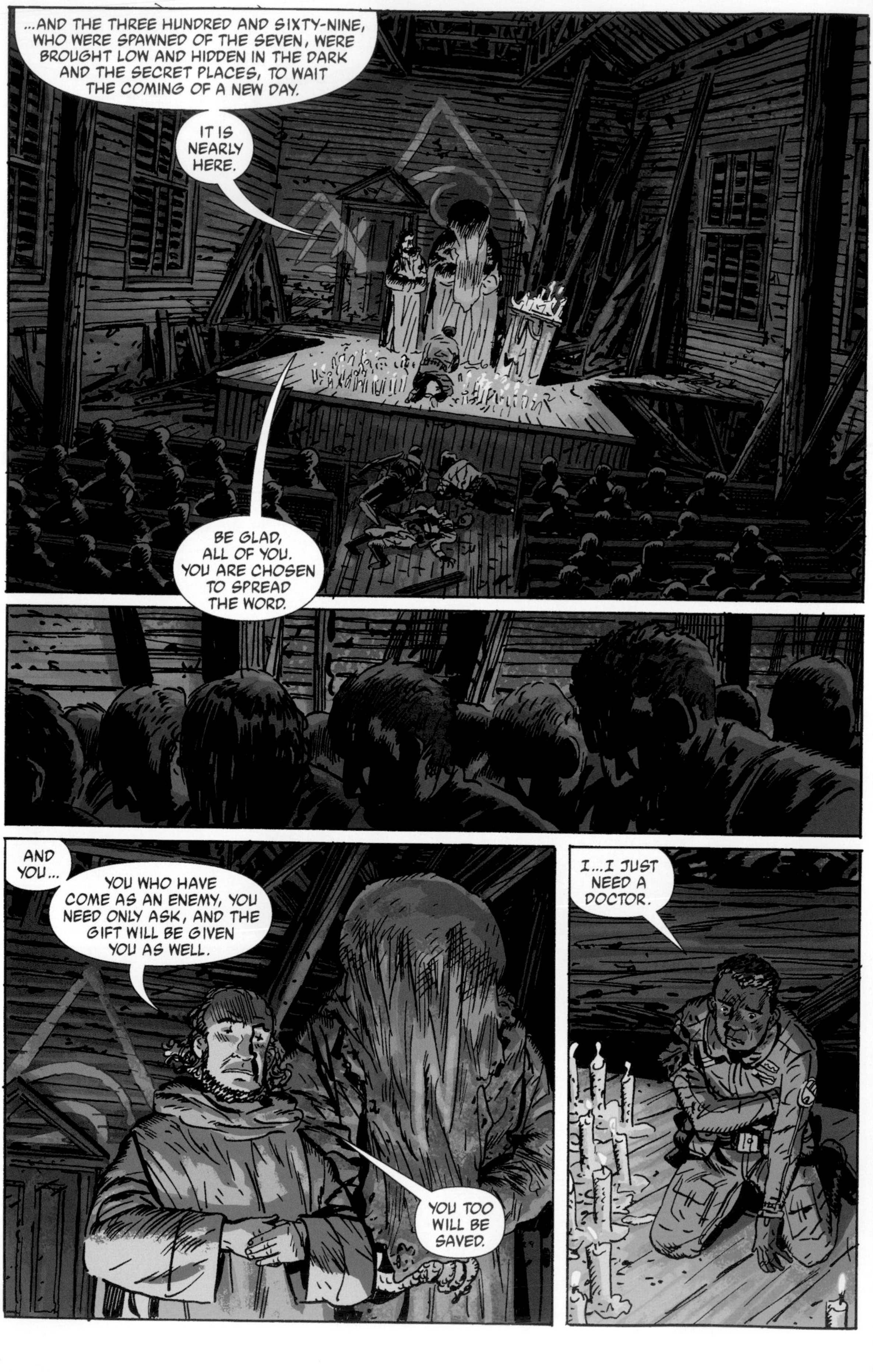
...AND THE THREE HUNDRED AND SIXTY-NINE, WHO WERE SPAWNED OF THE SEVEN, WERE BROUGHT LOW AND HIDDEN IN THE DARK AND THE SECRET PLACES, TO WAIT THE COMING OF A NEW DAY.
IT IS NEARLY HERE.
BE GLAD, ALL OF YOU. YOU ARE CHOSEN TO SPREAD THE WORD.
AND YOU...
YOU WHO HAVE COME AS AN ENEMY, YOU NEED ONLY ASK, AND THE GIFT WILL BE GIVEN YOU AS WELL.
YOU TOO WILL BE SAVED.
I...I JUST NEED A DOCTOR.

TO MEND FLESH AND BONE? MY OWN HANDS COULD ACCOMPLISH THAT. BUT WHY?

YOU WOULD STILL BE ONLY A MAN.

ABE...?

YEAH...

OPEN YOUR EYES.

I...

SEE THE THING THAT IS BEING OFFERED YOU...

TAKE IT.

FEEL THE EARTH TREMBLE BENEATH YOU. SMELL THE BLOOD ON THE WIND. *THE PLAGUE THAT IS COMING WILL PURGE THE EARTH OF MAN.*

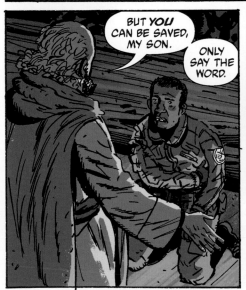

BUT *YOU* CAN BE SAVED, MY SON.

ONLY SAY THE WORD.

LEAVE HIM ALONE!

WILSON, DON'T LISTEN TO HIM!

QUIET. I WILL DEAL WITH YOU SOON ENOUGH.

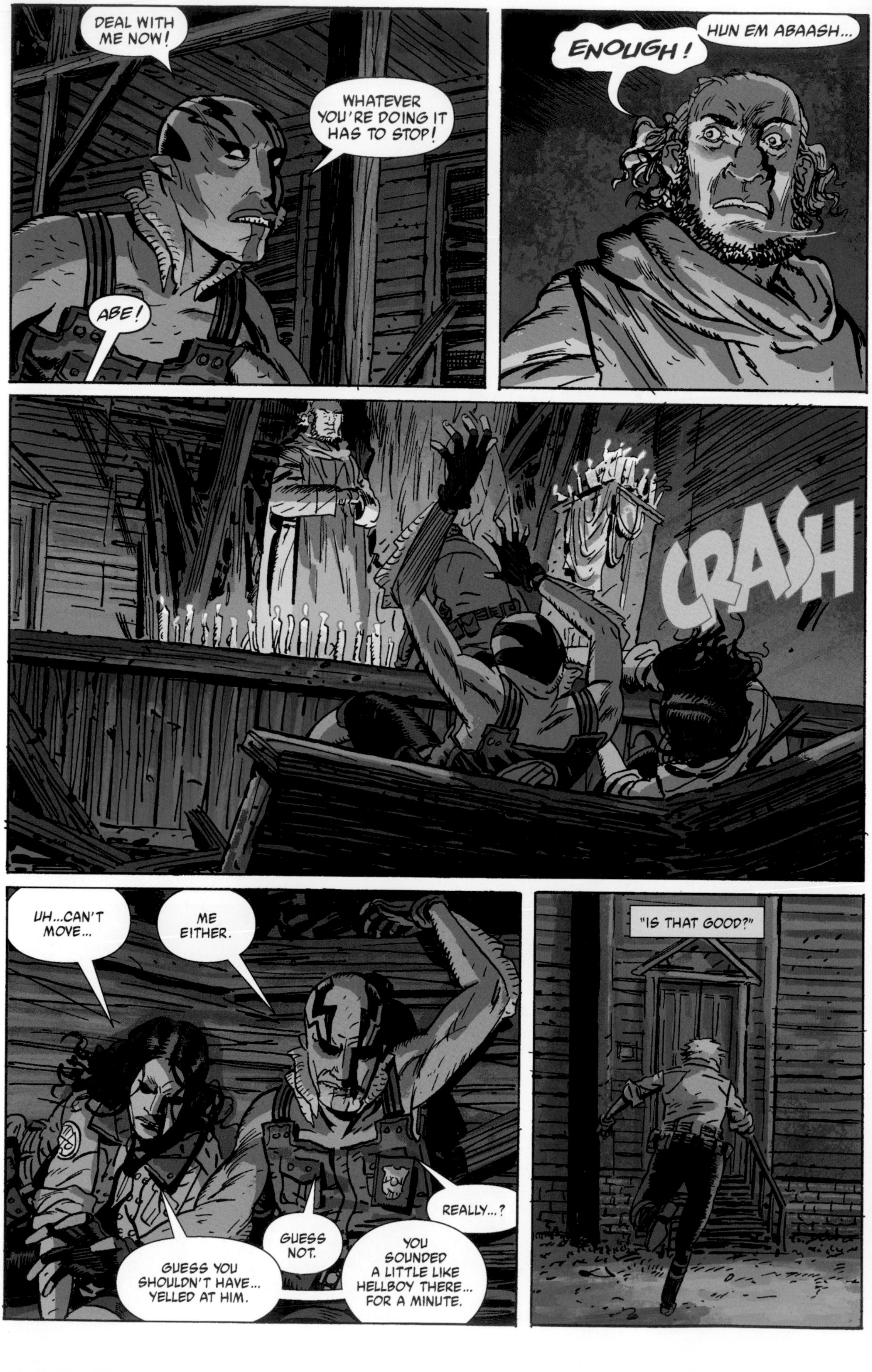
DEAL WITH ME NOW!
WHATEVER YOU'RE DOING IT HAS TO STOP!
ABE!
HUN EM ABAASH...
ENOUGH!
CRASH
UH...CAN'T MOVE...
ME EITHER.
GUESS YOU SHOULDN'T HAVE... YELLED AT HIM.
GUESS NOT.
REALLY...?
YOU SOUNDED A LITTLE LIKE HELLBOY THERE... FOR A MINUTE.
"IS THAT GOOD?"

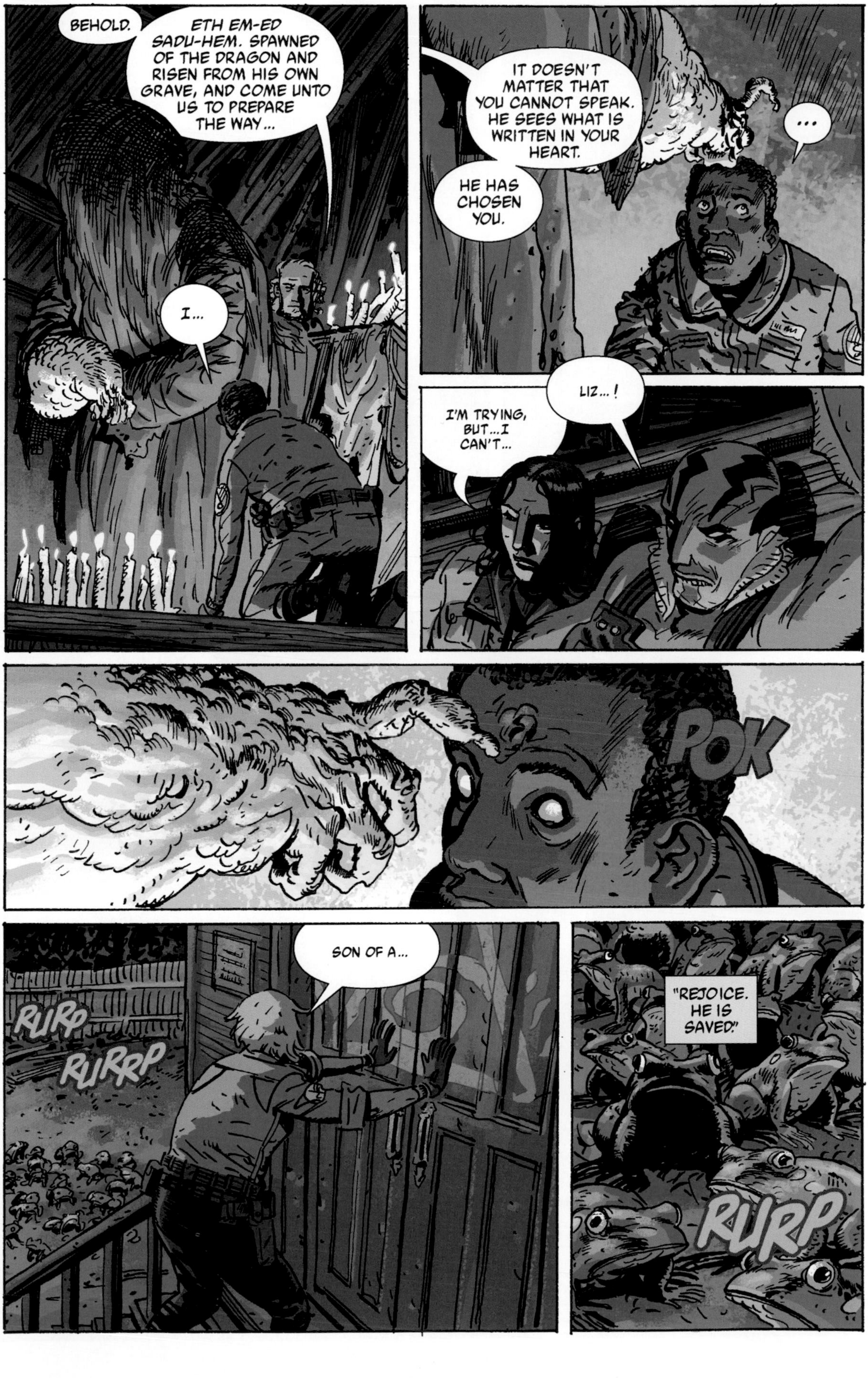
BEHOLD.
ETH EM-ED SADU-HEM. SPAWNED OF THE DRAGON AND RISEN FROM HIS OWN GRAVE, AND COME UNTO US TO PREPARE THE WAY...
I...
IT DOESN'T MATTER THAT YOU CANNOT SPEAK. HE SEES WHAT IS WRITTEN IN YOUR HEART.
HE HAS CHOSEN YOU.
...
I'M TRYING, BUT...I CAN'T...
LIZ...!
POK
RURP
RURRP
SON OF A...
"REJOICE. HE IS SAVED."
RURP

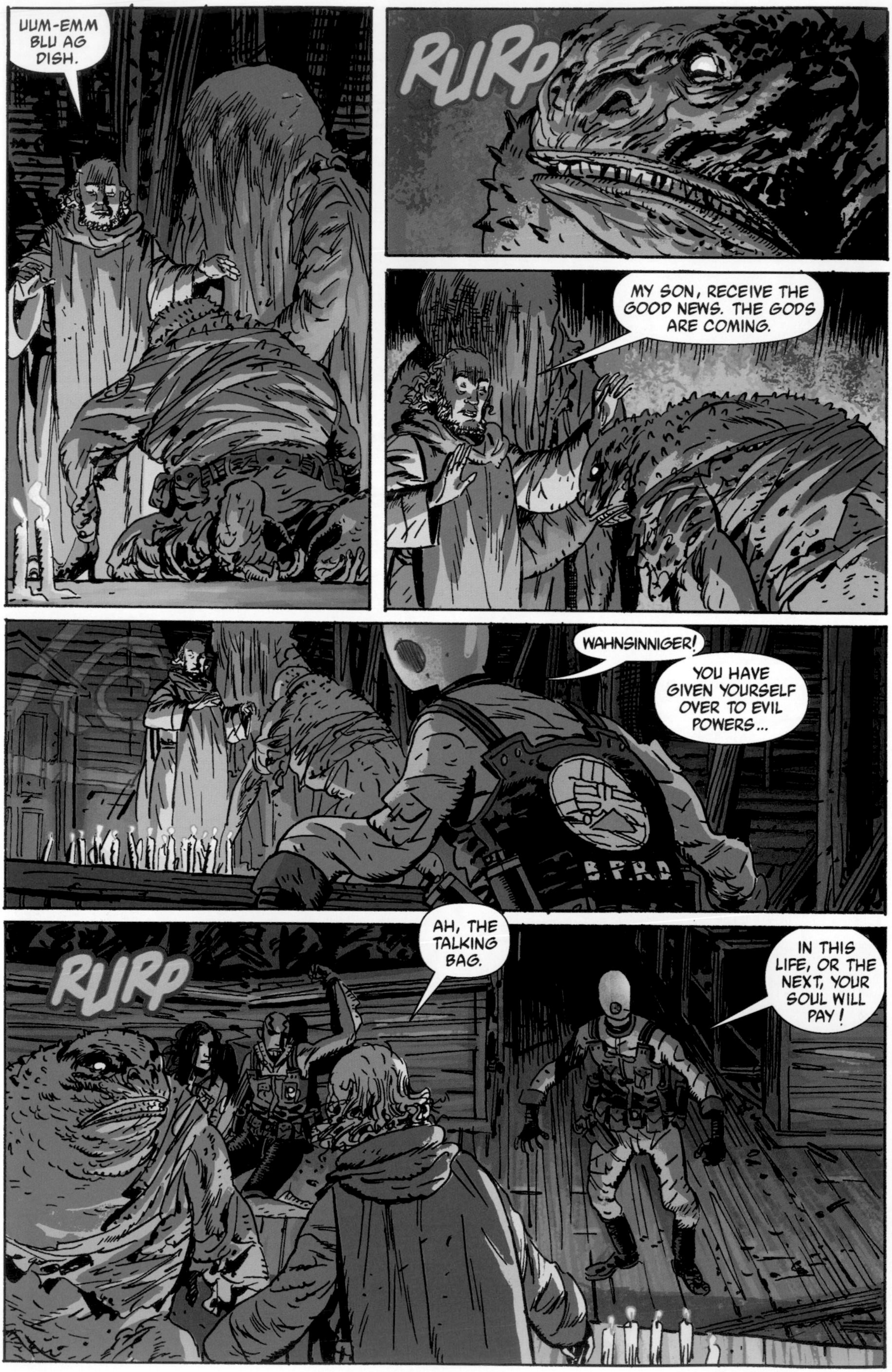
UUM-EMM BLU AG DISH.
RURP
MY SON, RECEIVE THE GOOD NEWS. THE GODS ARE COMING.
WAHNSINNIGER!
YOU HAVE GIVEN YOURSELF OVER TO EVIL POWERS...
B.P.R.D.
RURP
AH, THE TALKING BAG.
IN THIS LIFE, OR THE NEXT, YOUR SOUL WILL PAY!

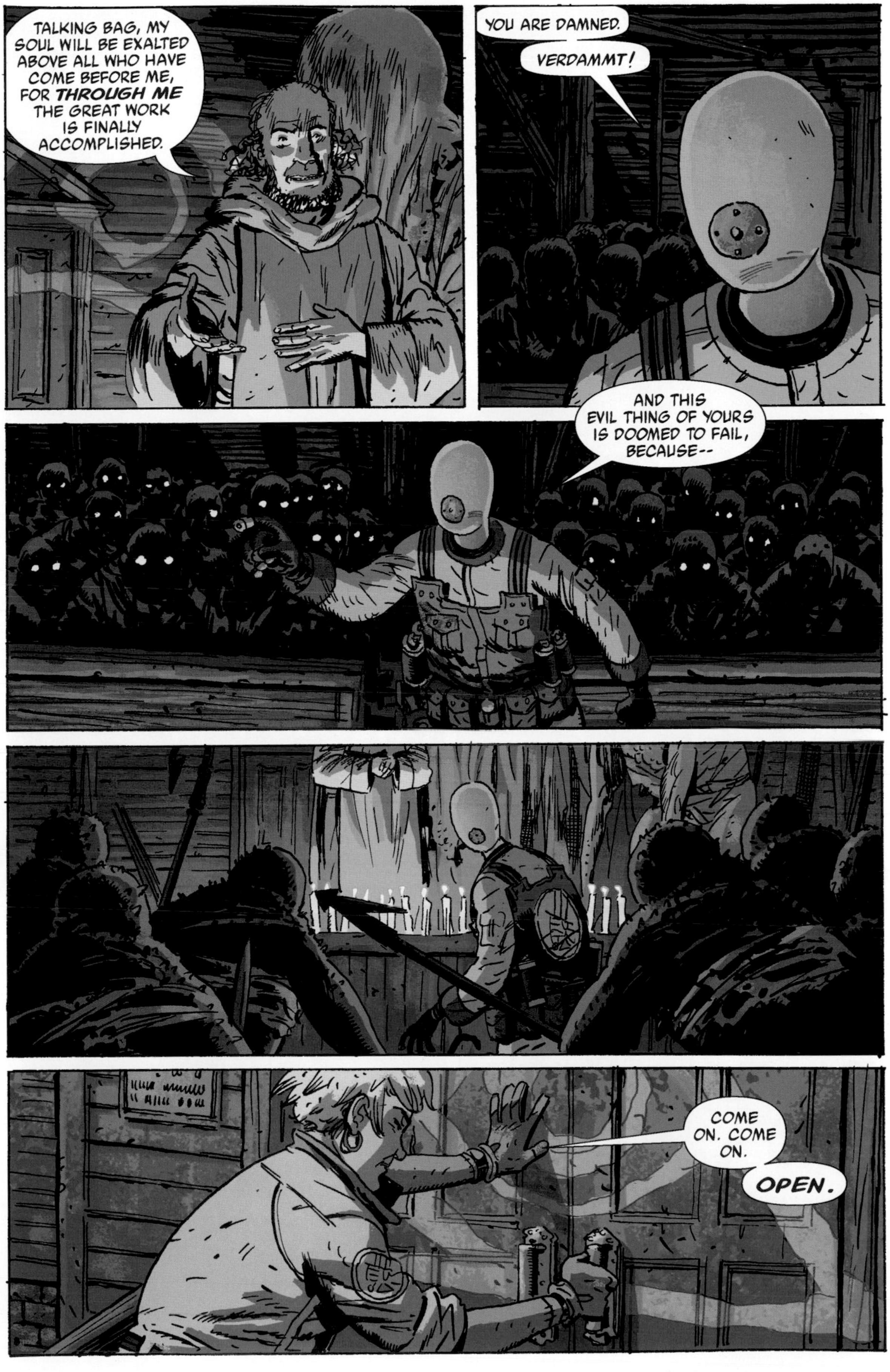
TALKING BAG, MY SOUL WILL BE EXALTED ABOVE ALL WHO HAVE COME BEFORE ME, FOR ***THROUGH ME*** THE GREAT WORK IS FINALLY ACCOMPLISHED.
YOU ARE DAMNED.
VERDAMMT!
AND THIS EVIL THING OF YOURS IS DOOMED TO FAIL, BECAUSE--
COME ON. COME ON.
OPEN.

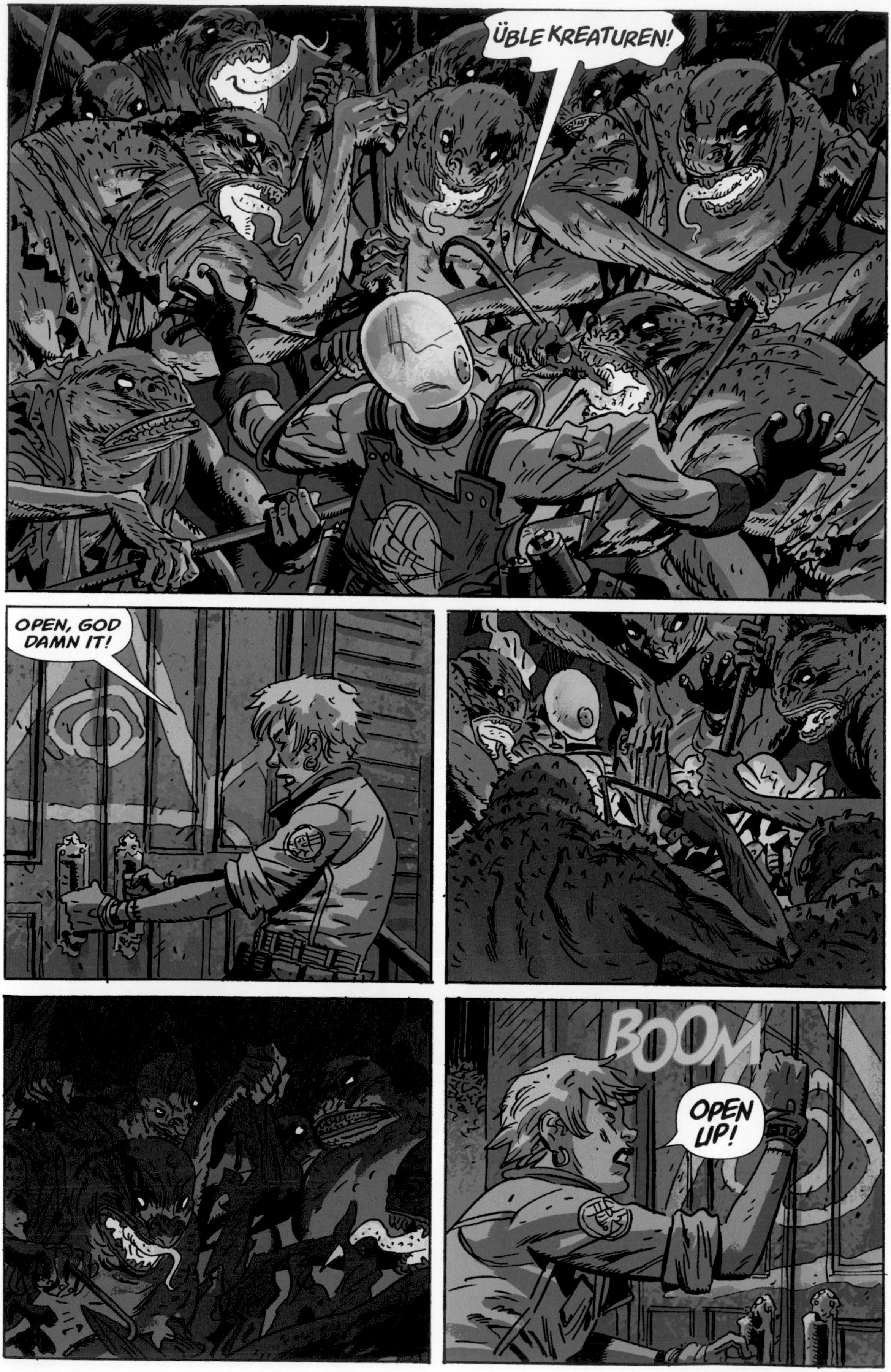
ÜBLE KREATUREN!
OPEN, GOD DAMN IT!
BOOM
OPEN UP!

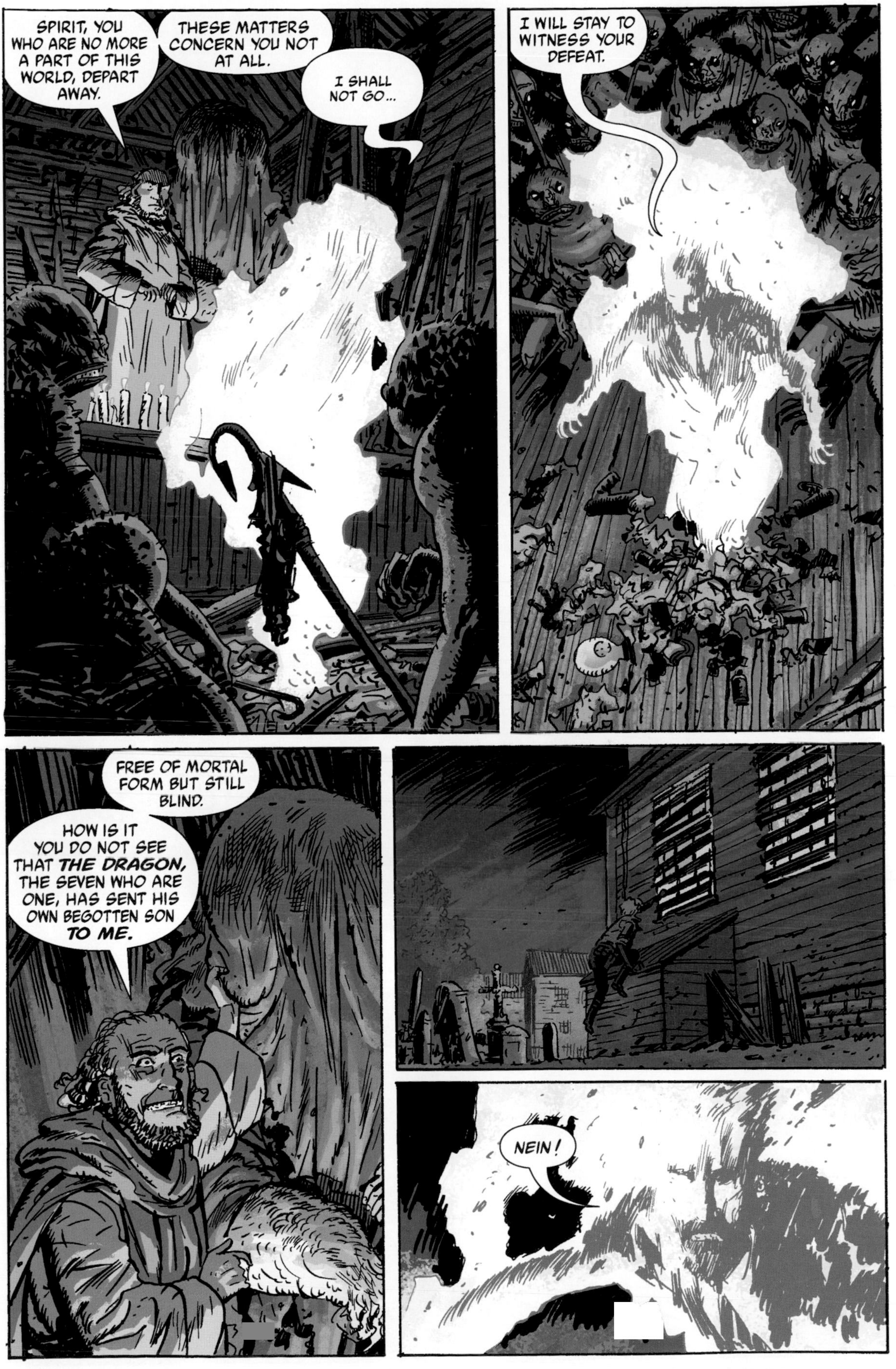
SPIRIT, YOU WHO ARE NO MORE A PART OF THIS WORLD, DEPART AWAY.
THESE MATTERS CONCERN YOU NOT AT ALL.
I SHALL NOT GO...
I WILL STAY TO WITNESS YOUR DEFEAT.
FREE OF MORTAL FORM BUT STILL BLIND.
HOW IS IT YOU DO NOT SEE THAT **THE DRAGON,** THE SEVEN WHO ARE ONE, HAS SENT HIS OWN BEGOTTEN SON **TO ME.**
NEIN!

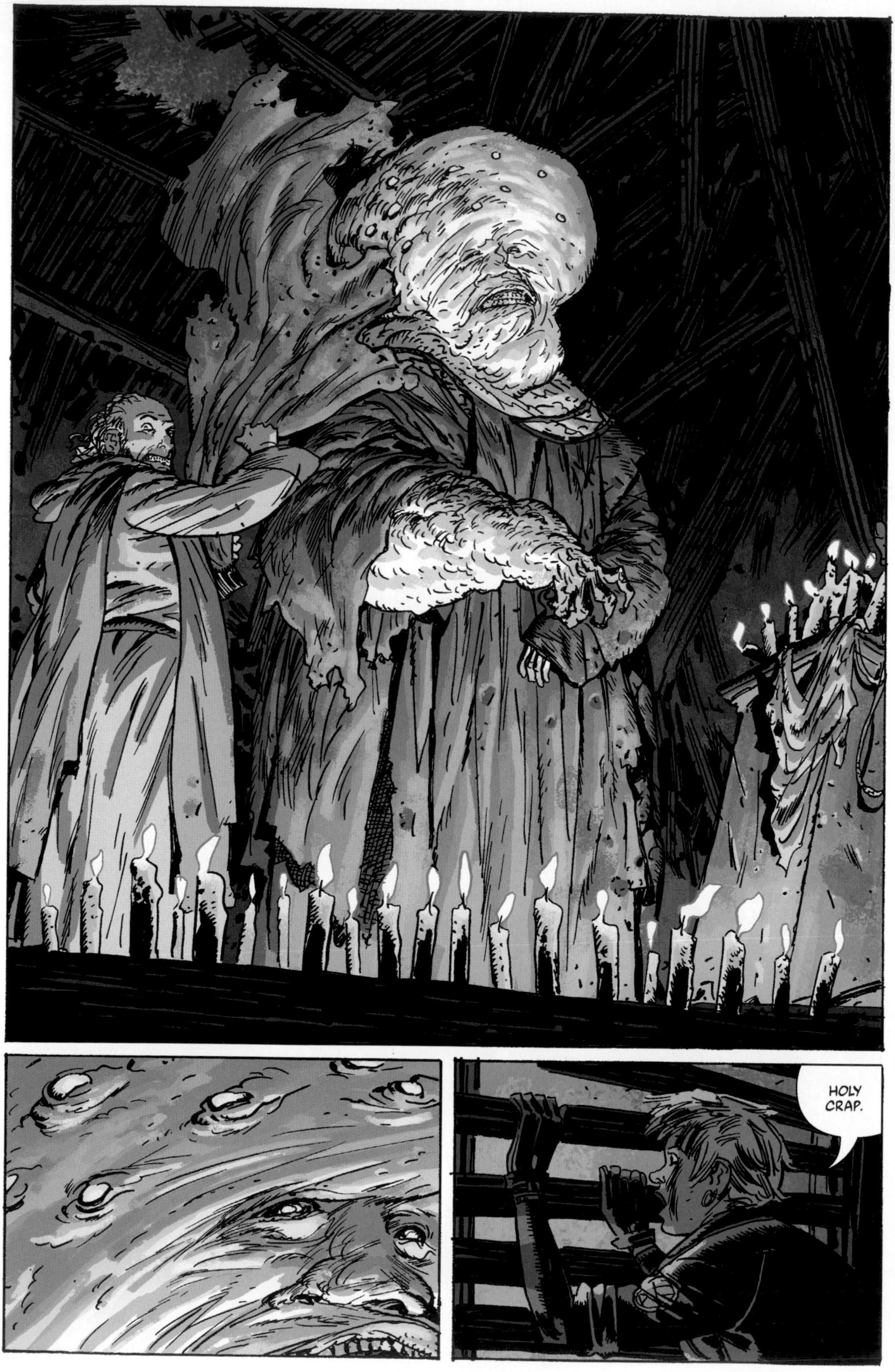
HOLY
CRAP.

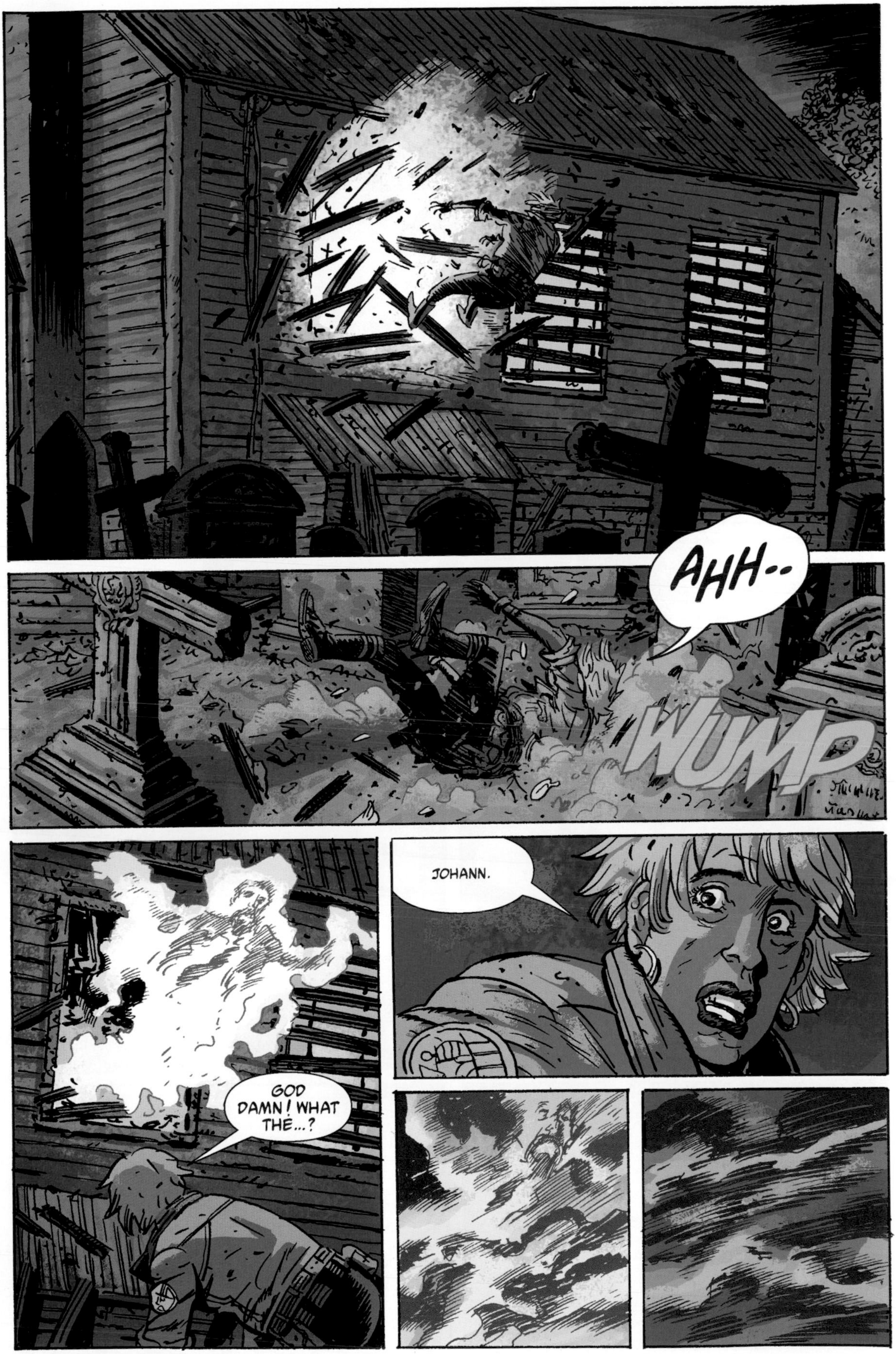
AHH..
WUMP
JOHANN.
GOD DAMN! WHAT THE...?

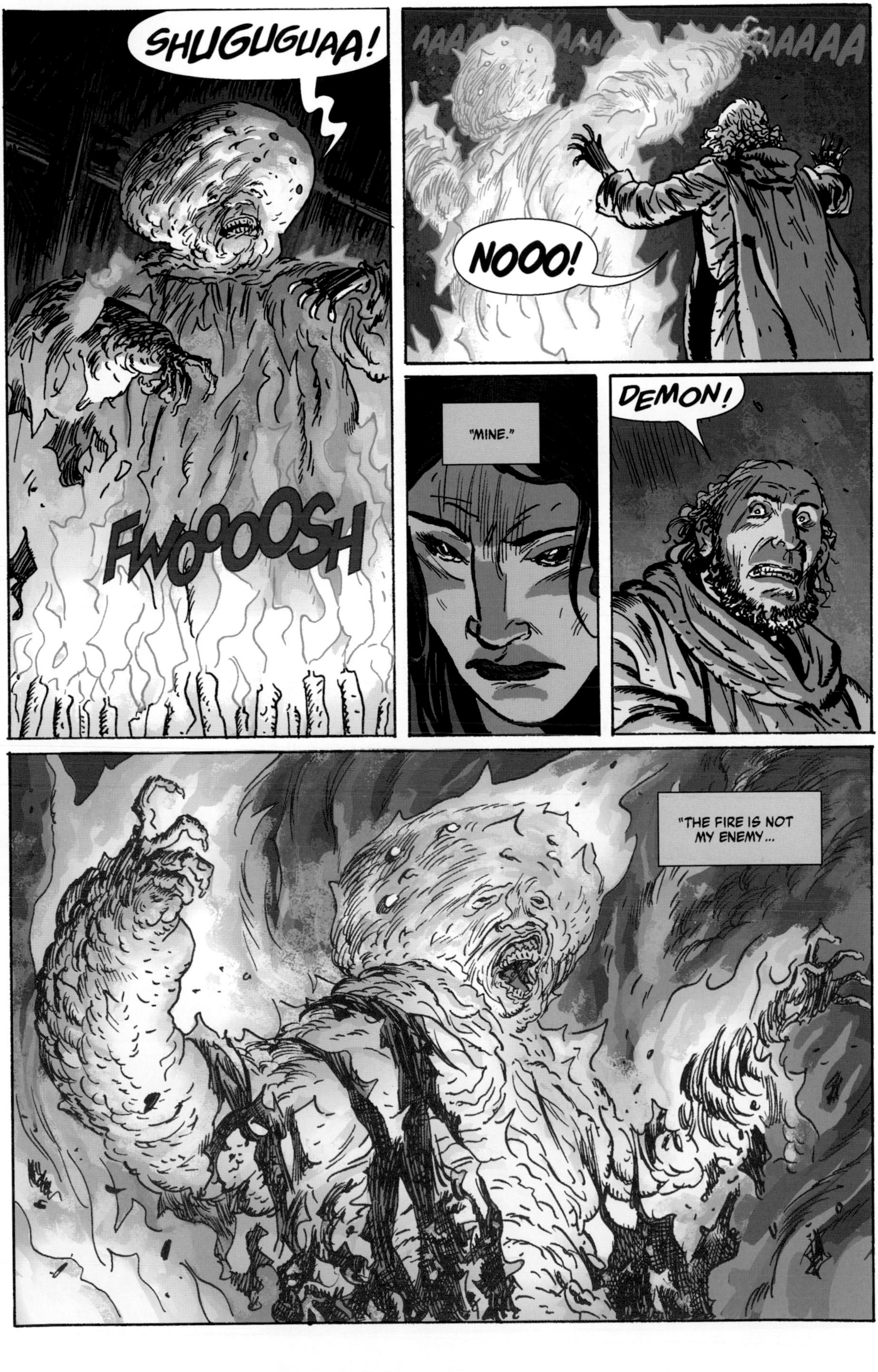
SHUGUGUAA!
FWOOOOOSH
AAAAAAAAAAAAAAAAAA
NOOO!
"MINE."
DEMON!
"THE FIRE IS NOT MY ENEMY...

"IT IS A PART OF ME..."

GREAT, LIZ, GREAT.

NOW REIN IT IN.

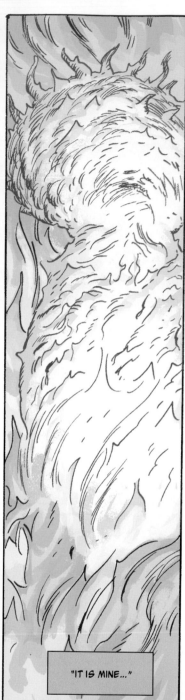

"IT IS MINE..."

A LITTLE MORE. A LITTLE MORE. A LITTLE--

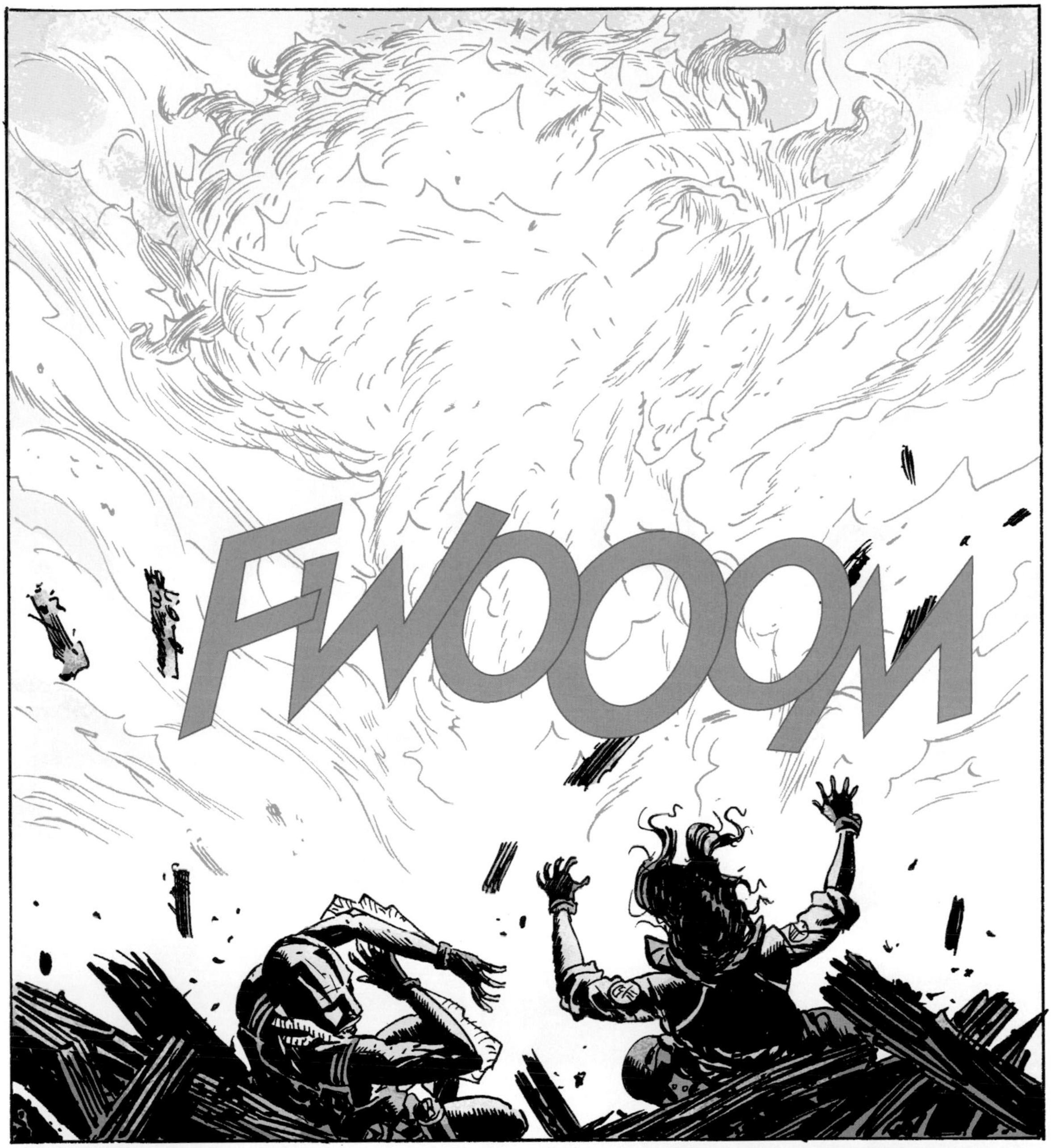
FWOOOM
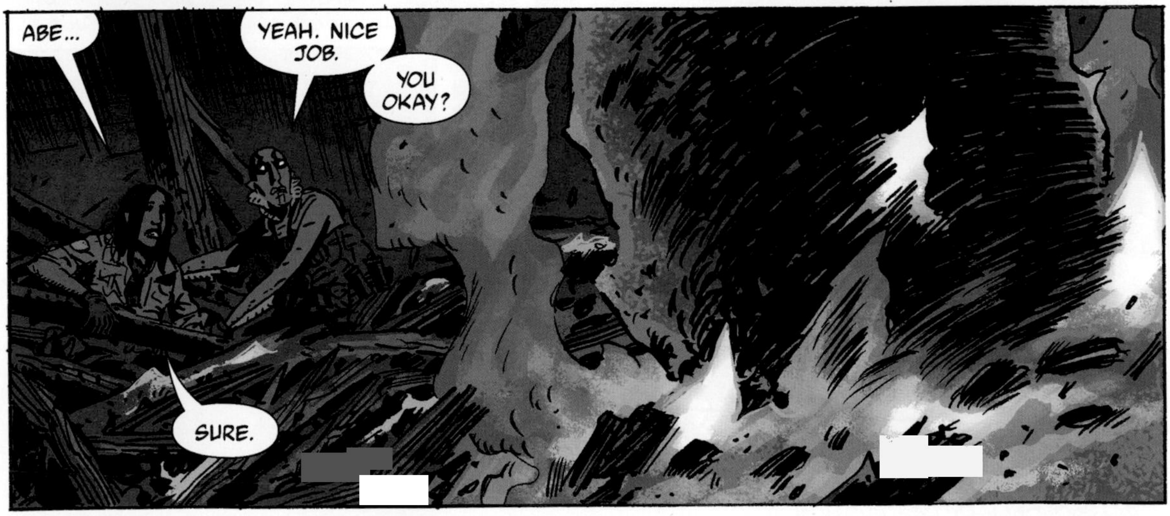
ABE...
YEAH. NICE JOB.
YOU OKAY?
SURE.

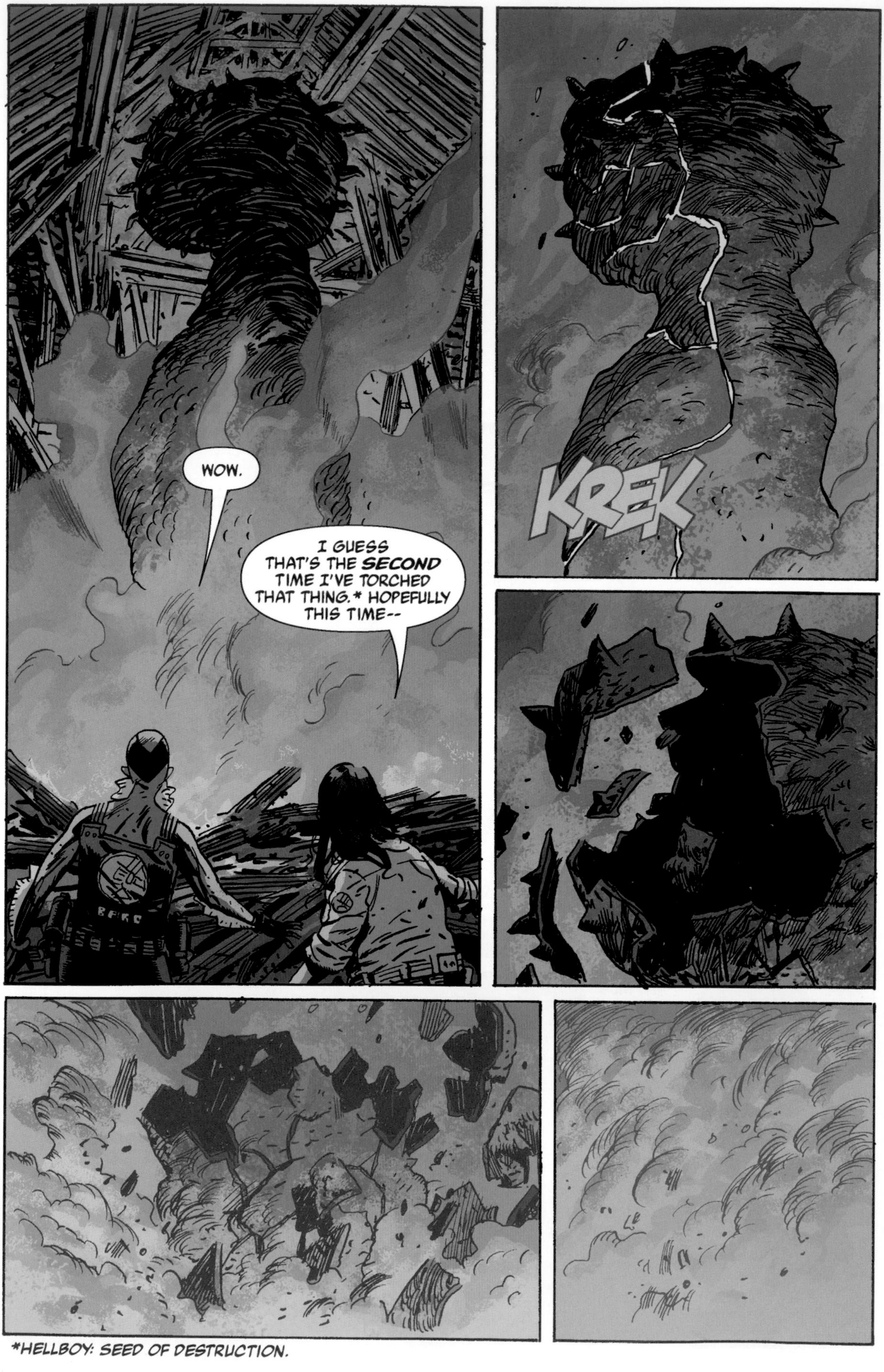
WOW.
I GUESS THAT'S THE SECOND TIME I'VE TORCHED THAT THING.* HOPEFULLY THIS TIME--
KREK

*HELLBOY: SEED OF DESTRUCTION.

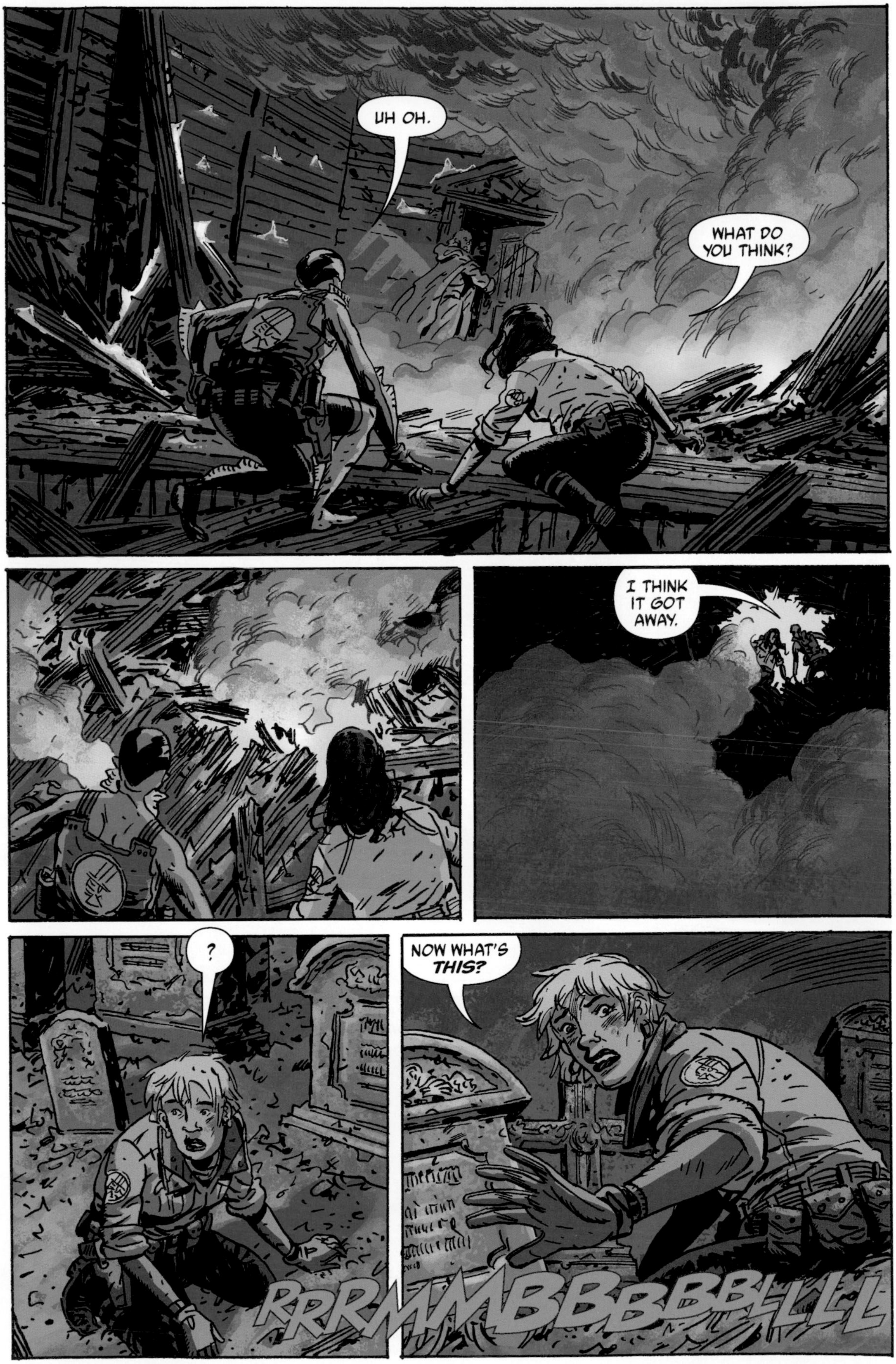
UH OH.
WHAT DO YOU THINK?
I THINK IT GOT AWAY.
?
NOW WHAT'S *THIS?*
RRRMMMBBBBBLLLL

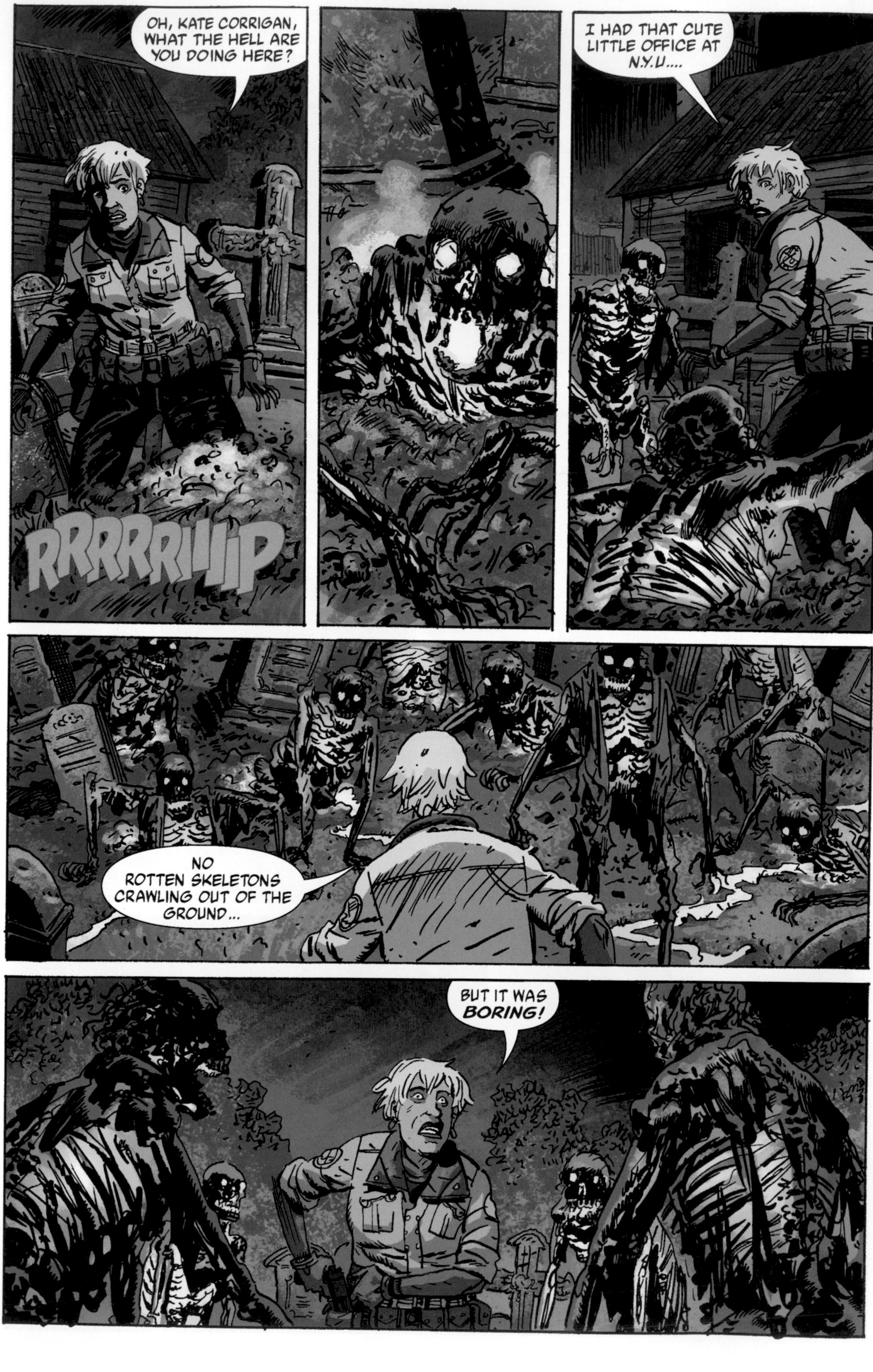
OH, KATE CORRIGAN, WHAT THE HELL ARE YOU DOING HERE?
RRRRRIIIIP
I HAD THAT CUTE LITTLE OFFICE AT N.Y.U....
NO ROTTEN SKELETONS CRAWLING OUT OF THE GROUND...
BUT IT WAS *BORING!*

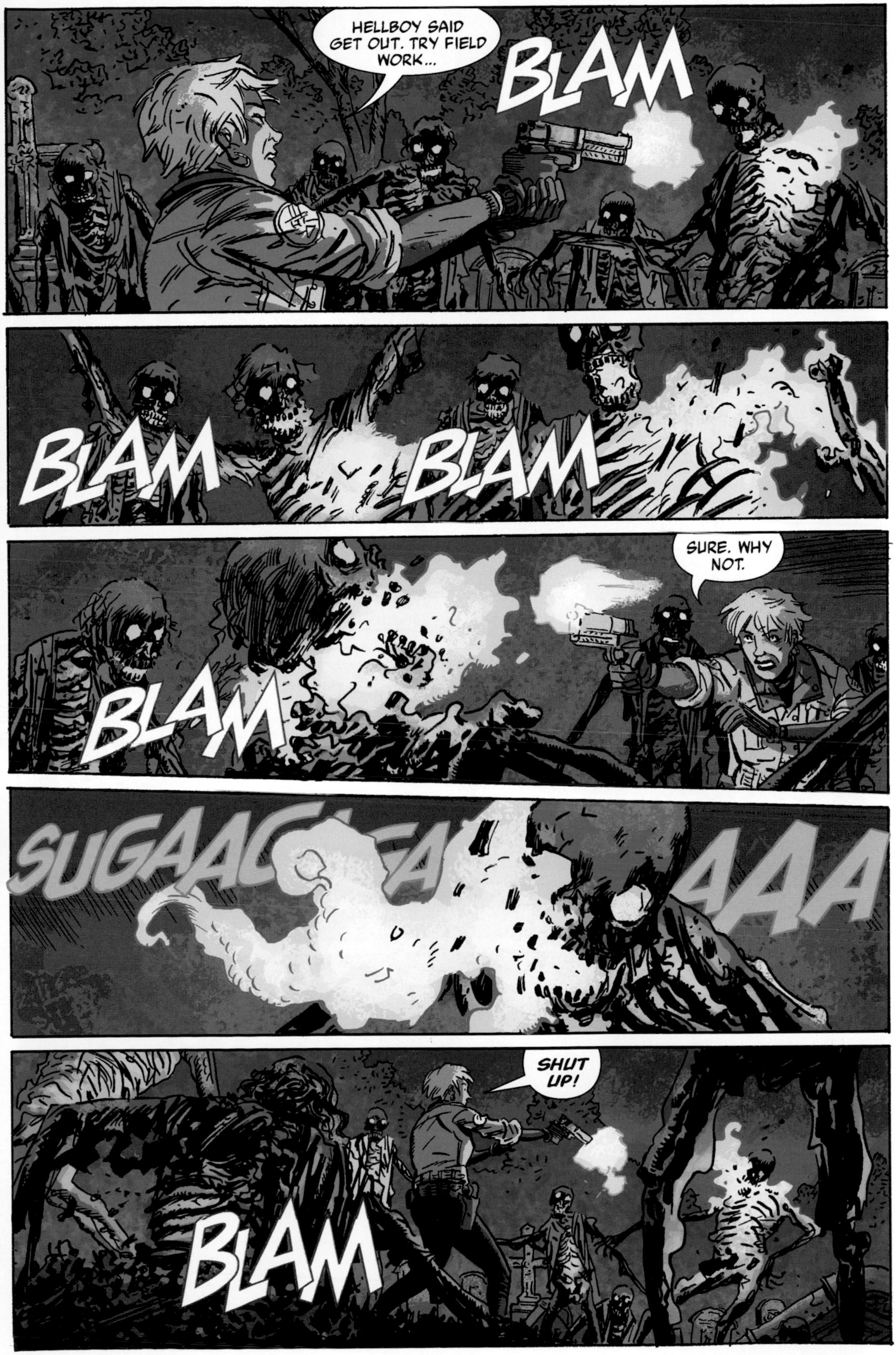
HELLBOY SAID GET OUT. TRY FIELD WORK...
BLAM
BLAM
BLAM
SURE. WHY NOT.
BLAM
SHUT UP!
BLAM

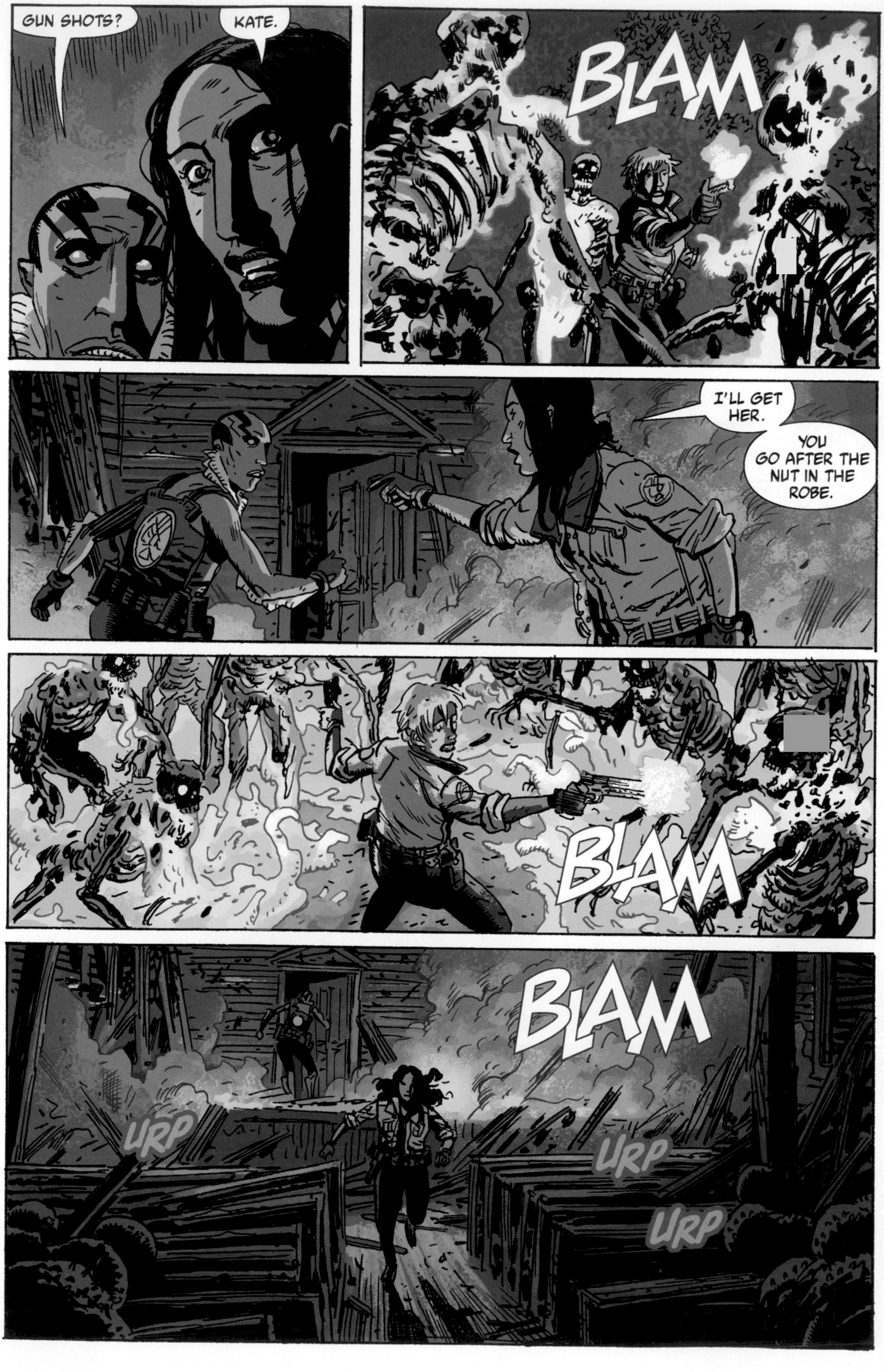
GUN SHOTS?
KATE.
BLAM
I'LL GET HER.
YOU GO AFTER THE NUT IN THE ROBE.
BLAM
BLAM
URP
URP
URP

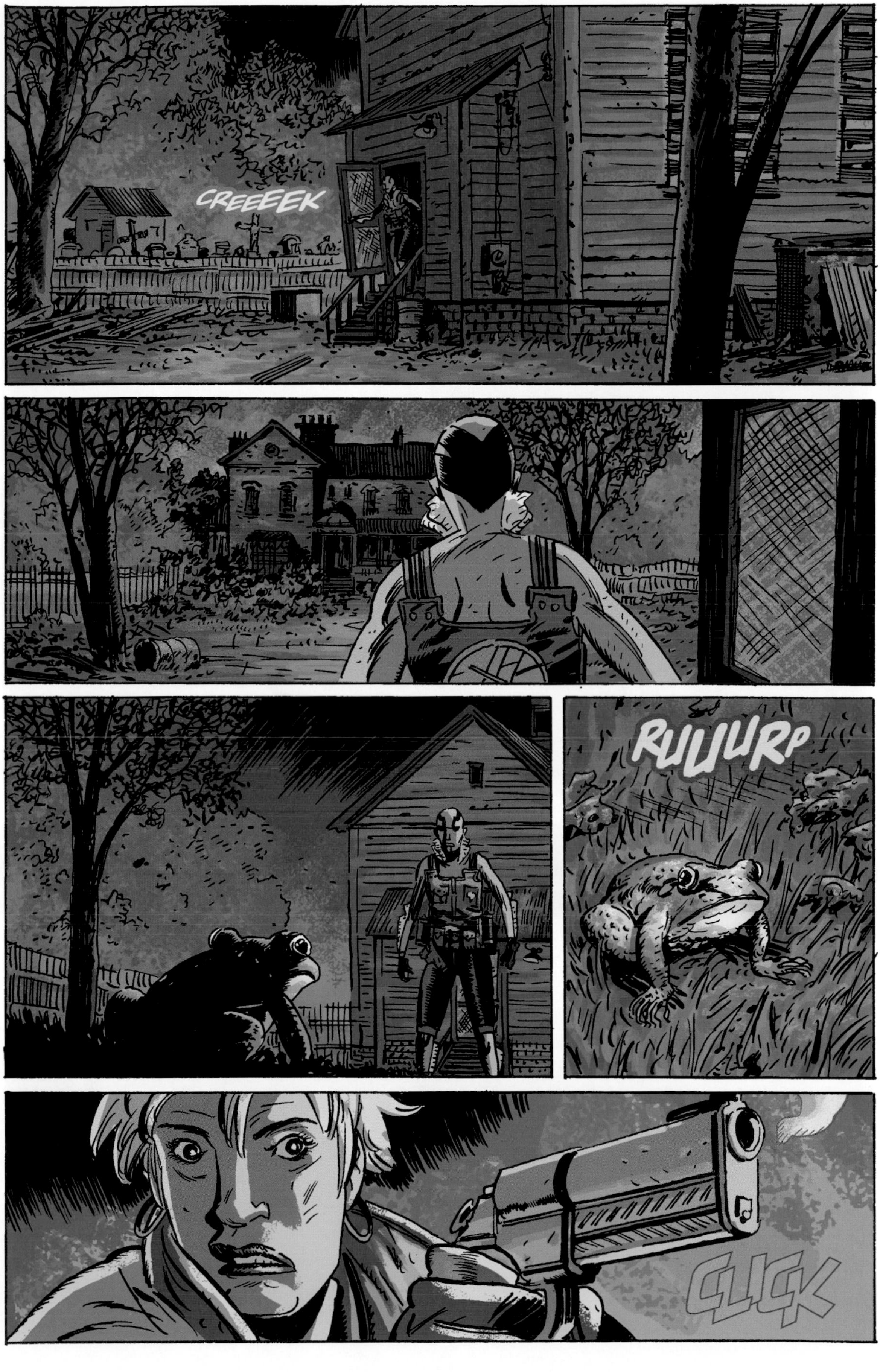
CREEEEK
RUUURP
CLICK

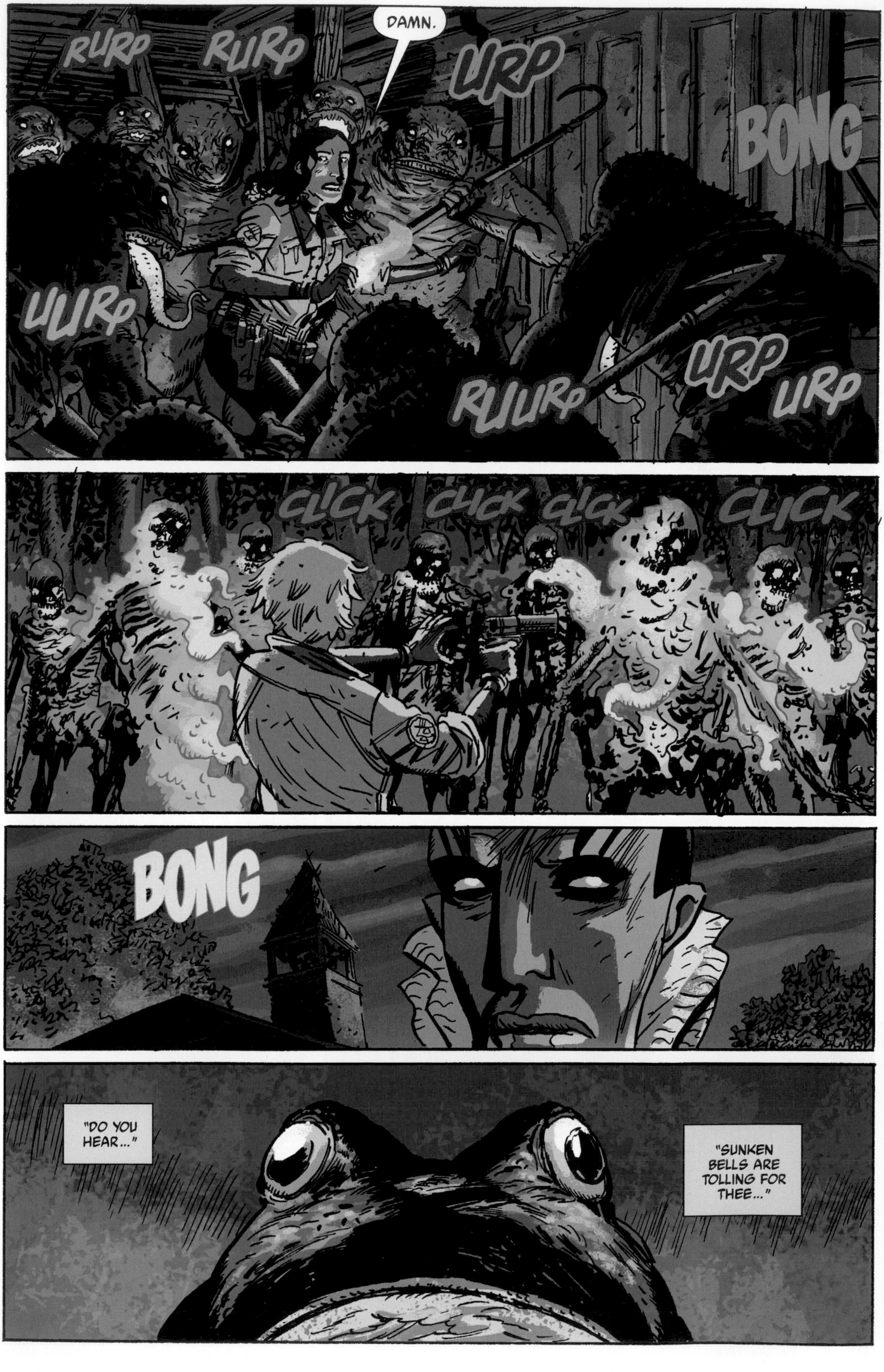
RURP
RURP
DAMN.
URP
BONG
UURP
RUURP
URP
URP
CLICK
CLICK
CLICK
CLICK
BONG
"DO YOU HEAR..."
"SUNKEN BELLS ARE TOLLING FOR THEE..."

CHAPTER FOUR

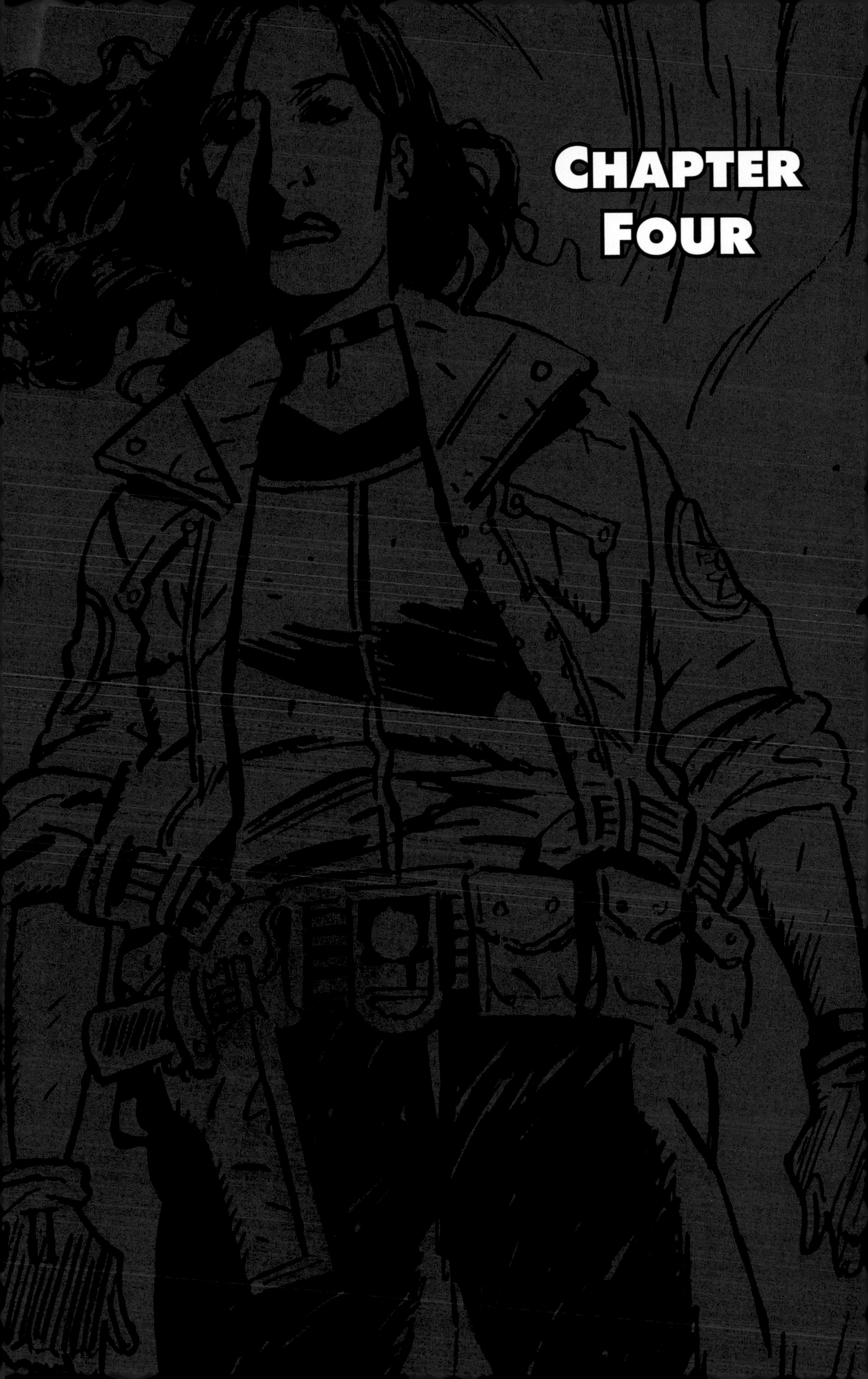

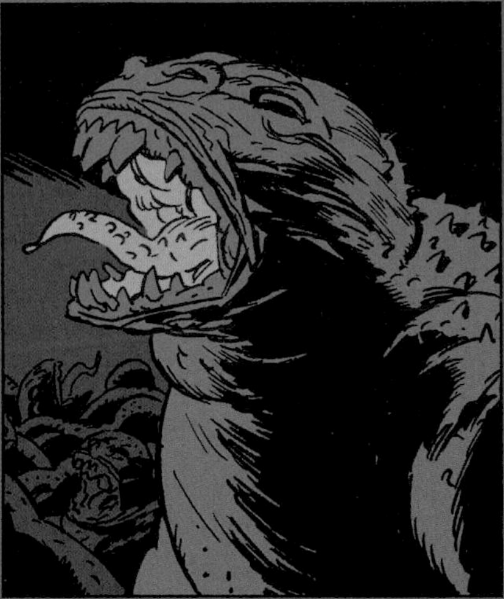

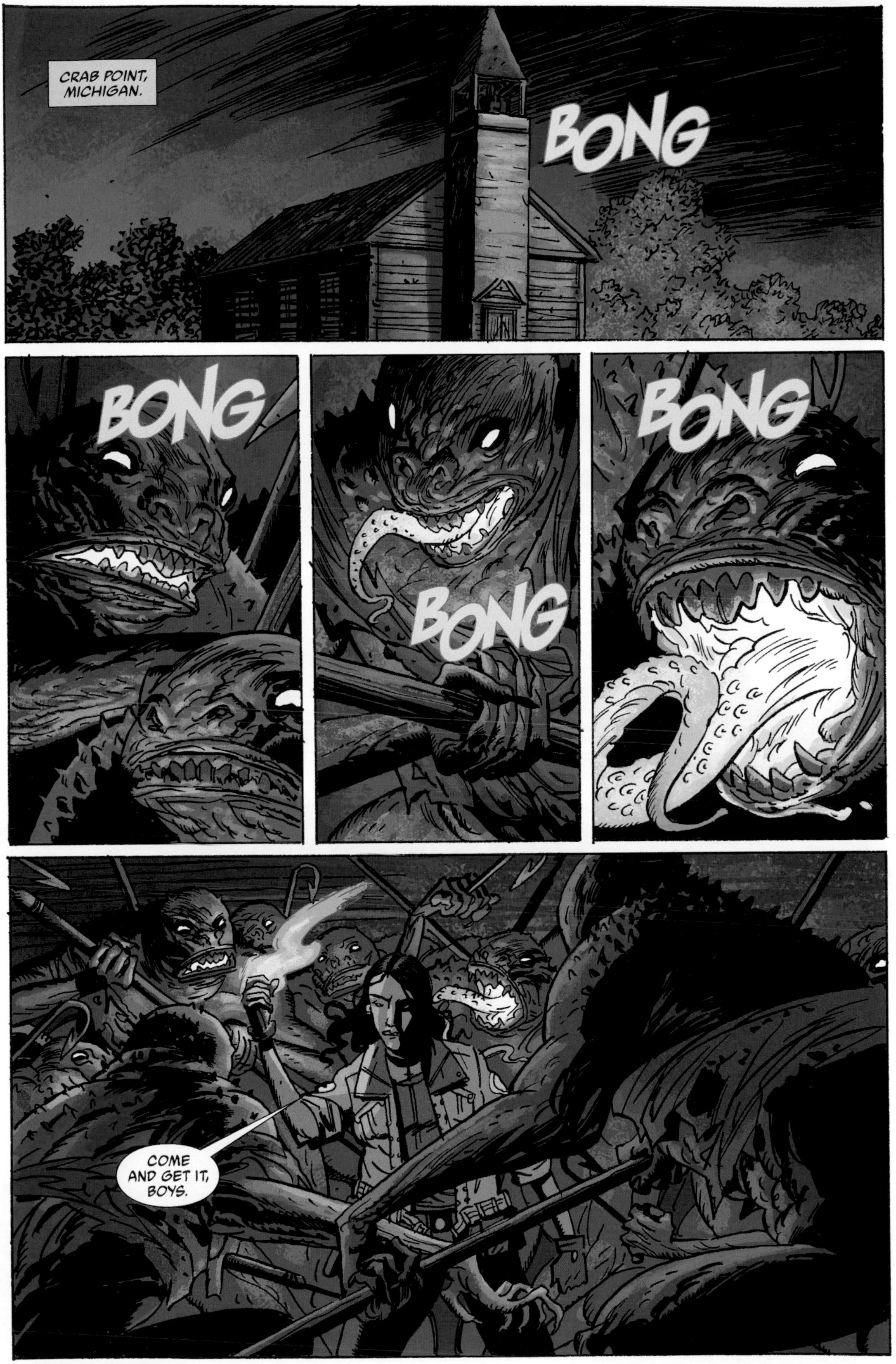
CRAB POINT, MICHIGAN.
BONG
BONG
BONG
BONG
BONG
COME AND GET IT, BOYS.

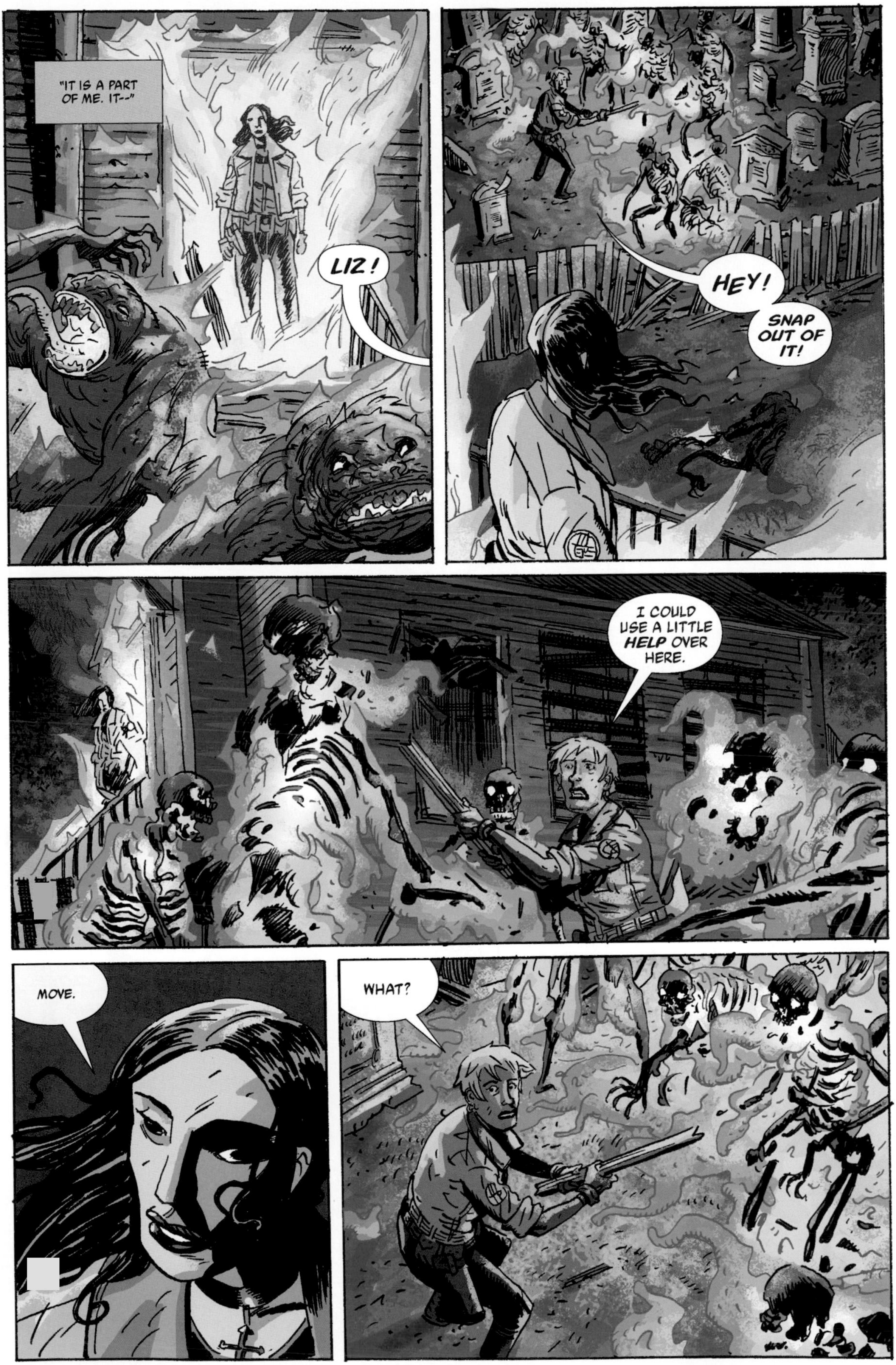
"IT IS A PART OF ME. IT--"
LIZ!
HEY!
SNAP OUT OF IT!
I COULD USE A LITTLE **HELP** OVER HERE.
MOVE.
WHAT?

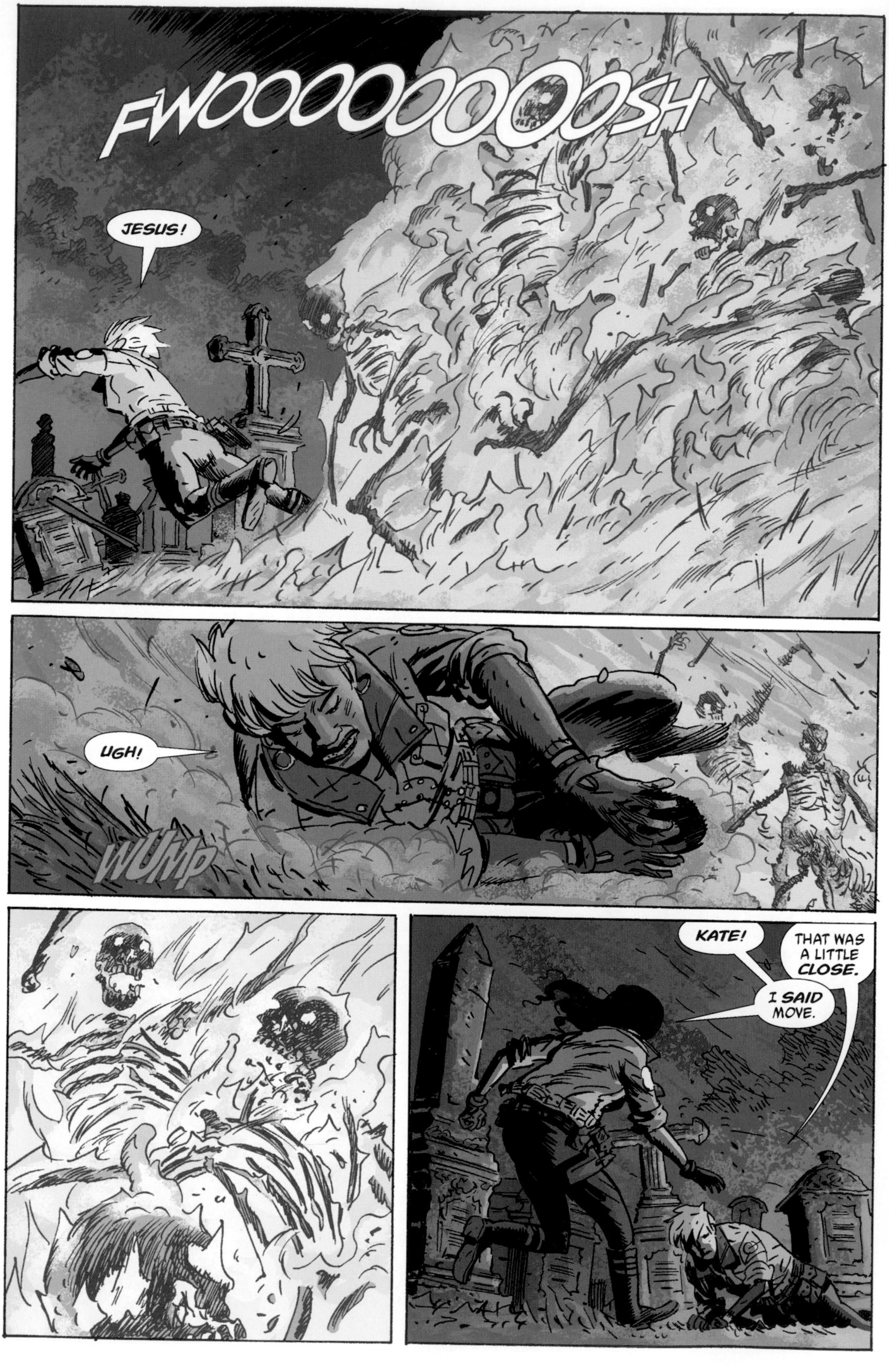
FWOOOOOOOOOSH
JESUS!
UGH!
WUMP
KATE!
THAT WAS A LITTLE CLOSE.
I SAID MOVE.

IT'S OKAY.

SO WHAT DID I MISS?

DOCTOR-WHAT'S-HIS-NAME APPARENTLY TURNED INTO A GIANT ELEPHANT-MAN FUNGUS GUY, AND HE'S MIXED UP WITH A CRAZY DOOMSDAY-CULT PRIEST GUY...

AND BETWEEN THE TWO OF THEM IT LOOKS LIKE THEY TURNED THE WHOLE TOWN INTO FROG MONSTERS.

THE WHOLE TOWN...

JOHANN...?

TORN UP BY THE FROG GUYS AND BLOWN OUT THE WINDOW BY THE PRIEST.

I SAW THAT.

YEAH...

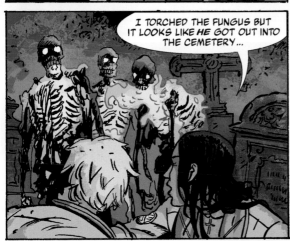

I TORCHED THE FUNGUS BUT IT LOOKS LIKE *HE* GOT OUT INTO THE CEMETERY...

NOT GOING TO BE A PROBLEM THOUGH...

"THE FIRE IS A PART OF ME..."

WOOOOOOSH

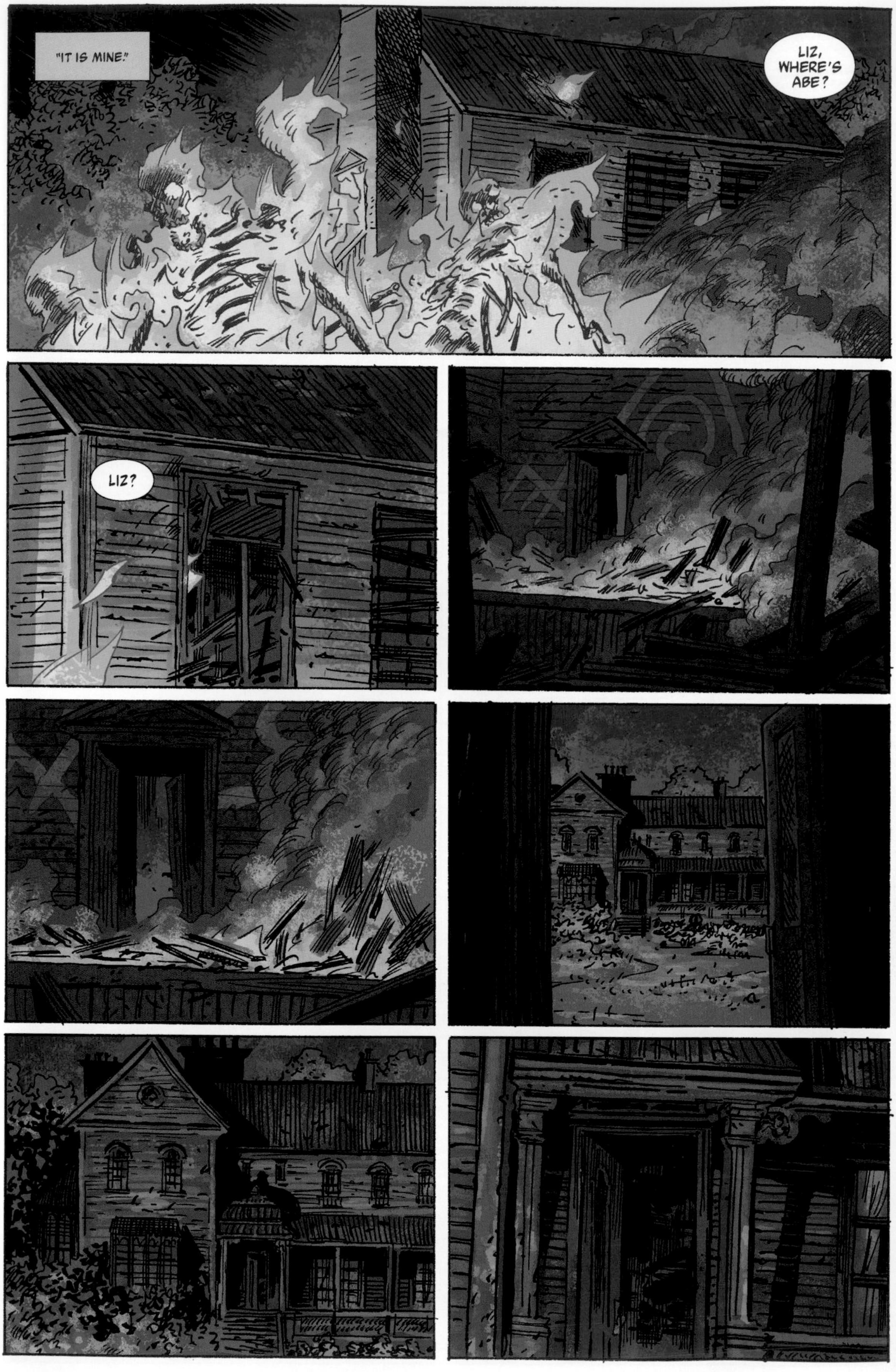
"IT IS MINE."
LIZ, WHERE'S ABE?
LIZ?

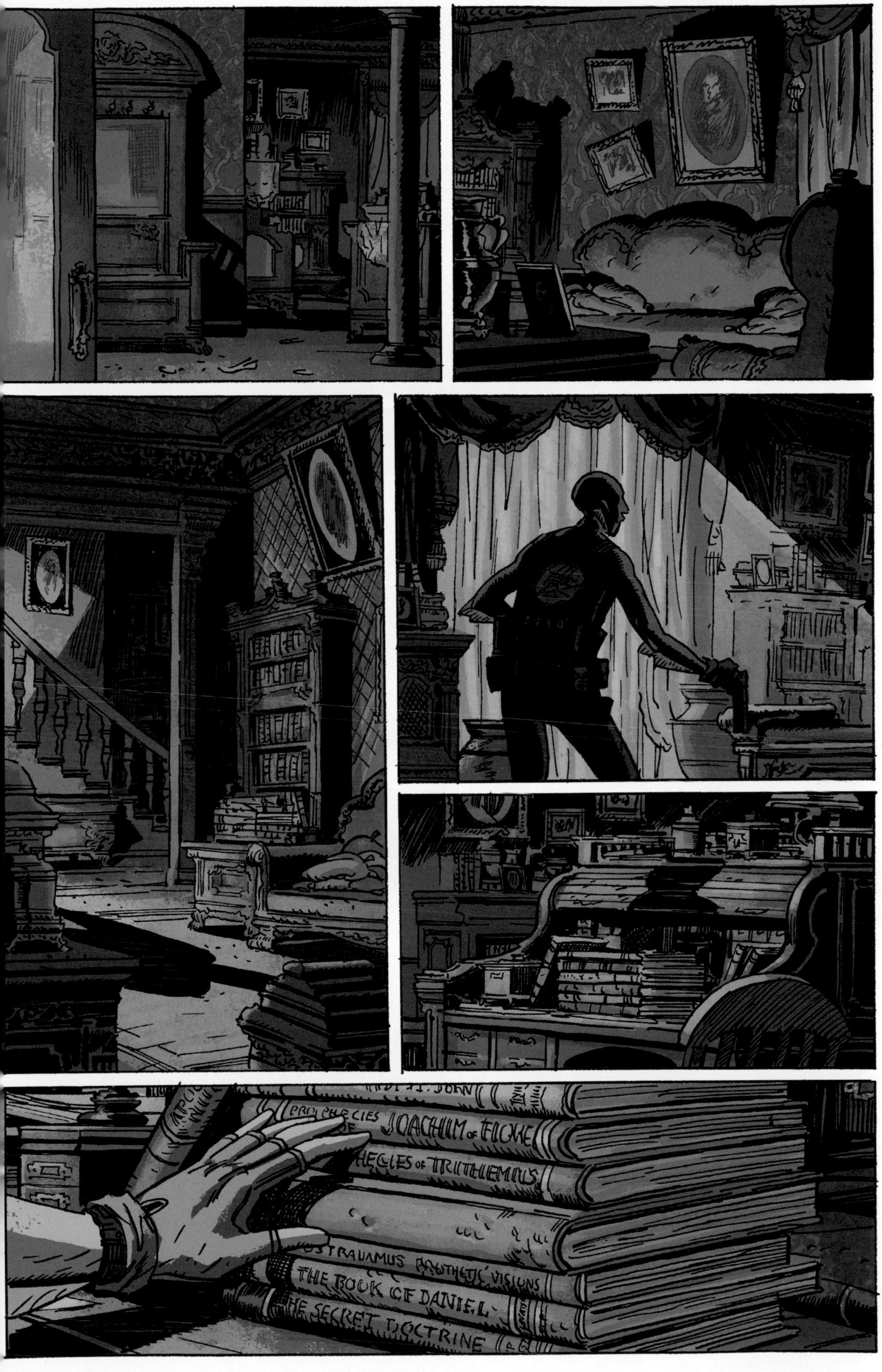
JOACHIM of FIORE
TRITHEMIUS
VISIONS
THE BOOK OF DANIEL
SECRET DOCTRINE

?

SCRAPBOOK.

"MIRACLE BOY"

DOZENS CLAIM CURED BY MIRACLE BOY

"NINE-YEAR-OLD HUMBERT T. JONES, OF MARNET, WEST VIRGINIA, APPARENTLY HEALED THE BROKEN ARM OF A CLASSMATE..."

I WAS CURED BY WEST VIRGINIA MIRACLE BOY

"DOCTORS CONFIRM THAT TUMORS HAVE VANISHED..."

HEALING POWER BAFFLES EXPERTS

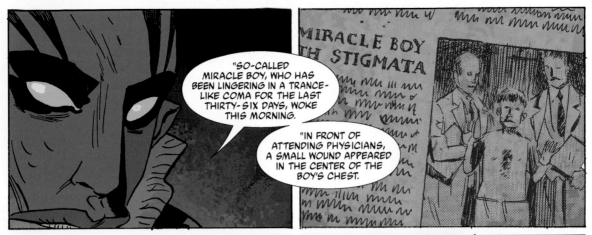

"SO-CALLED MIRACLE BOY, WHO HAS BEEN LINGERING IN A TRANCE-LIKE COMA FOR THE LAST THIRTY-SIX DAYS, WOKE THIS MORNING.
"IN FRONT OF ATTENDING PHYSICIANS, A SMALL WOUND APPEARED IN THE CENTER OF THE BOY'S CHEST.
MIRACLE BOY
TH STIGMATA
"THOUGH THE WOUND COUNTINUED TO BLEED FOR SEVERAL HOURS, NO CAUSE COULD BE DETERMINED..."
MAY 11, 1994
MAY 11, 1994...
CAVENDISH HALL...*
THE CAVENDISH BROTHERS...
FROG MONSTERS...

* CAVENDISH HALL WAS DESTROYED BY AN EXPLOSION ON MAY 11, 1994.

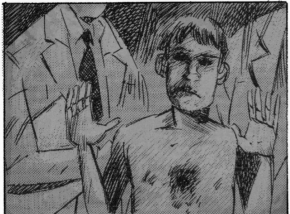

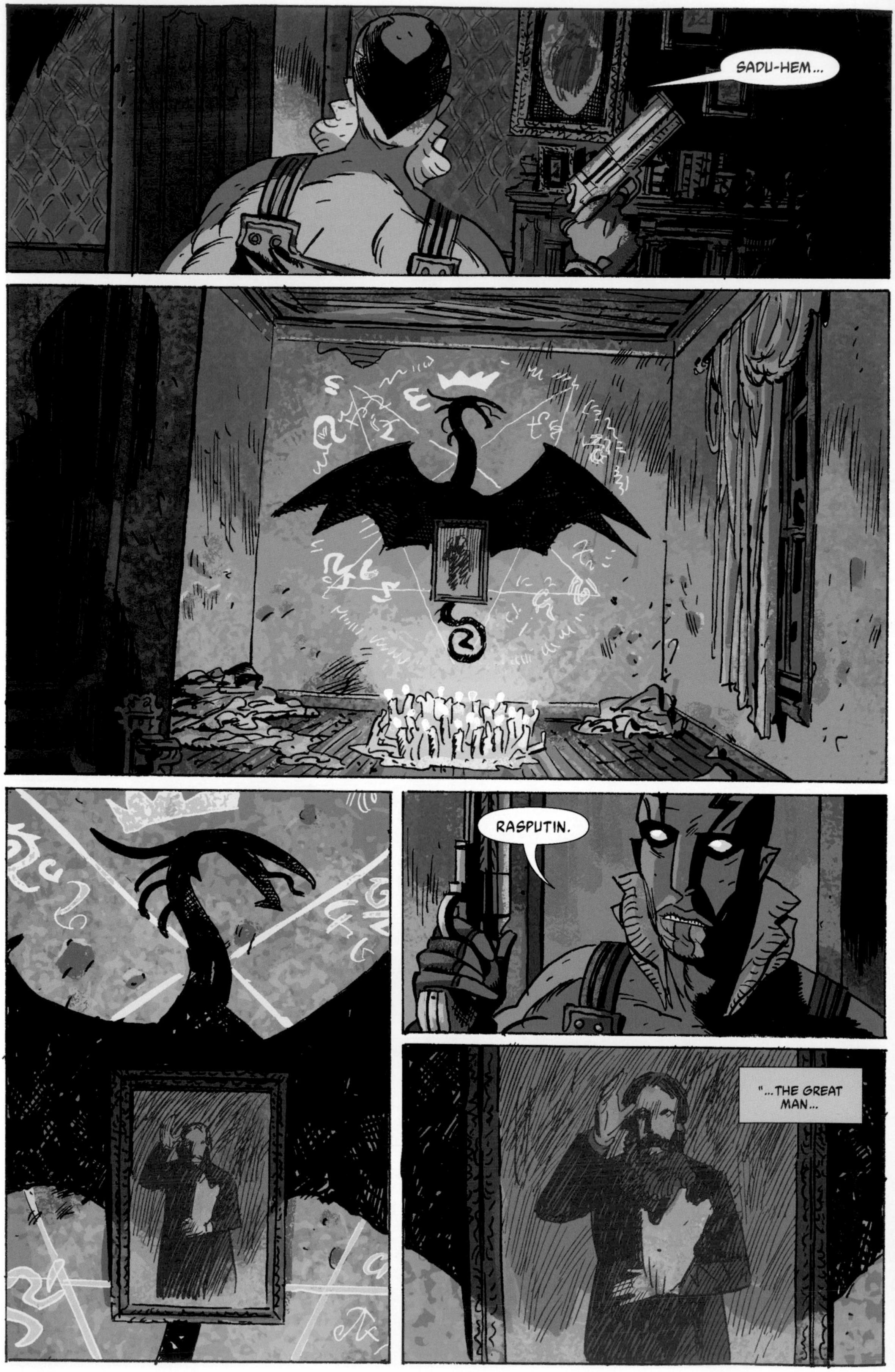
SADU-HEM...
RASPUTIN.
"...THE GREAT MAN...

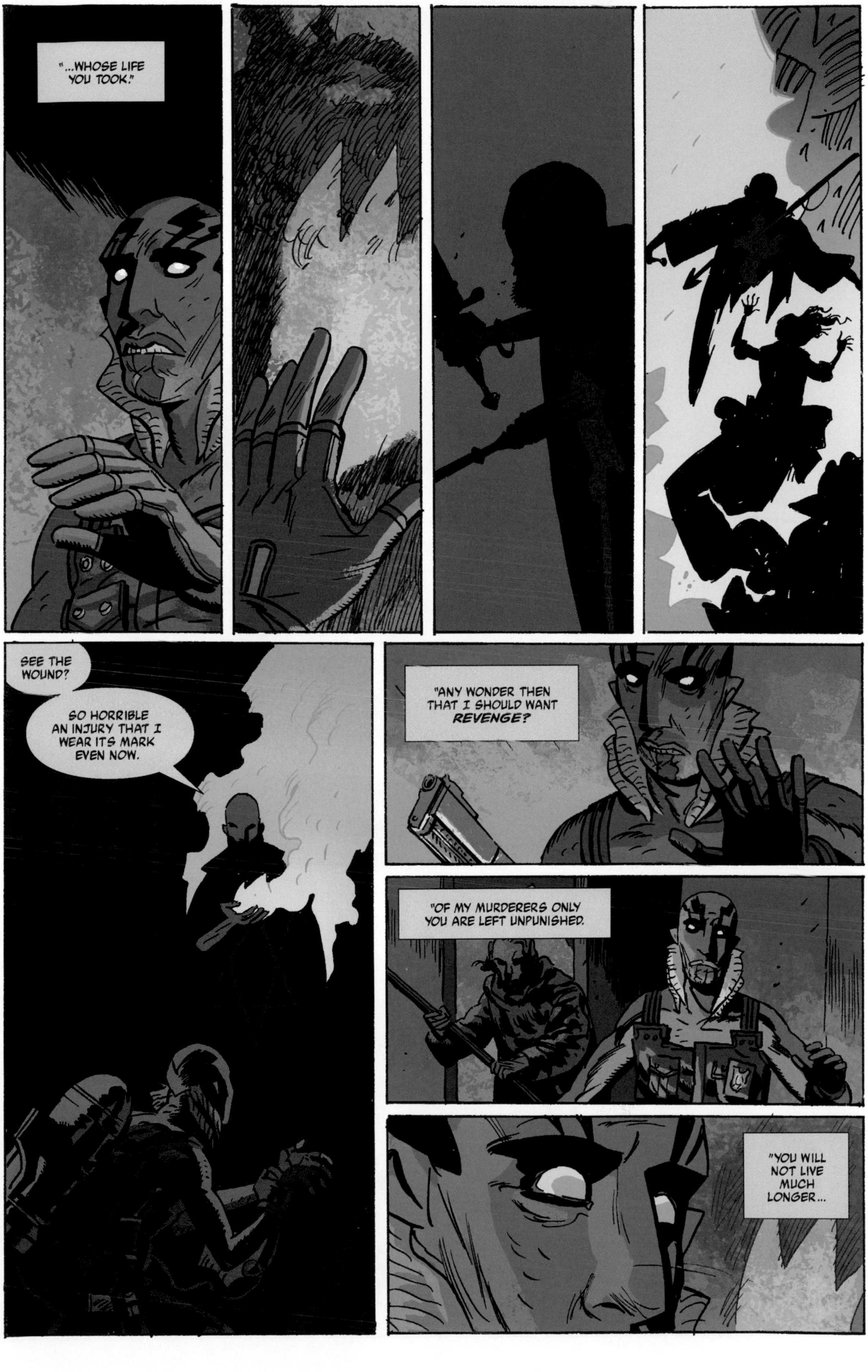
"...WHOSE LIFE YOU TOOK."
SEE THE WOUND?
SO HORRIBLE AN INJURY THAT I WEAR ITS MARK EVEN NOW.
"ANY WONDER THEN THAT I SHOULD WANT REVENGE?
"OF MY MURDERERS ONLY YOU ARE LEFT UNPUNISHED.
"YOU WILL NOT LIVE MUCH LONGER...

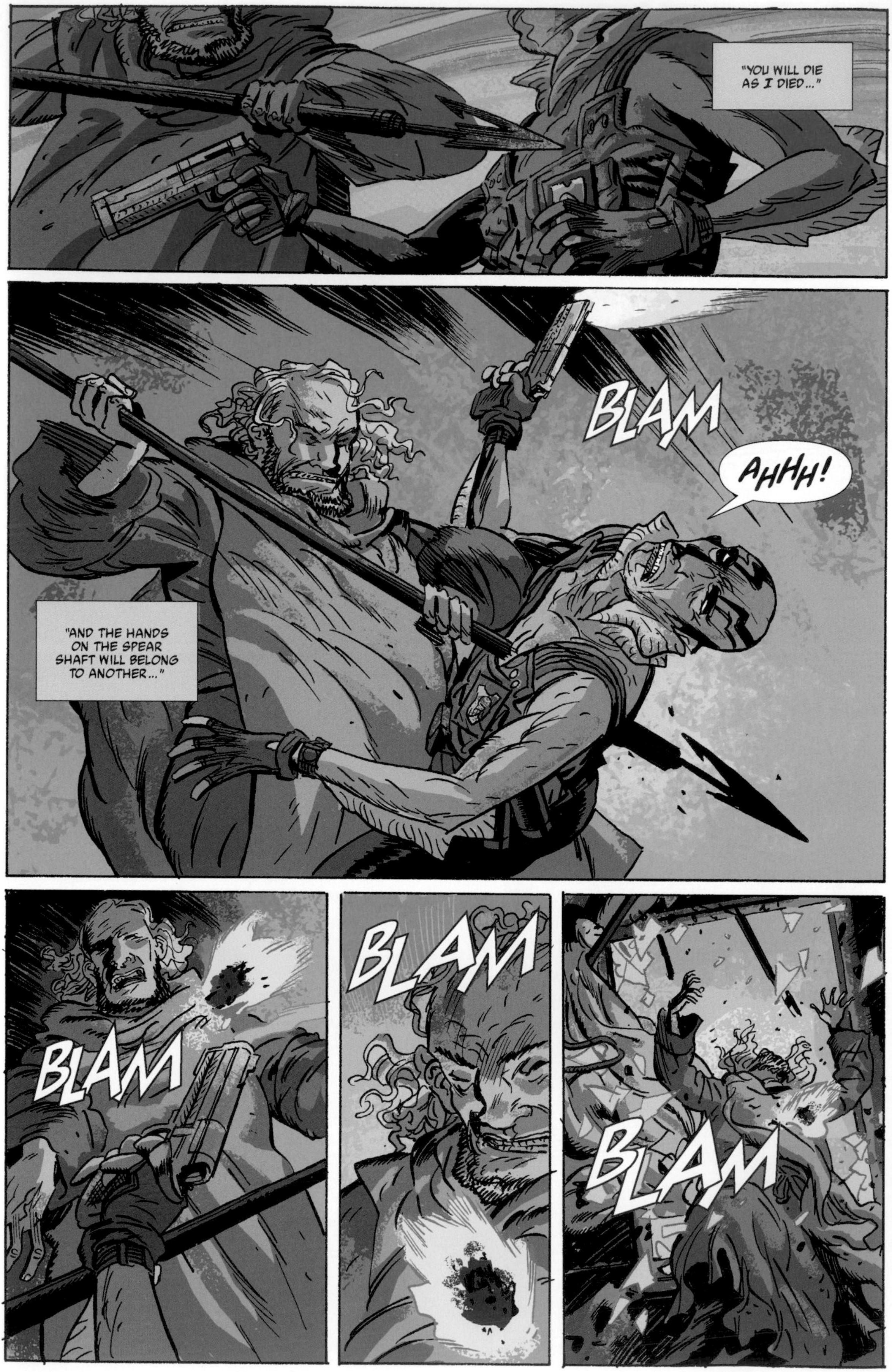
"YOU WILL DIE AS I DIED..."
BLAM
AHHH!
"AND THE HANDS ON THE SPEAR SHAFT WILL BELONG TO ANOTHER..."
BLAM
BLAM
BLAM

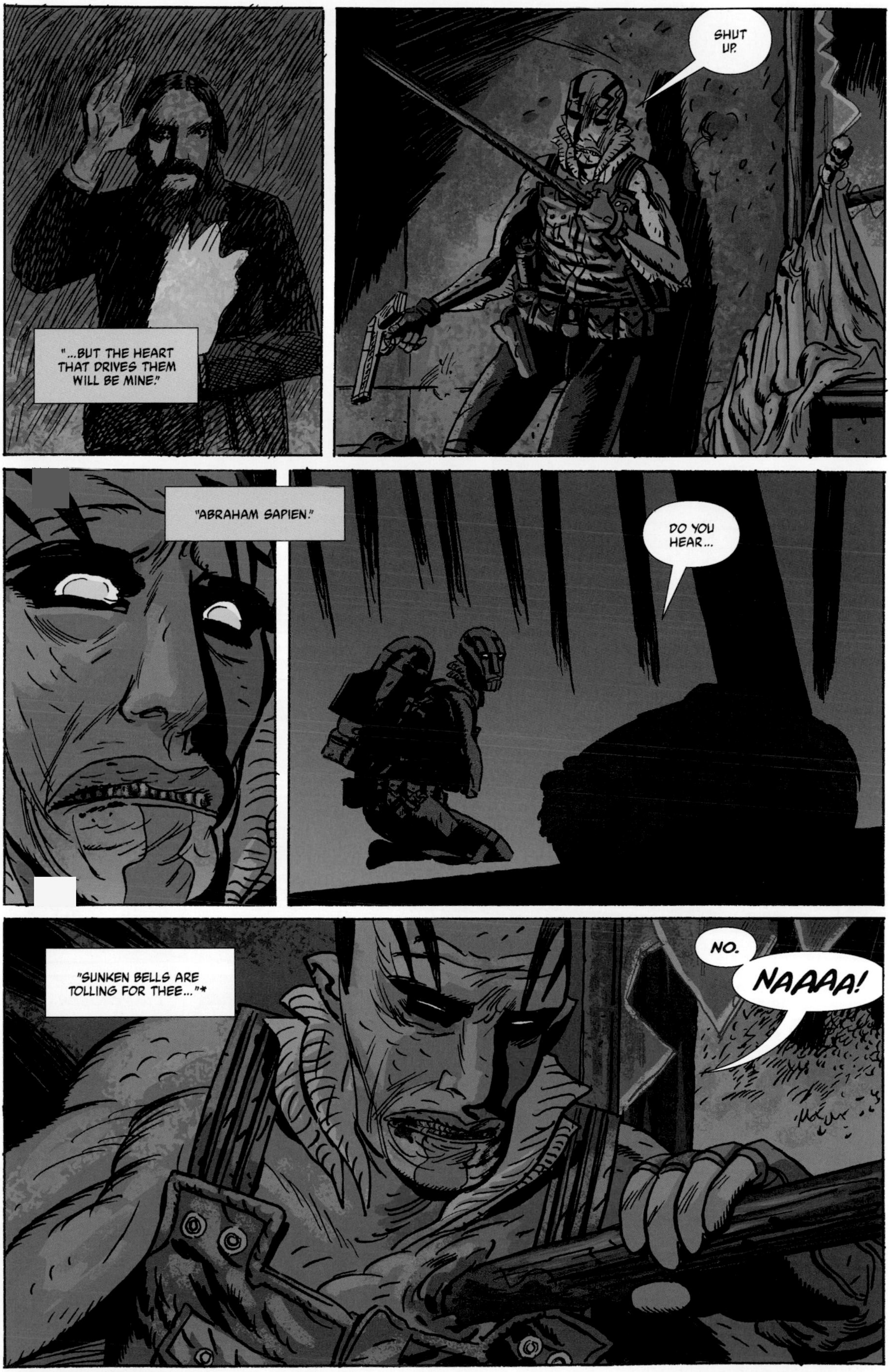
"...BUT THE HEART THAT DRIVES THEM WILL BE MINE."
SHUT UP.
"ABRAHAM SAPIEN."
DO YOU HEAR...
"SUNKEN BELLS ARE TOLLING FOR THEE..."*
NO.
NAAAA!

* FROM HELLBOY: WAKE THE DEVIL

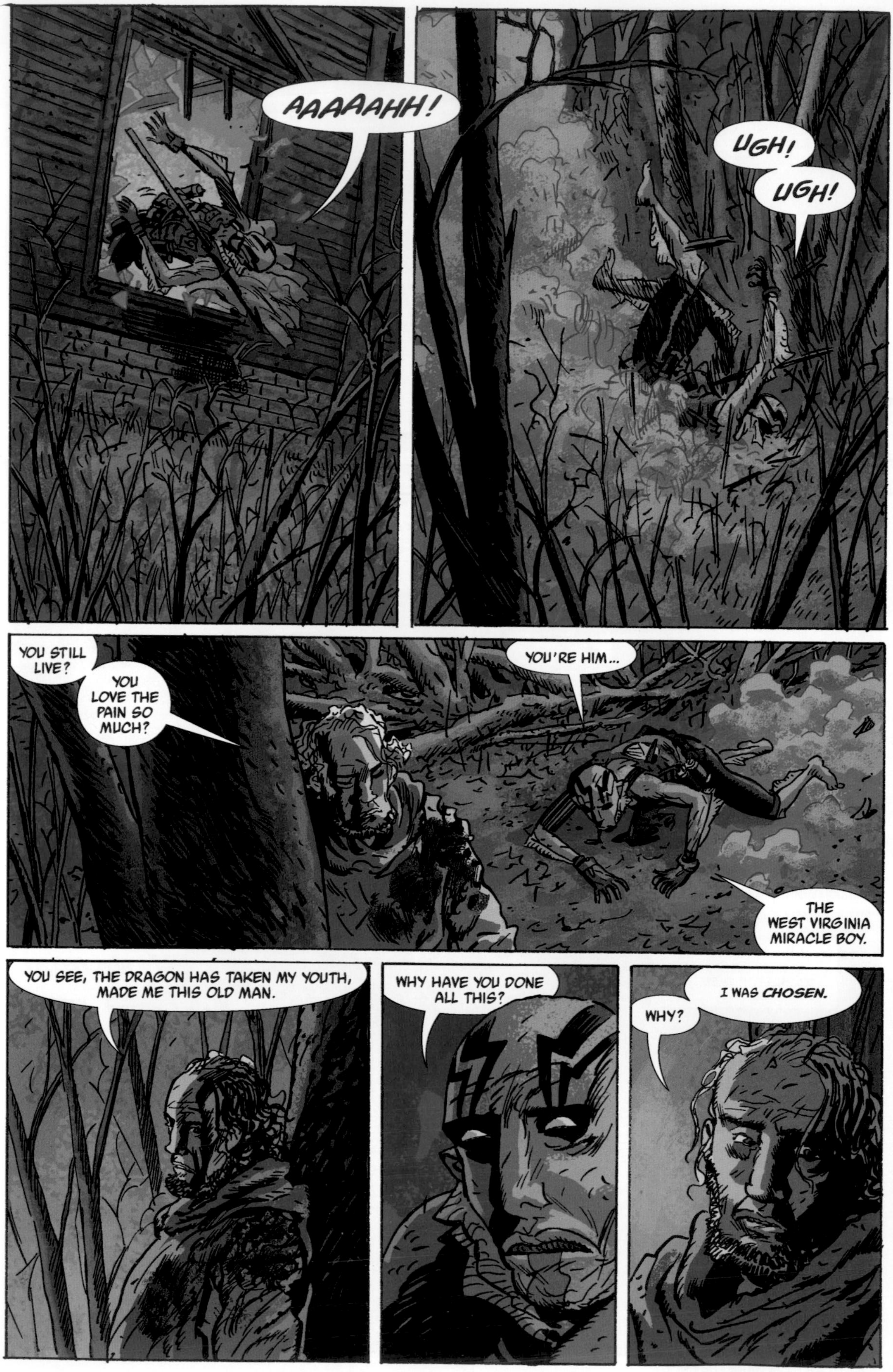
AAAAAHH!
UGH!
UGH!
YOU STILL LIVE?
YOU LOVE THE PAIN SO MUCH?
YOU'RE HIM...
THE WEST VIRGINIA MIRACLE BOY.
YOU SEE, THE DRAGON HAS TAKEN MY YOUTH, MADE ME THIS OLD MAN.
WHY HAVE YOU DONE ALL THIS?
I WAS CHOSEN.
WHY?

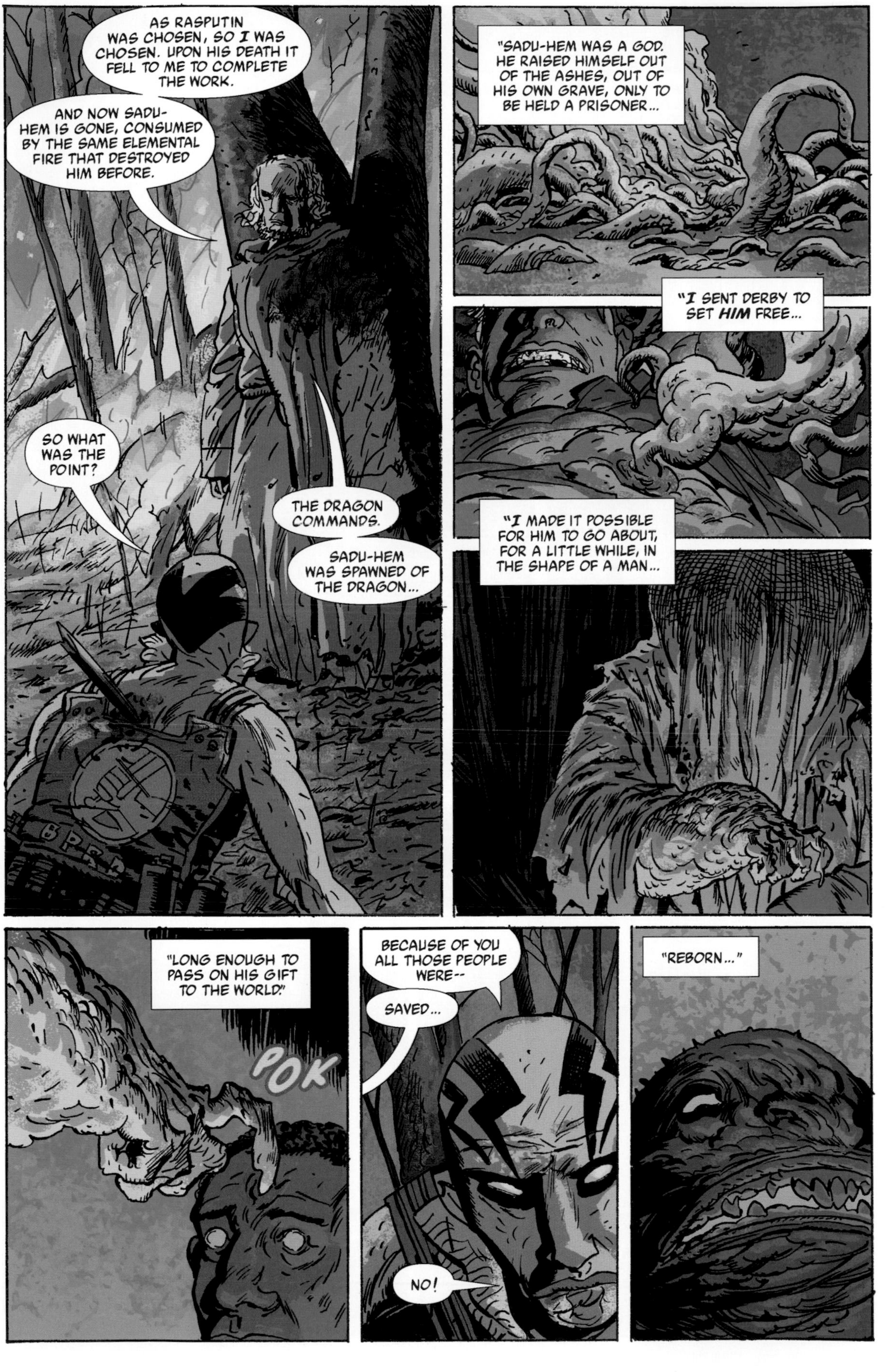
AS RASPUTIN WAS CHOSEN, SO I WAS CHOSEN. UPON HIS DEATH IT FELL TO ME TO COMPLETE THE WORK.
AND NOW SADU-HEM IS GONE, CONSUMED BY THE SAME ELEMENTAL FIRE THAT DESTROYED HIM BEFORE.
SO WHAT WAS THE POINT?
THE DRAGON COMMANDS.
SADU-HEM WAS SPAWNED OF THE DRAGON...
"SADU-HEM WAS A GOD. HE RAISED HIMSELF OUT OF THE ASHES, OUT OF HIS OWN GRAVE, ONLY TO BE HELD A PRISONER...
"I SENT DERBY TO SET HIM FREE...
"I MADE IT POSSIBLE FOR HIM TO GO ABOUT, FOR A LITTLE WHILE, IN THE SHAPE OF A MAN...
"LONG ENOUGH TO PASS ON HIS GIFT TO THE WORLD."
POK
BECAUSE OF YOU ALL THOSE PEOPLE WERE--
SAVED...
NO!
"REBORN..."

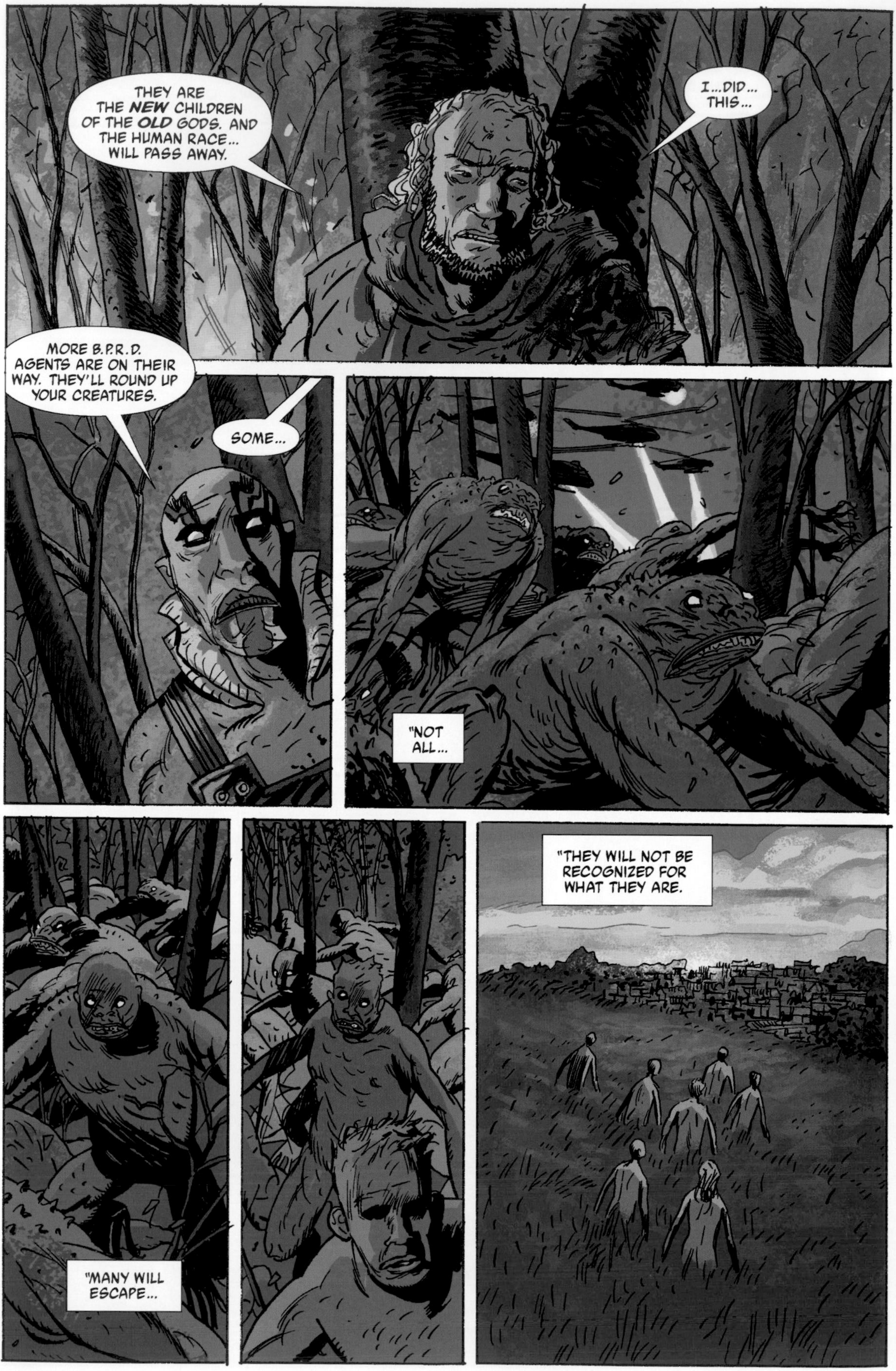
THEY ARE THE *NEW* CHILDREN OF THE *OLD* GODS. AND THE HUMAN RACE... WILL PASS AWAY.
I...DID... THIS...
MORE B.P.R.D. AGENTS ARE ON THEIR WAY. THEY'LL ROUND UP YOUR CREATURES.
SOME...
"NOT ALL...
"MANY WILL ESCAPE...
"THEY WILL NOT BE RECOGNIZED FOR WHAT THEY ARE.

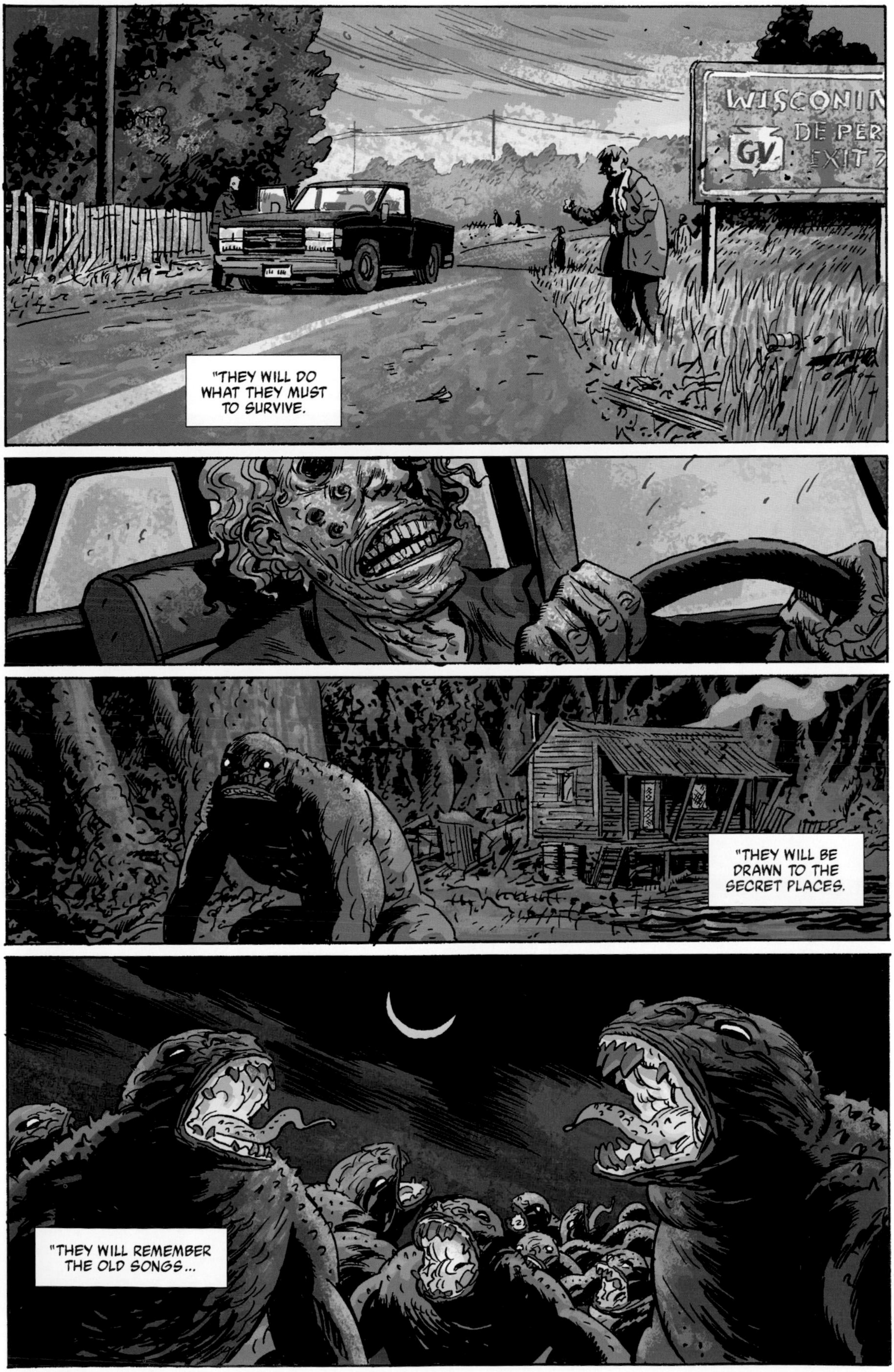
GV
"THEY WILL DO WHAT THEY MUST TO SURVIVE.
"THEY WILL BE DRAWN TO THE SECRET PLACES.
"THEY WILL REMEMBER THE OLD SONGS...

"...PRAYERS NOT HEARD IN A MILLION YEARS ON THIS EARTH...

"...AND THEY WILL SING...AND PRAY...

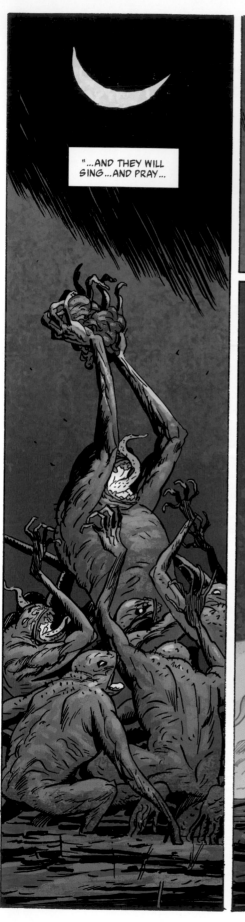

"...AND THE OLD GODS **WILL** WAKE..."

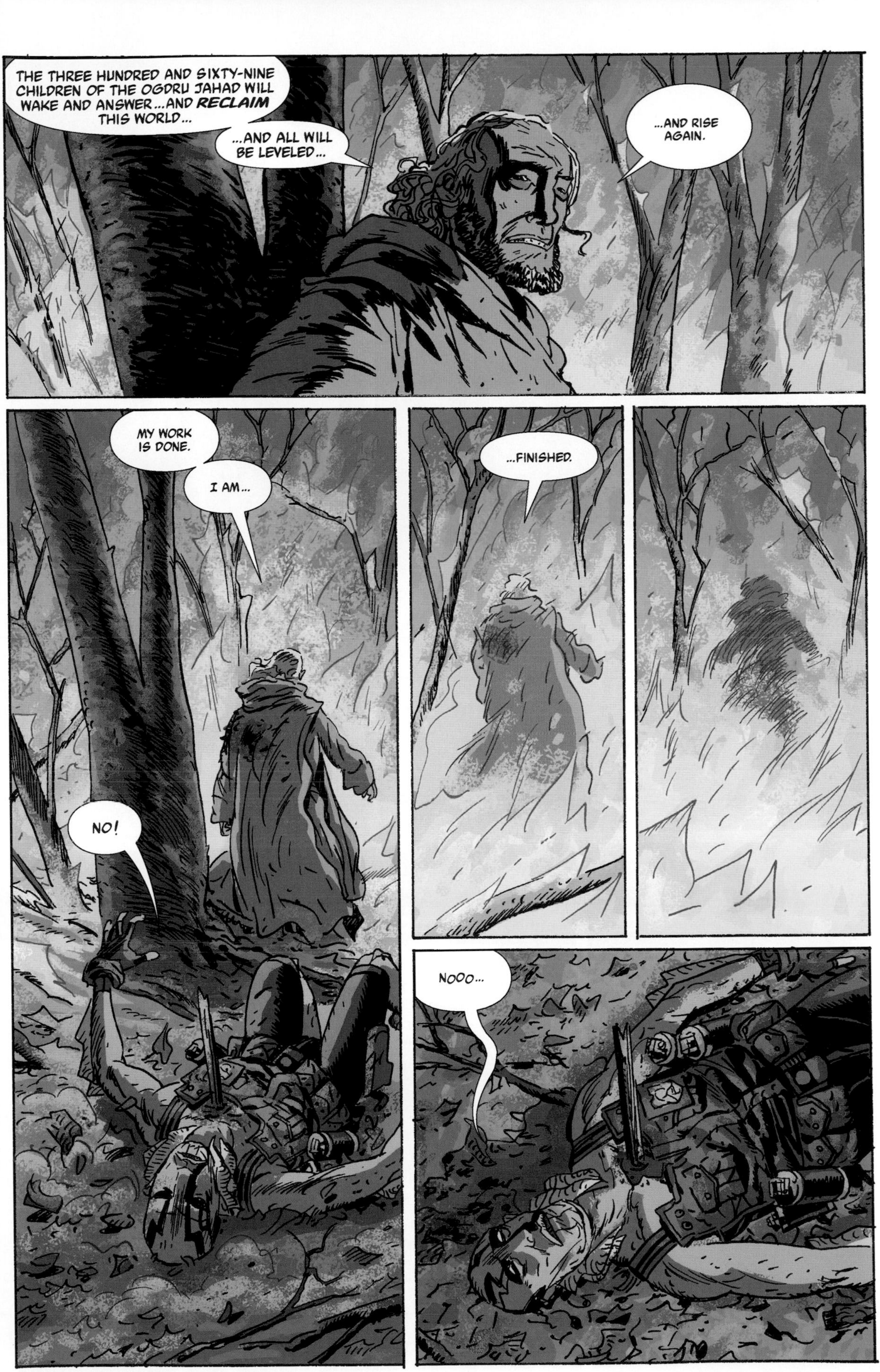
THE THREE HUNDRED AND SIXTY-NINE CHILDREN OF THE OGDRU JAHAD WILL WAKE AND ANSWER...AND RECLAIM THIS WORLD...
...AND ALL WILL BE LEVELED...
...AND RISE AGAIN.
MY WORK IS DONE.
I AM...
...FINISHED.
NO!
NOOO...

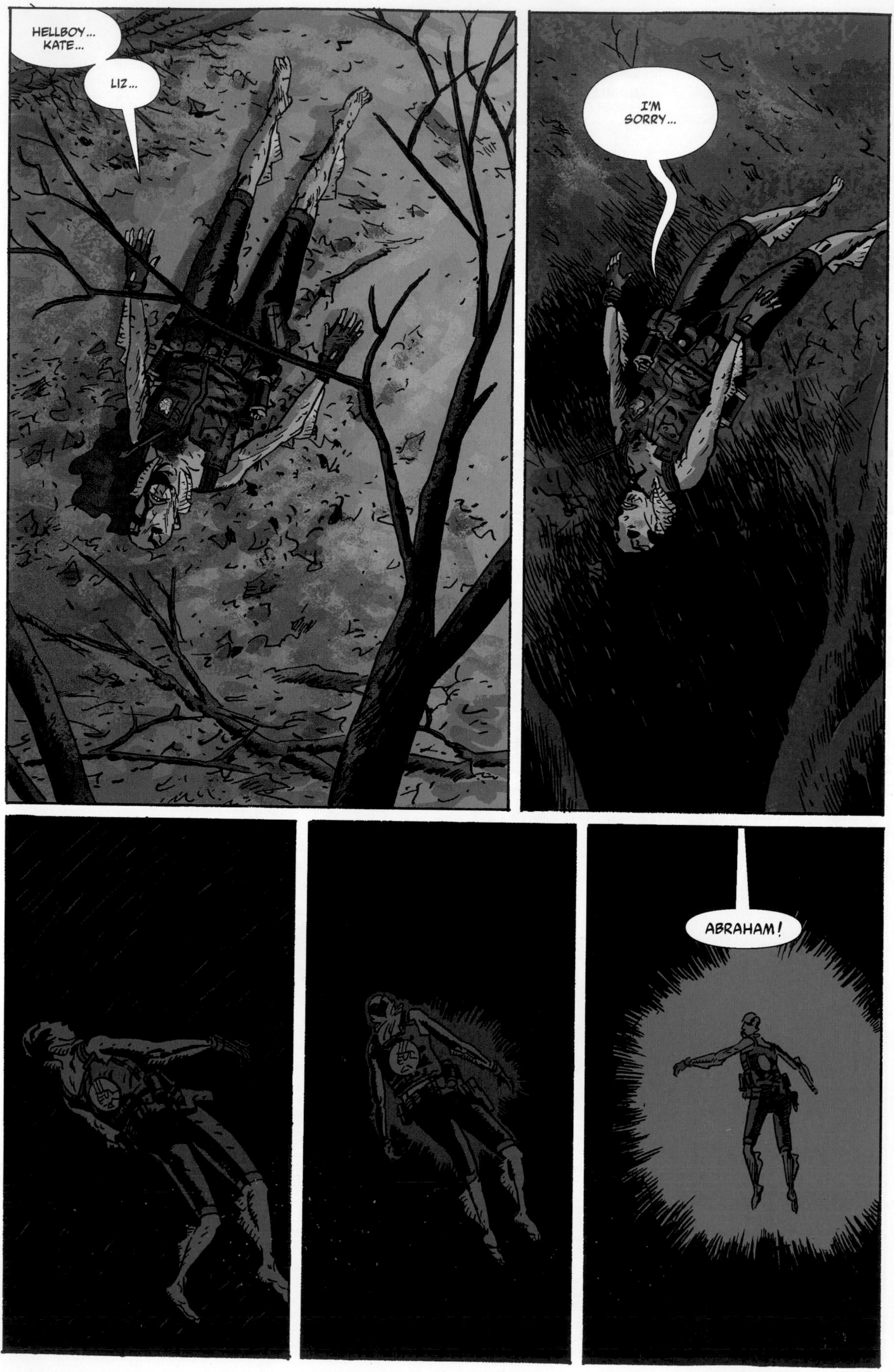
HELLBOY... KATE...
LIZ...
I'M SORRY...
ABRAHAM!

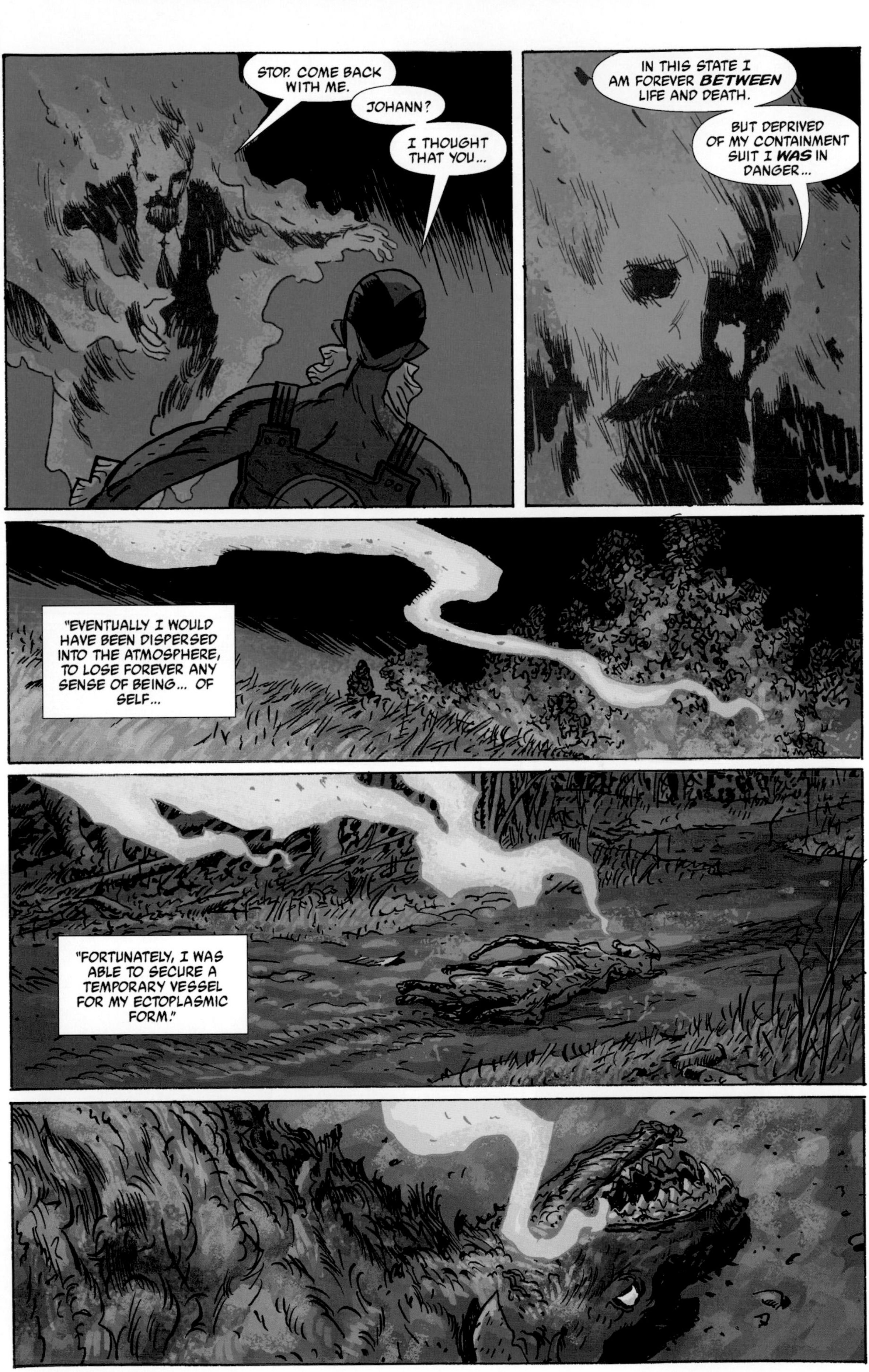
STOP. COME BACK WITH ME.
JOHANN?
I THOUGHT THAT YOU...
IN THIS STATE I AM FOREVER **BETWEEN** LIFE AND DEATH.
BUT DEPRIVED OF MY CONTAINMENT SUIT I **WAS** IN DANGER...
"EVENTUALLY I WOULD HAVE BEEN DISPERSED INTO THE ATMOSPHERE, TO LOSE FOREVER ANY SENSE OF BEING... OF SELF...
"FORTUNATELY, I WAS ABLE TO SECURE A TEMPORARY VESSEL FOR MY ECTOPLASMIC FORM."

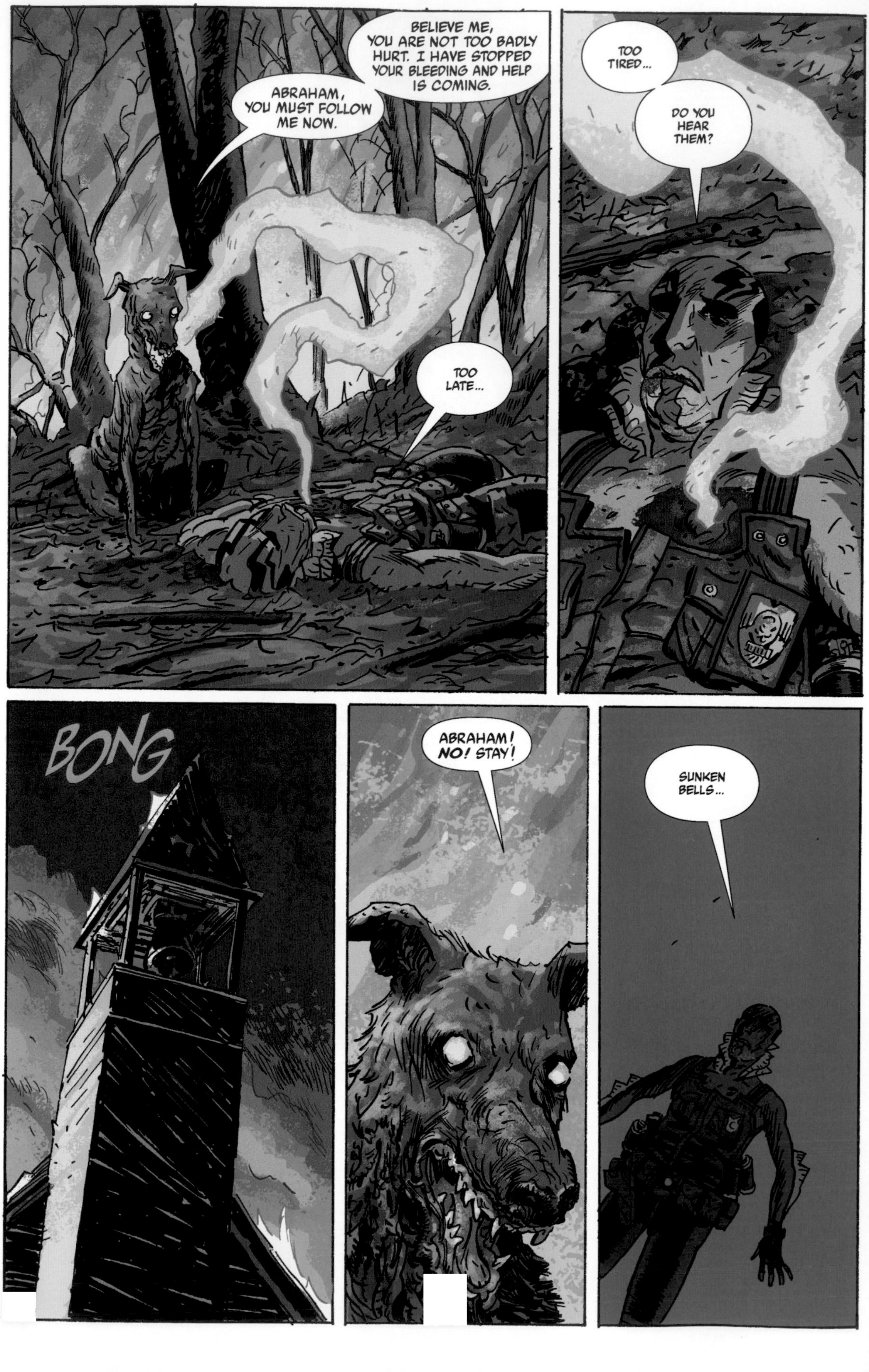
ABRAHAM, YOU MUST FOLLOW ME NOW.
BELIEVE ME, YOU ARE NOT TOO BADLY HURT. I HAVE STOPPED YOUR BLEEDING AND HELP IS COMING.
TOO LATE...
TOO TIRED...
DO YOU HEAR THEM?
BONG
ABRAHAM! NO! STAY!
SUNKEN BELLS...

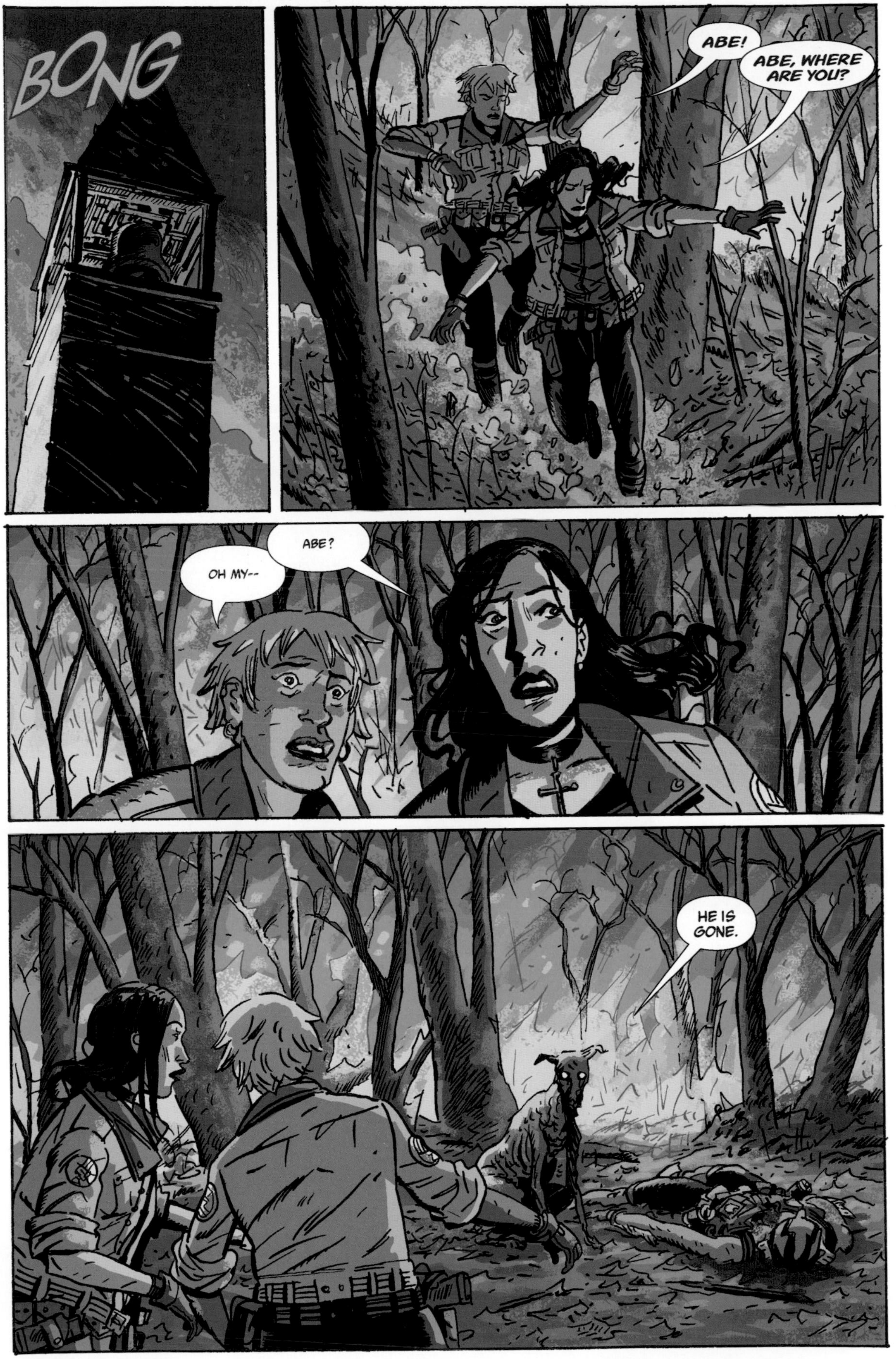
BONG
ABE!
ABE, WHERE ARE YOU?
OH MY--
ABE?
HE IS GONE.

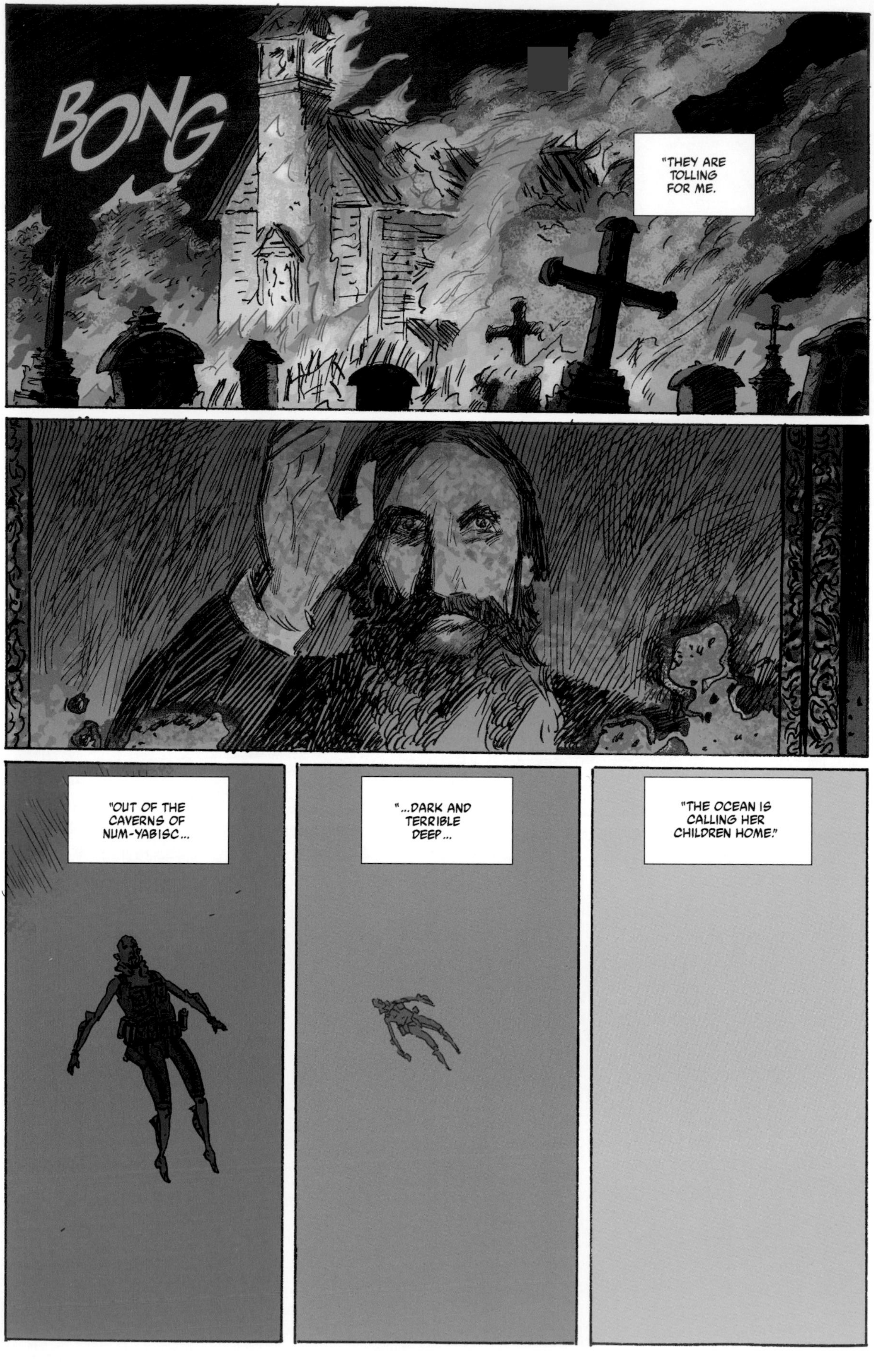
BONG
"THEY ARE TOLLING FOR ME.
"OUT OF THE CAVERNS OF NUM-YABISC...
"...DARK AND TERRIBLE DEEP...
"THE OCEAN IS CALLING HER CHILDREN HOME."

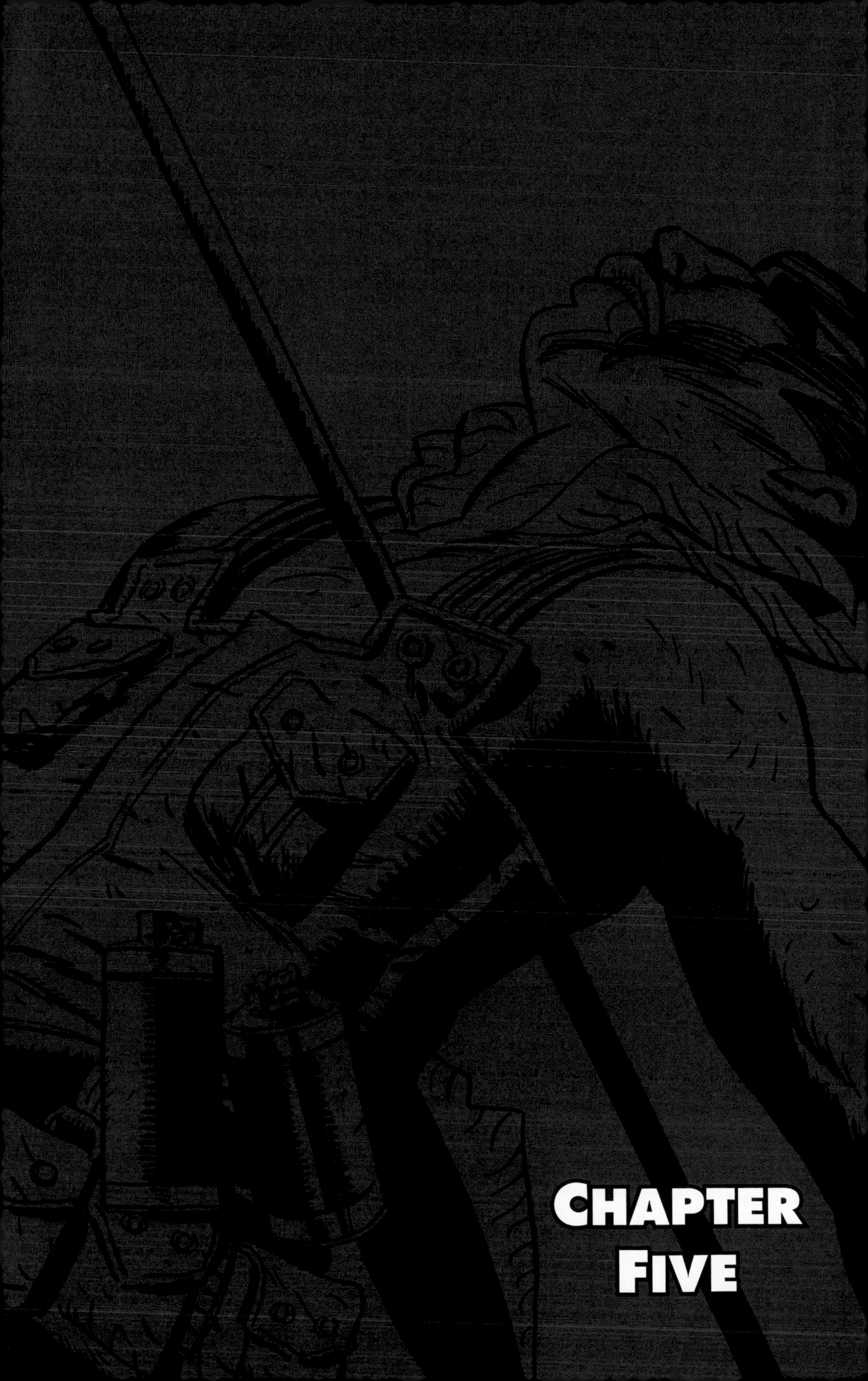

CHAPTER FIVE

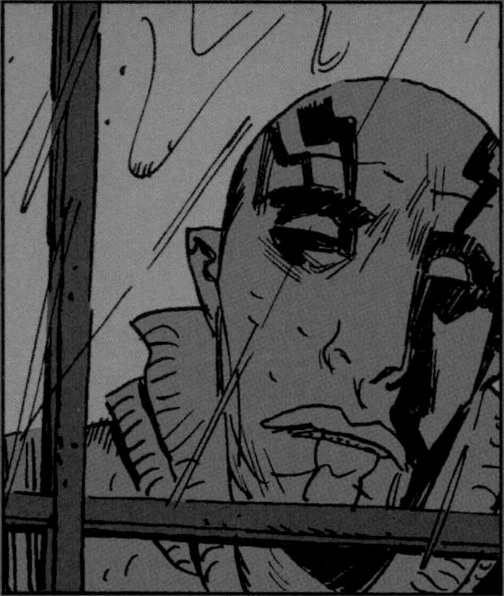

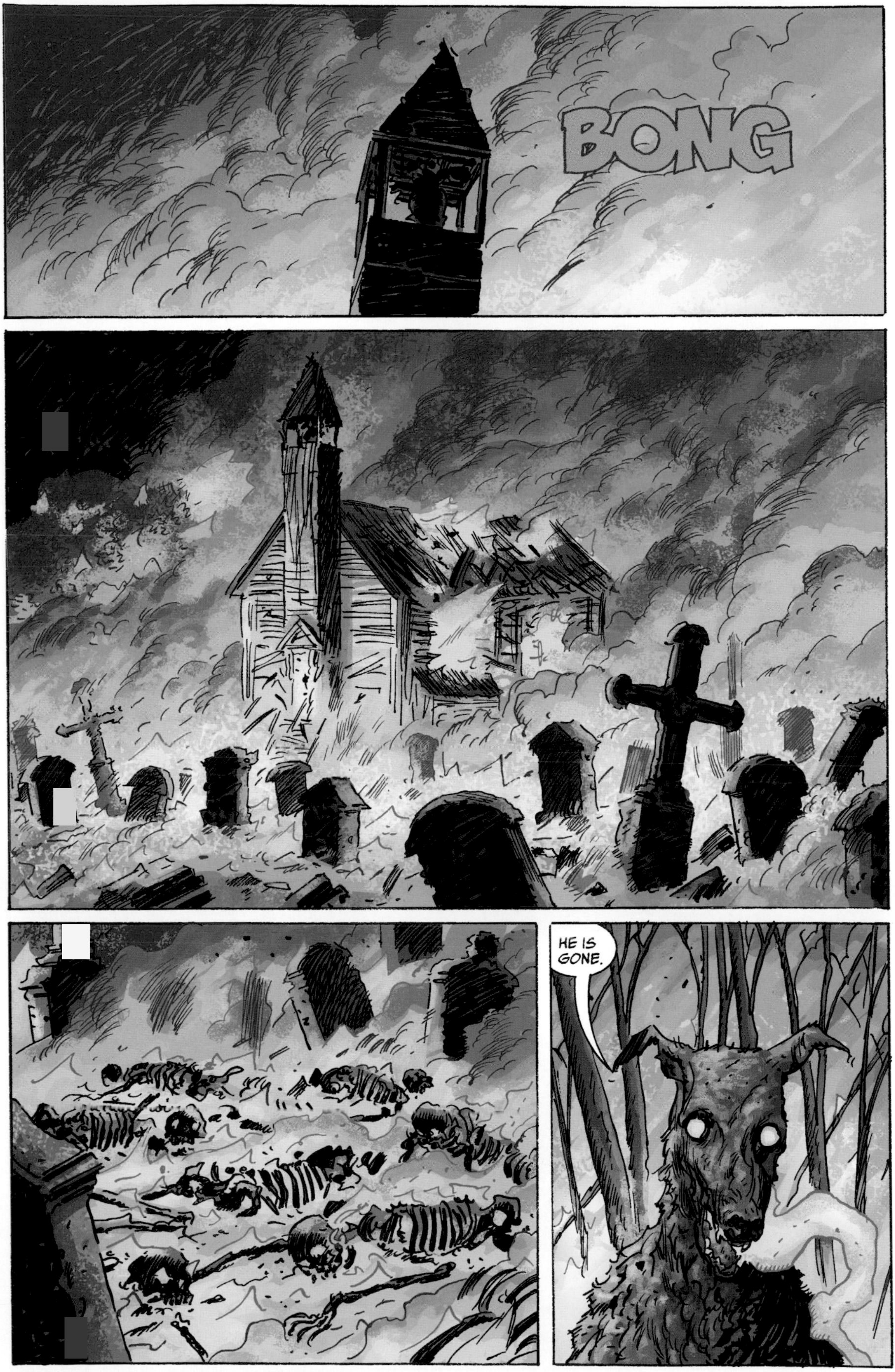
BONG
HE IS GONE.

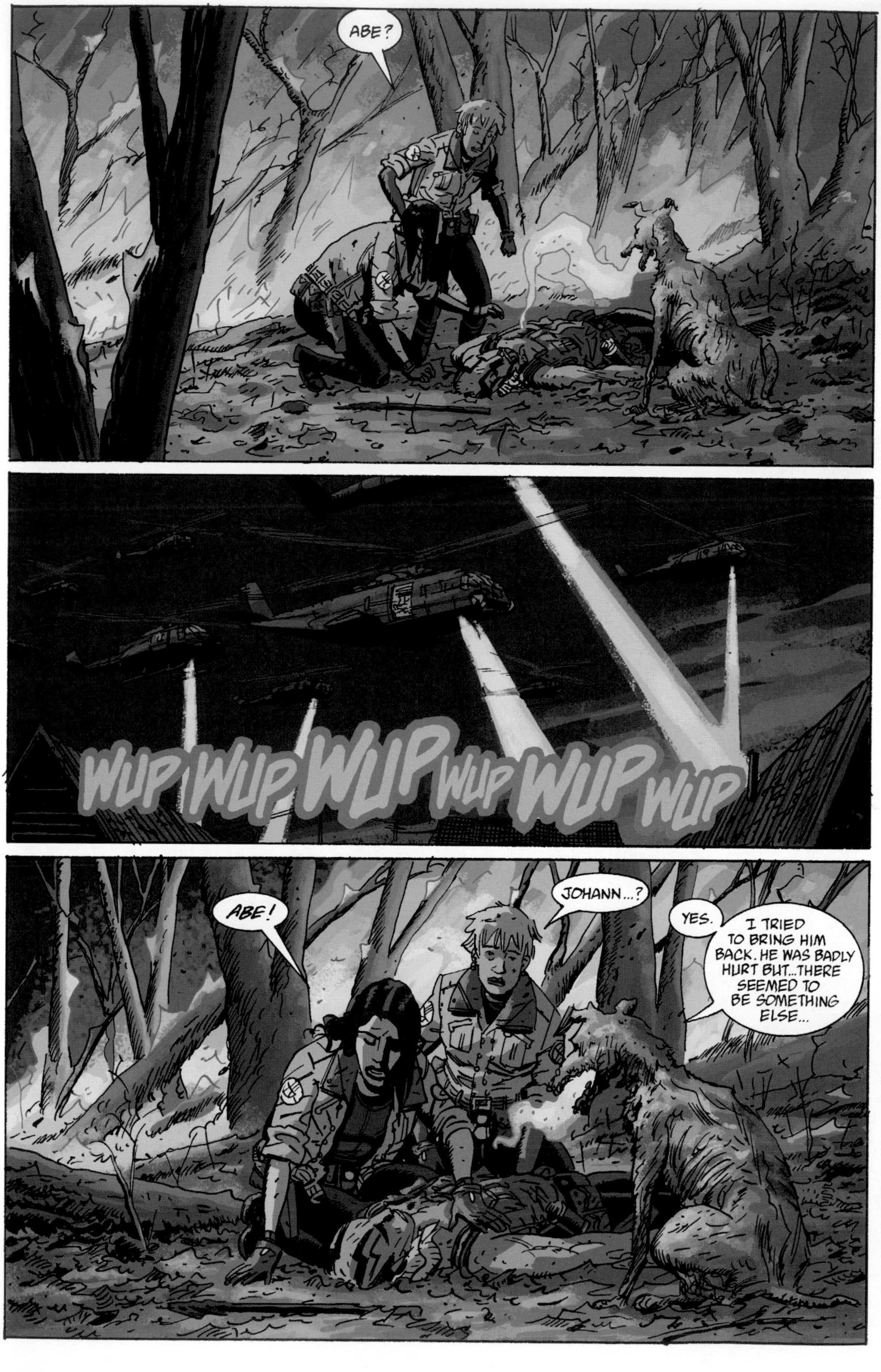
ABE?
WUP WUP WUP WUP WUP WUP
ABE!
JOHANN...?
YES.
I TRIED TO BRING HIM BACK. HE WAS BADLY HURT BUT...THERE SEEMED TO BE SOMETHING ELSE...

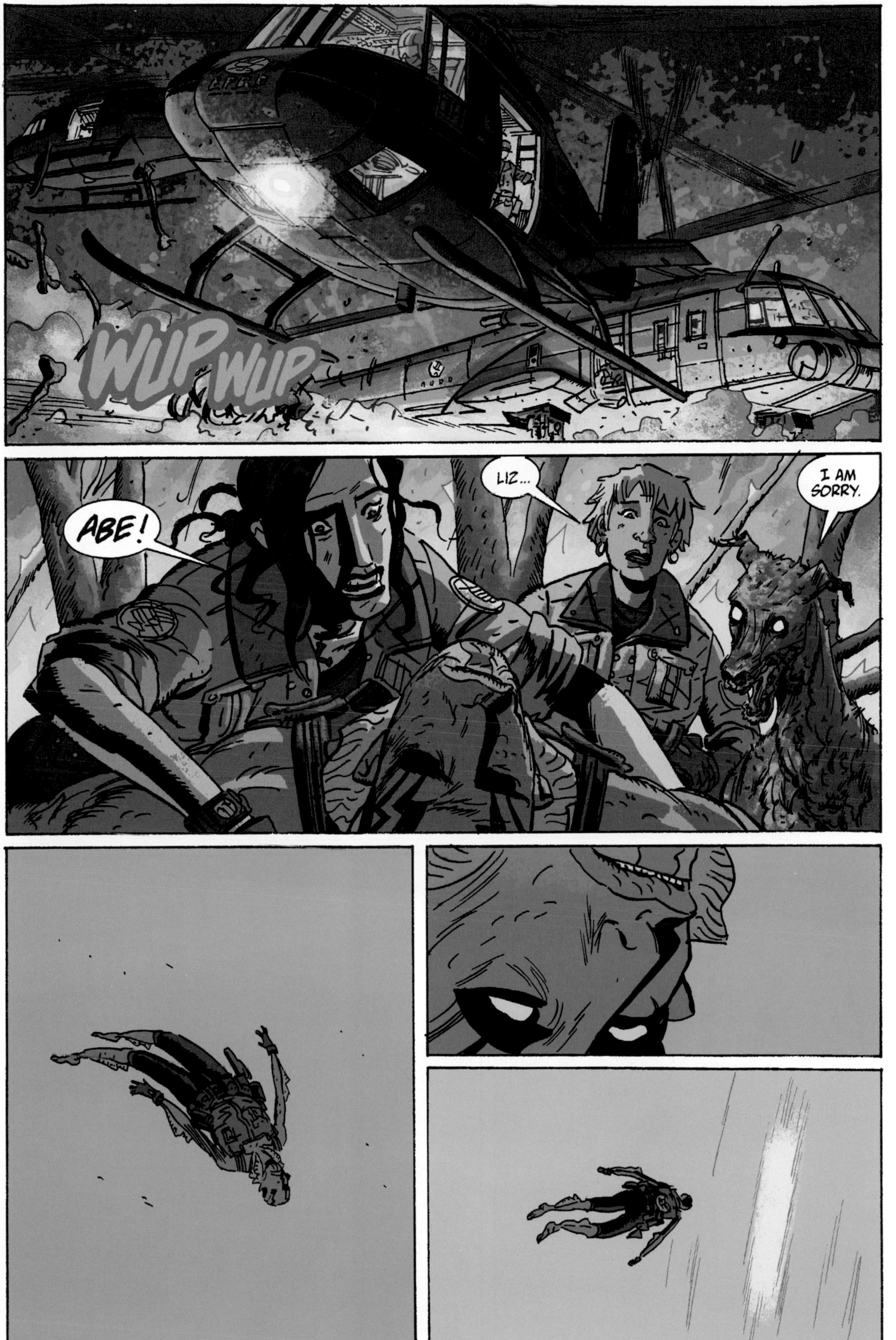
WUP WUP
ABE!
LIZ...
I AM SORRY.

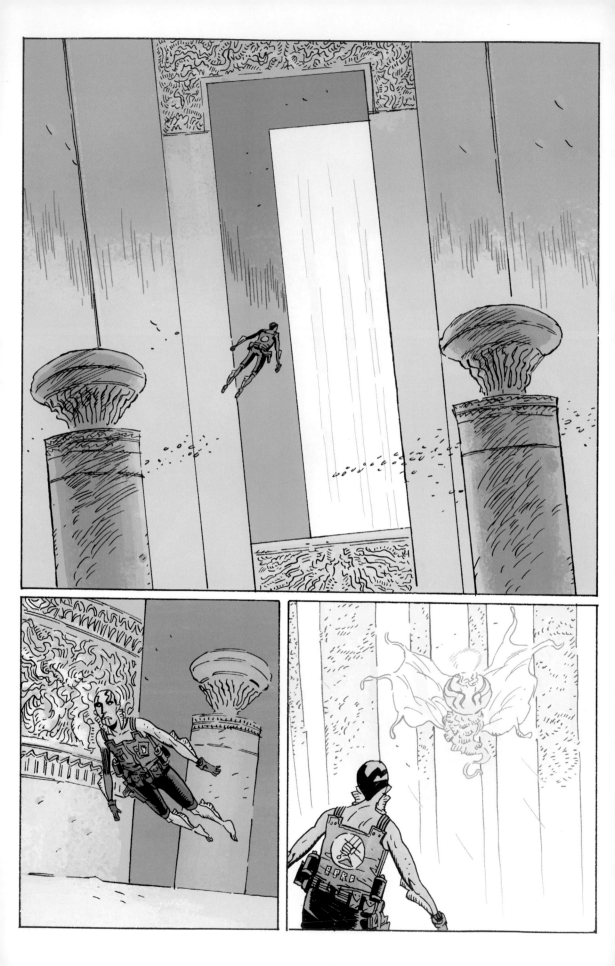

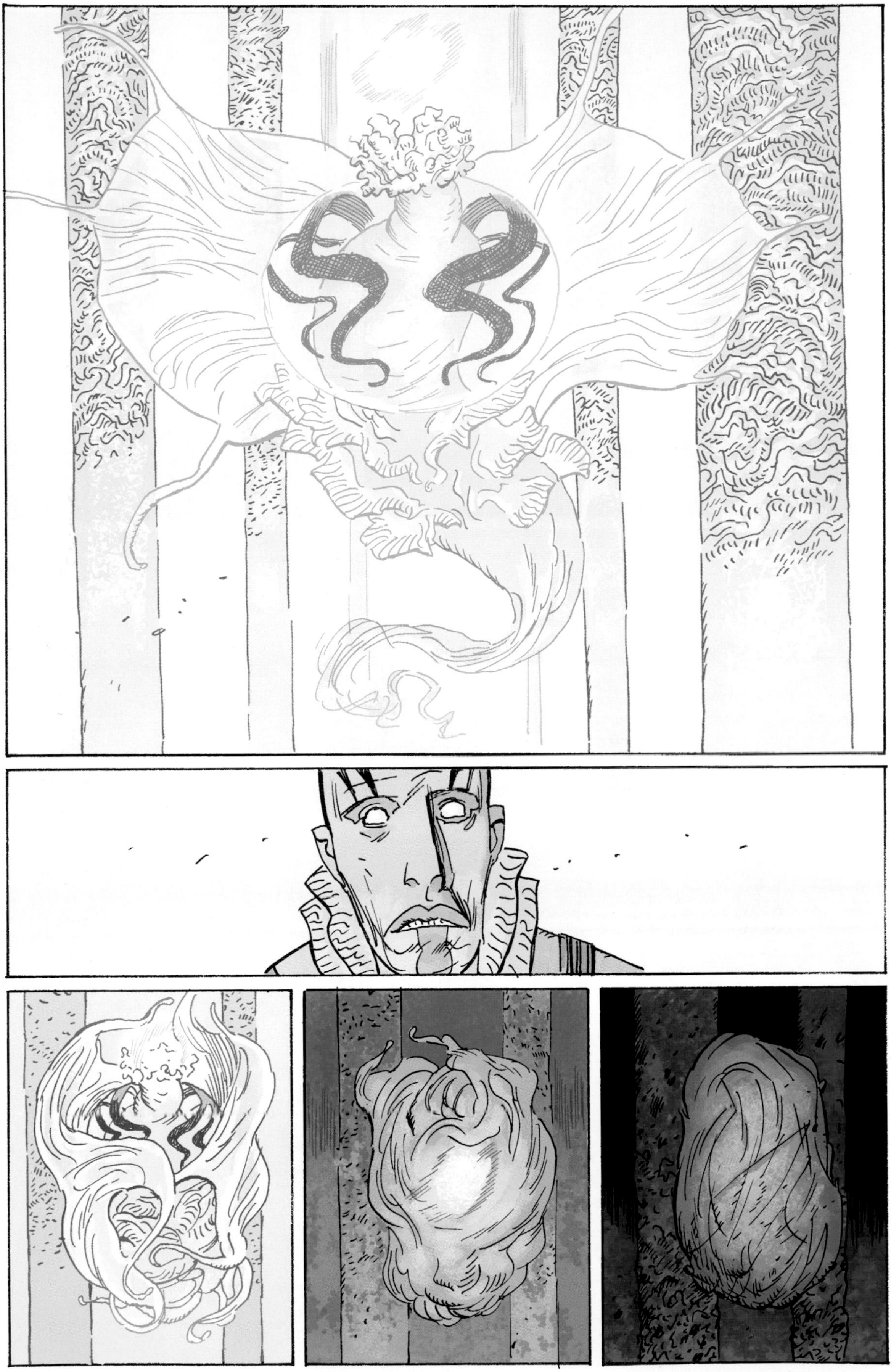

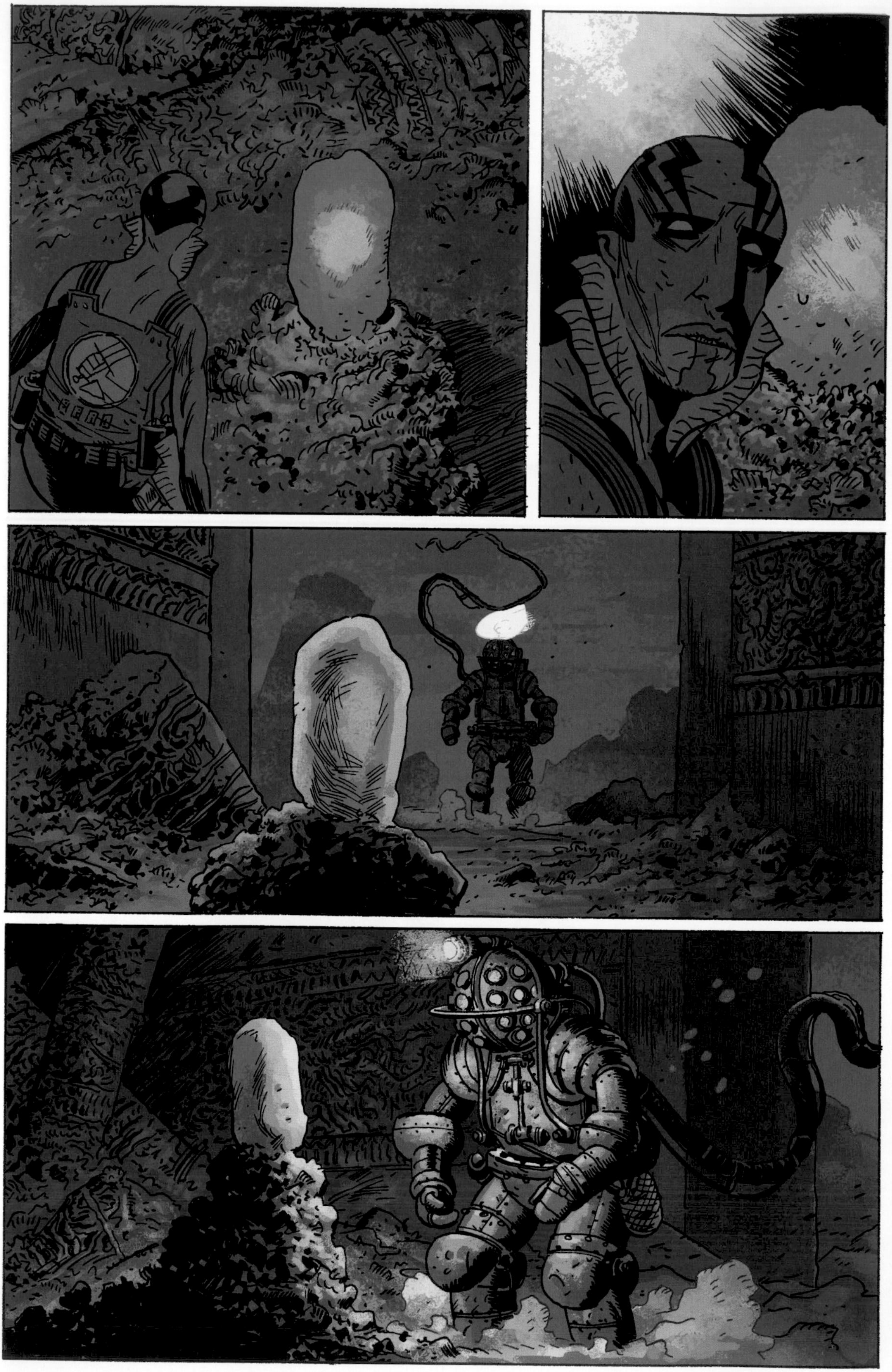

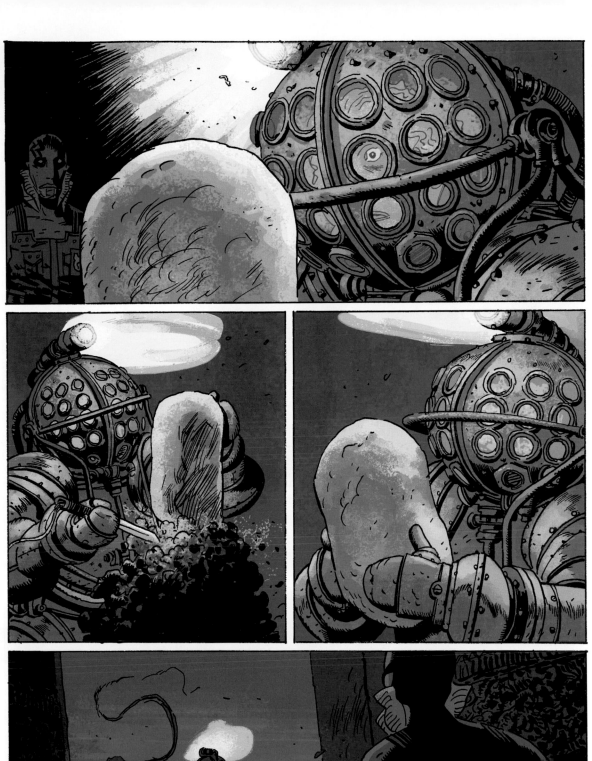

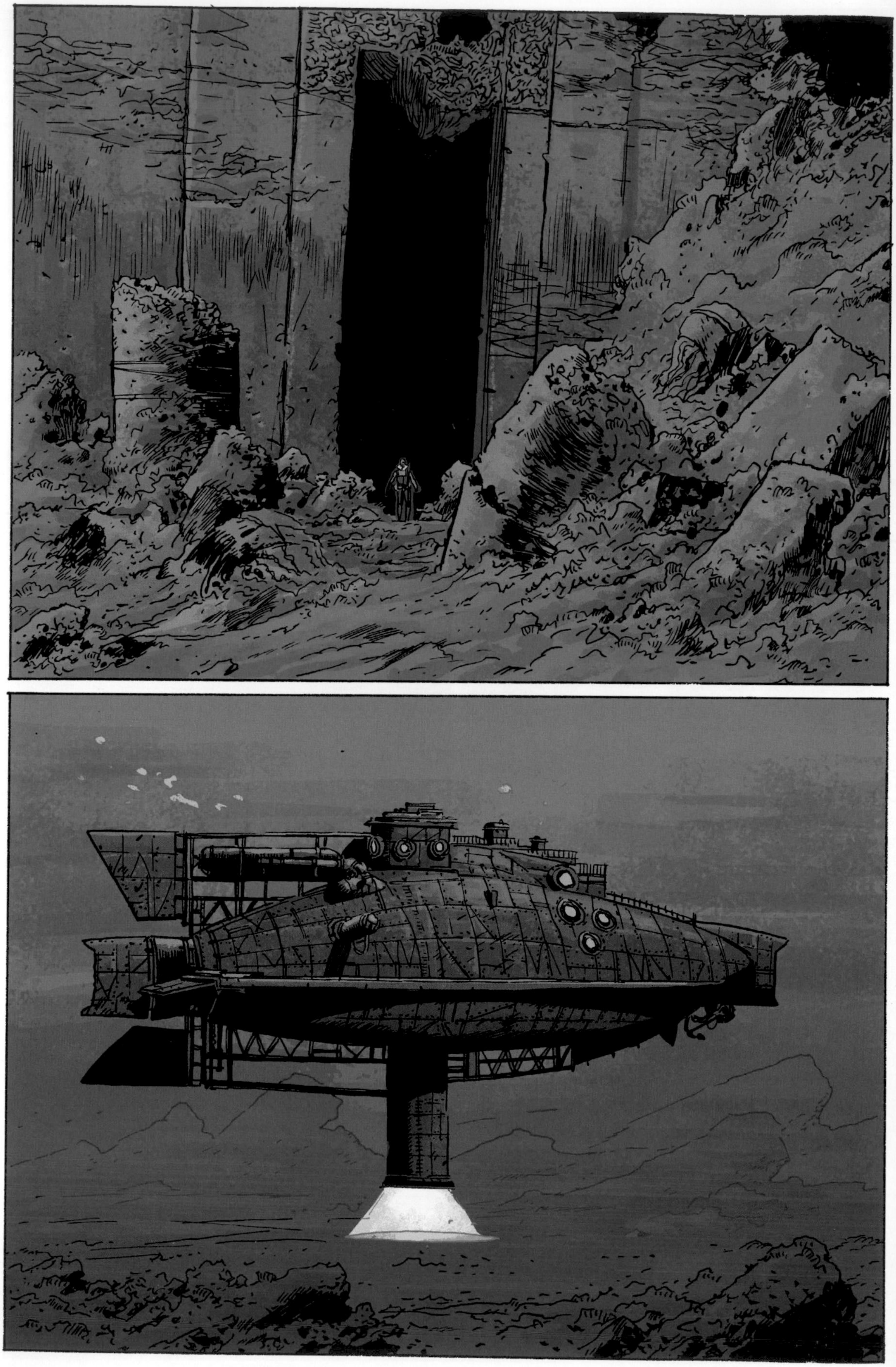

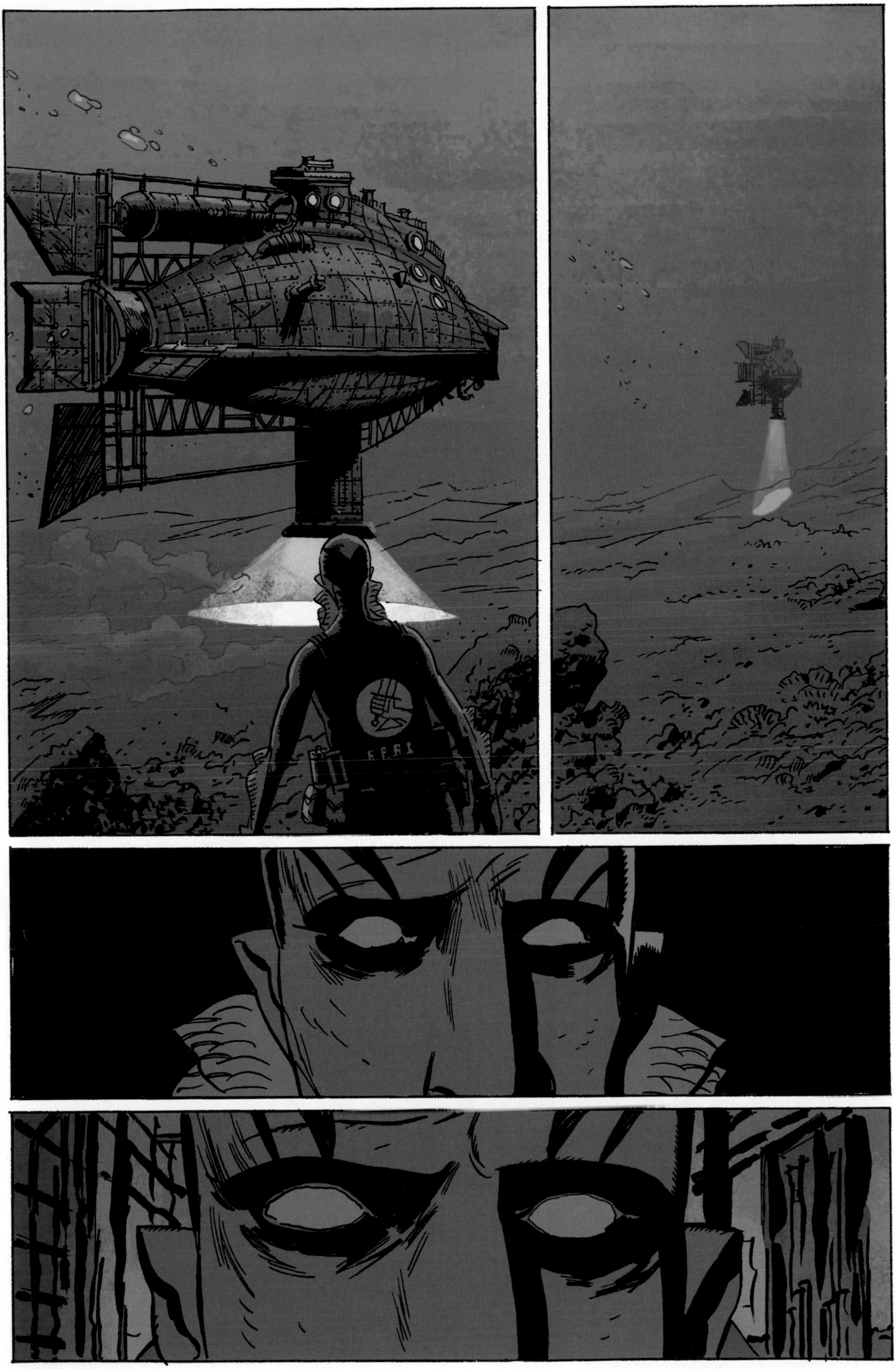

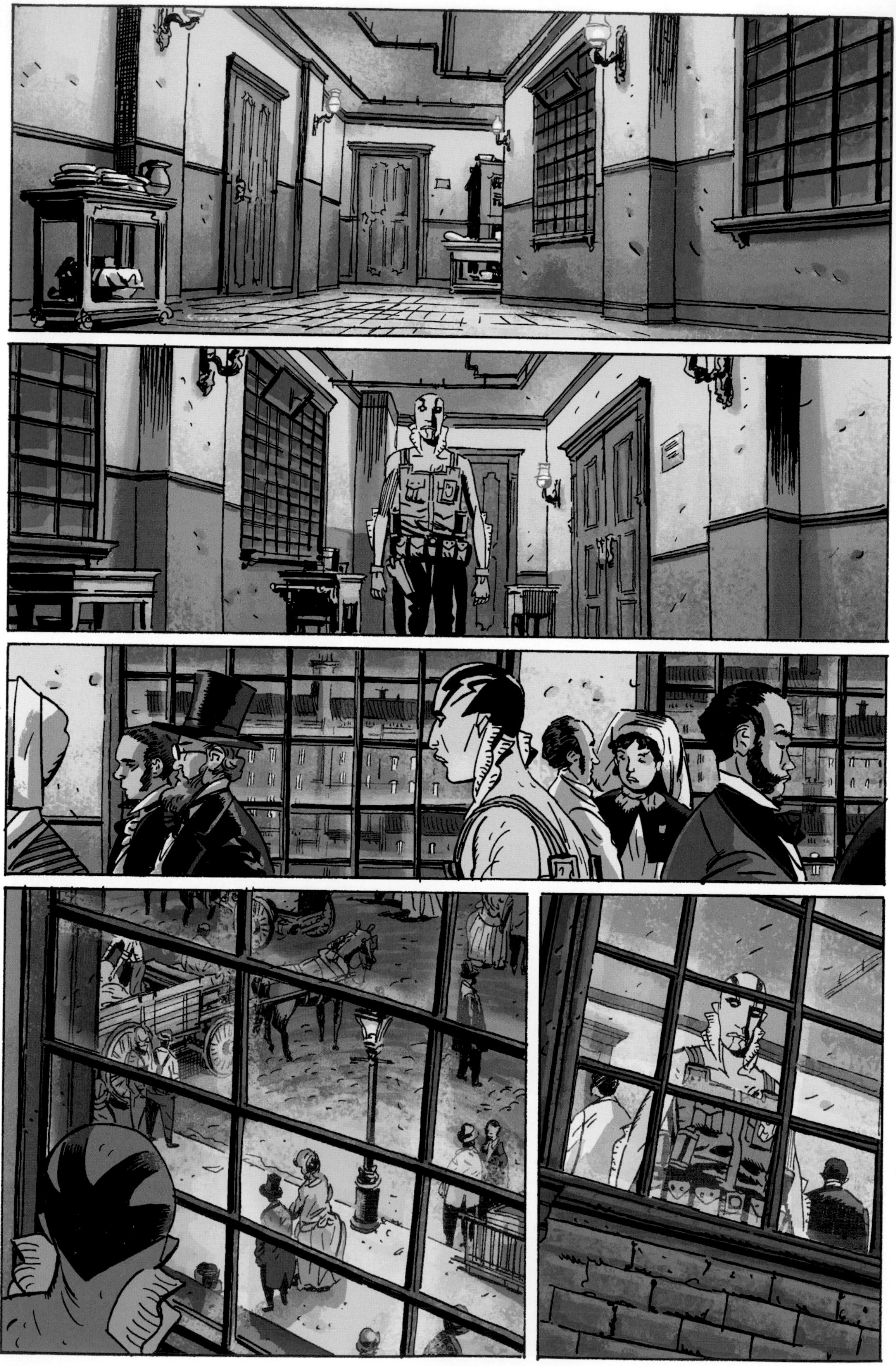

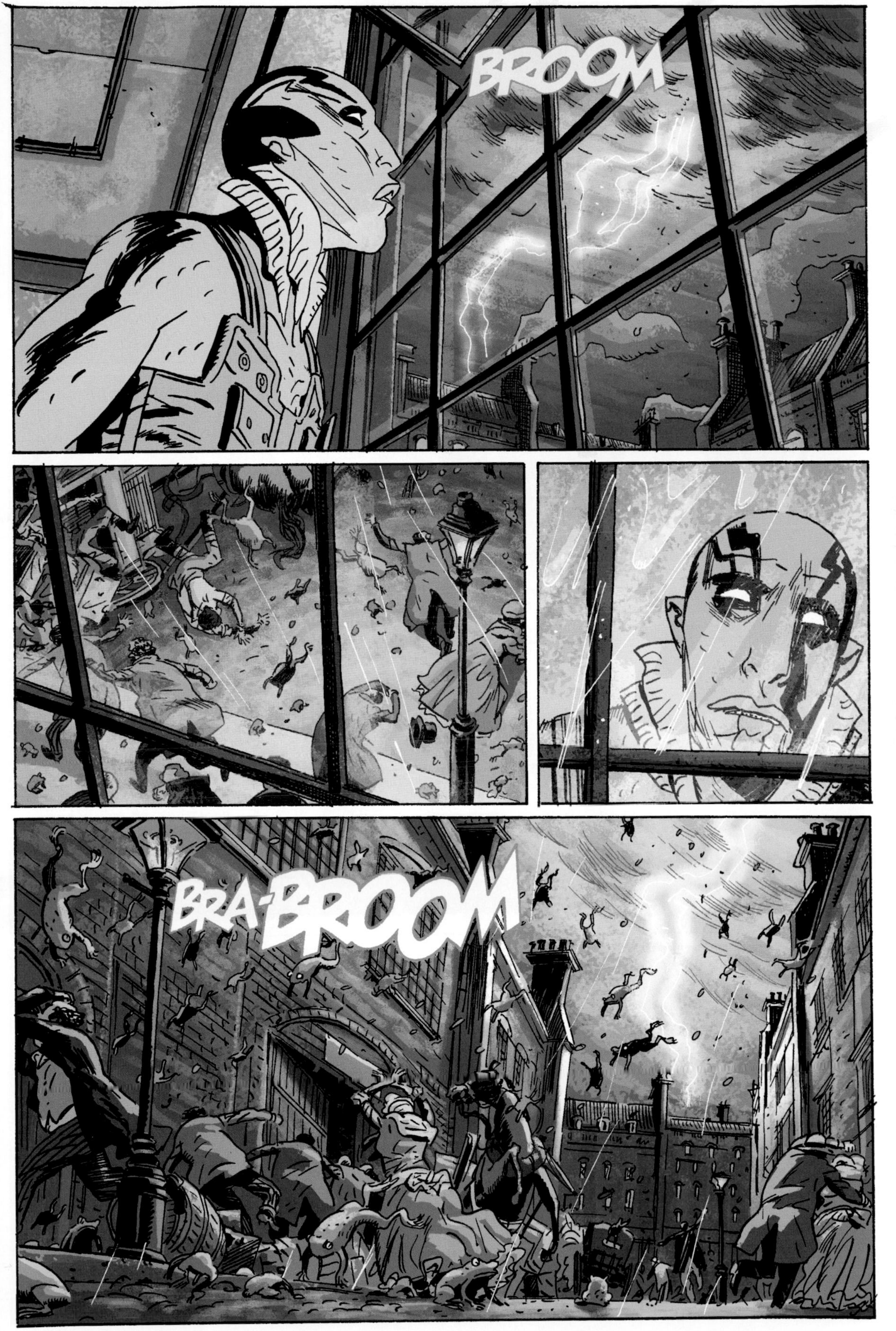
BROOM
BRA-BROOM

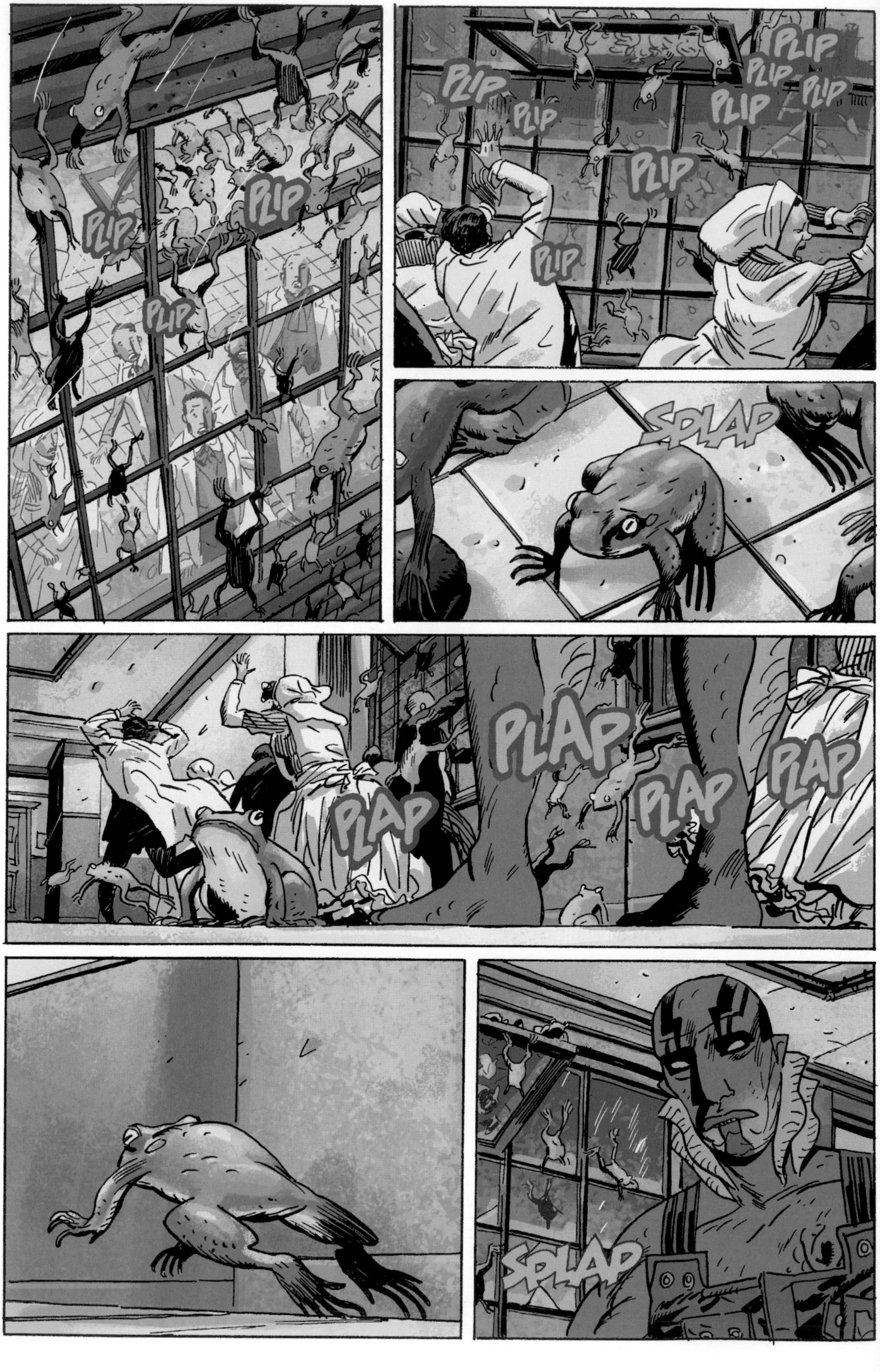
PLIP
PLIP
PLIP
PLIP
PLIP
PLIP
PLIP
PLIP
PLIP
PLIP
PLIP
SPLAP
PLAP
PLAP
PLAP
PLAP
SPLAP

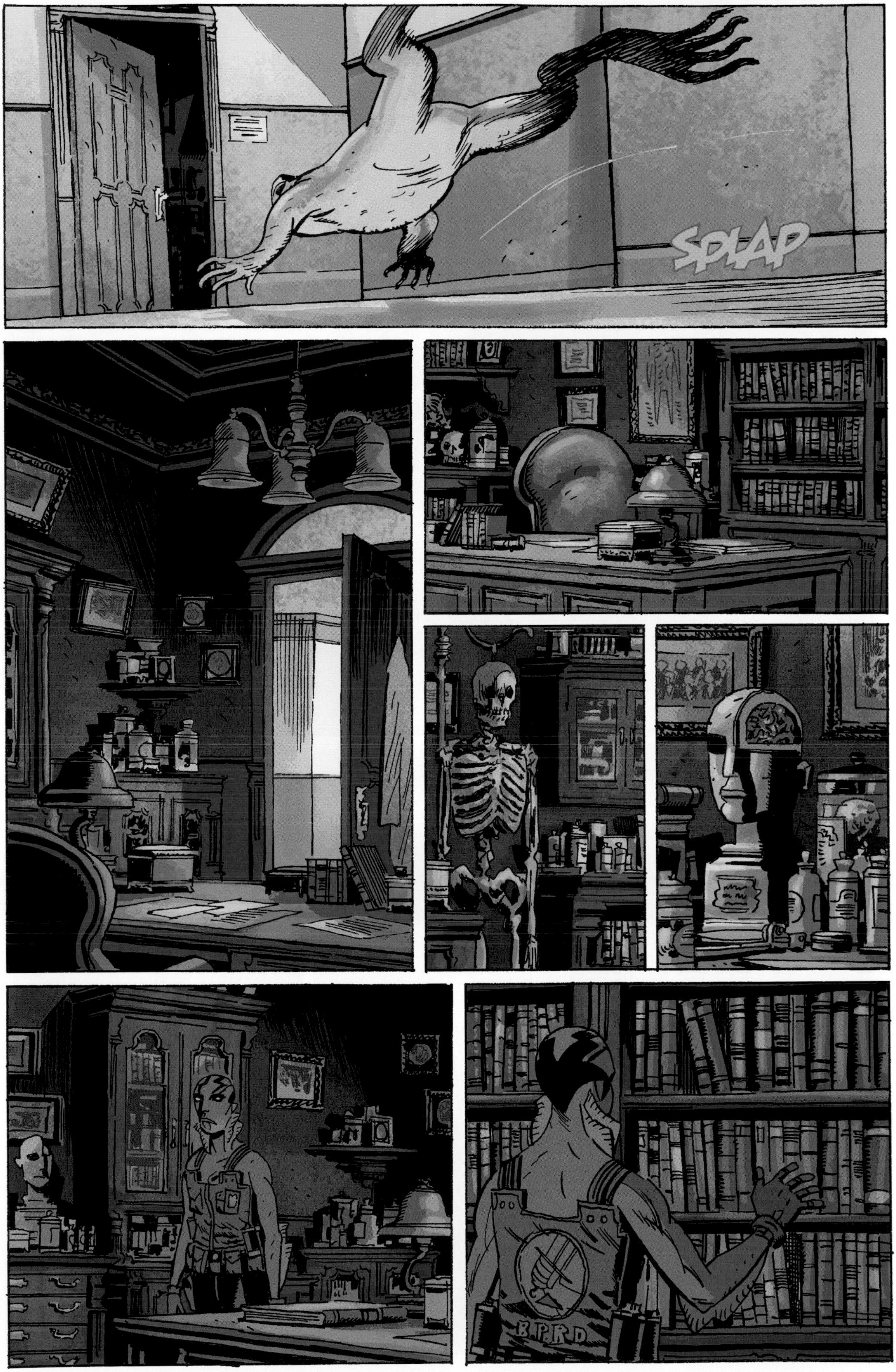
SPLAP
B.P.R.D.

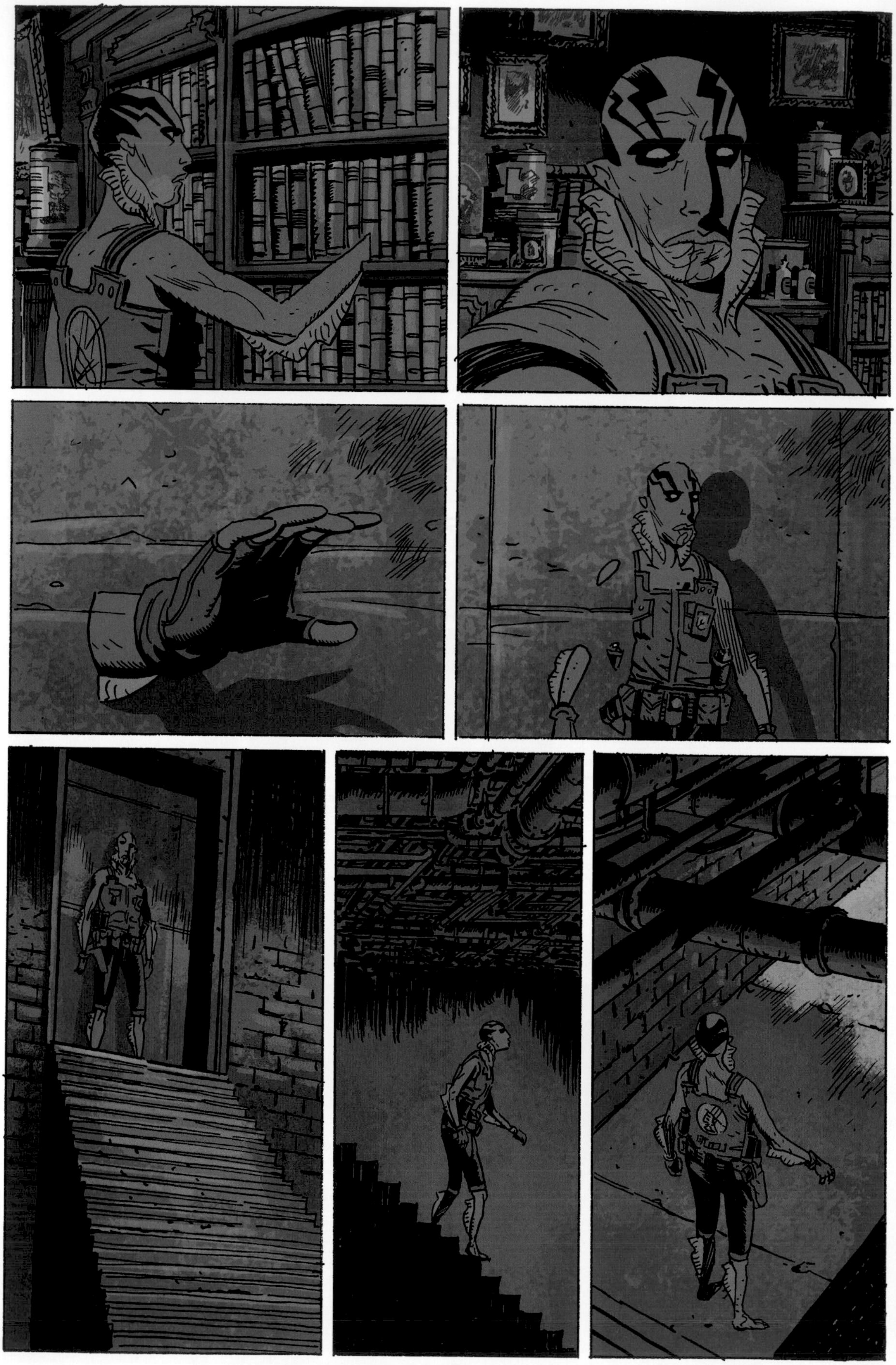

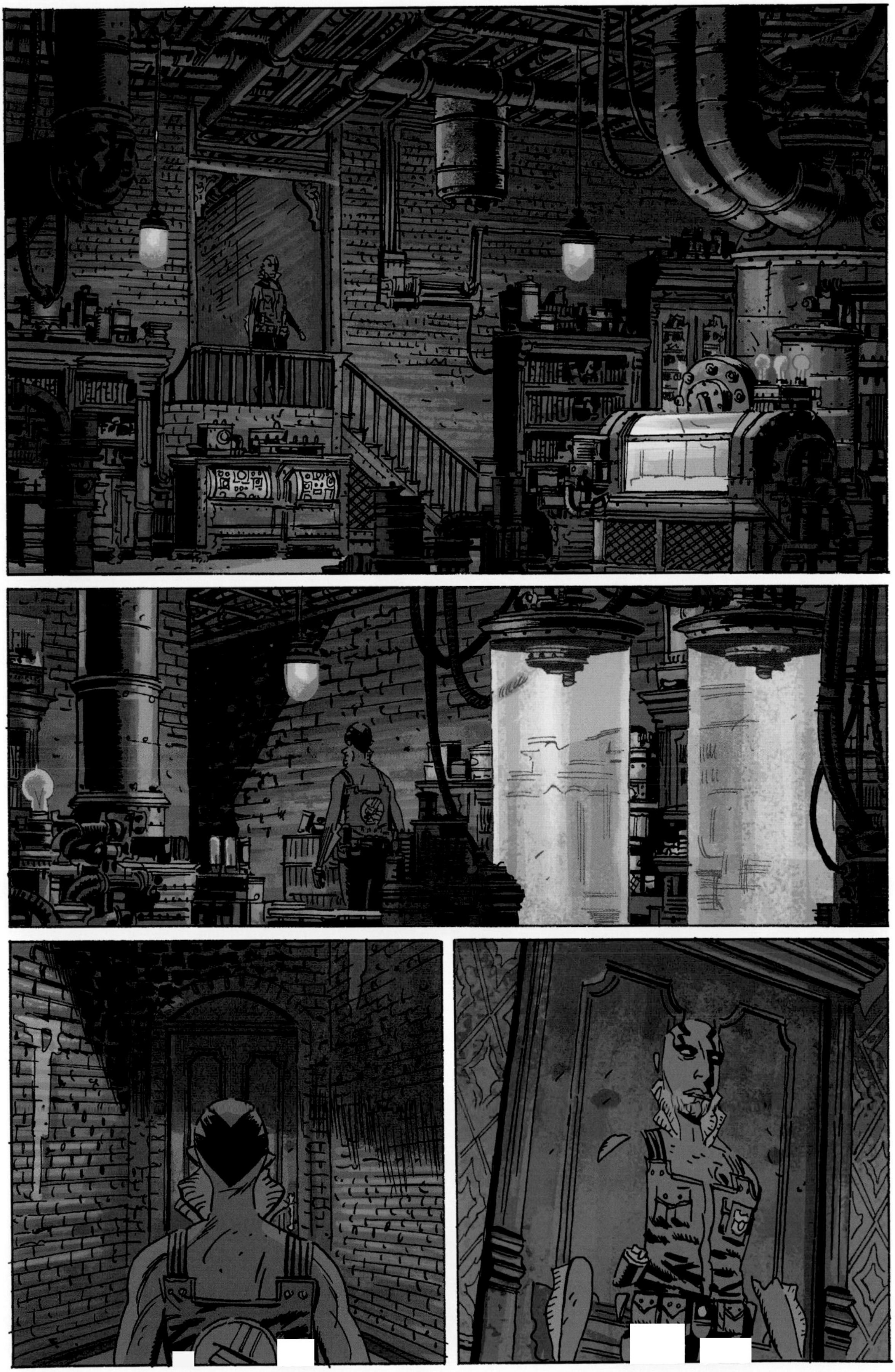

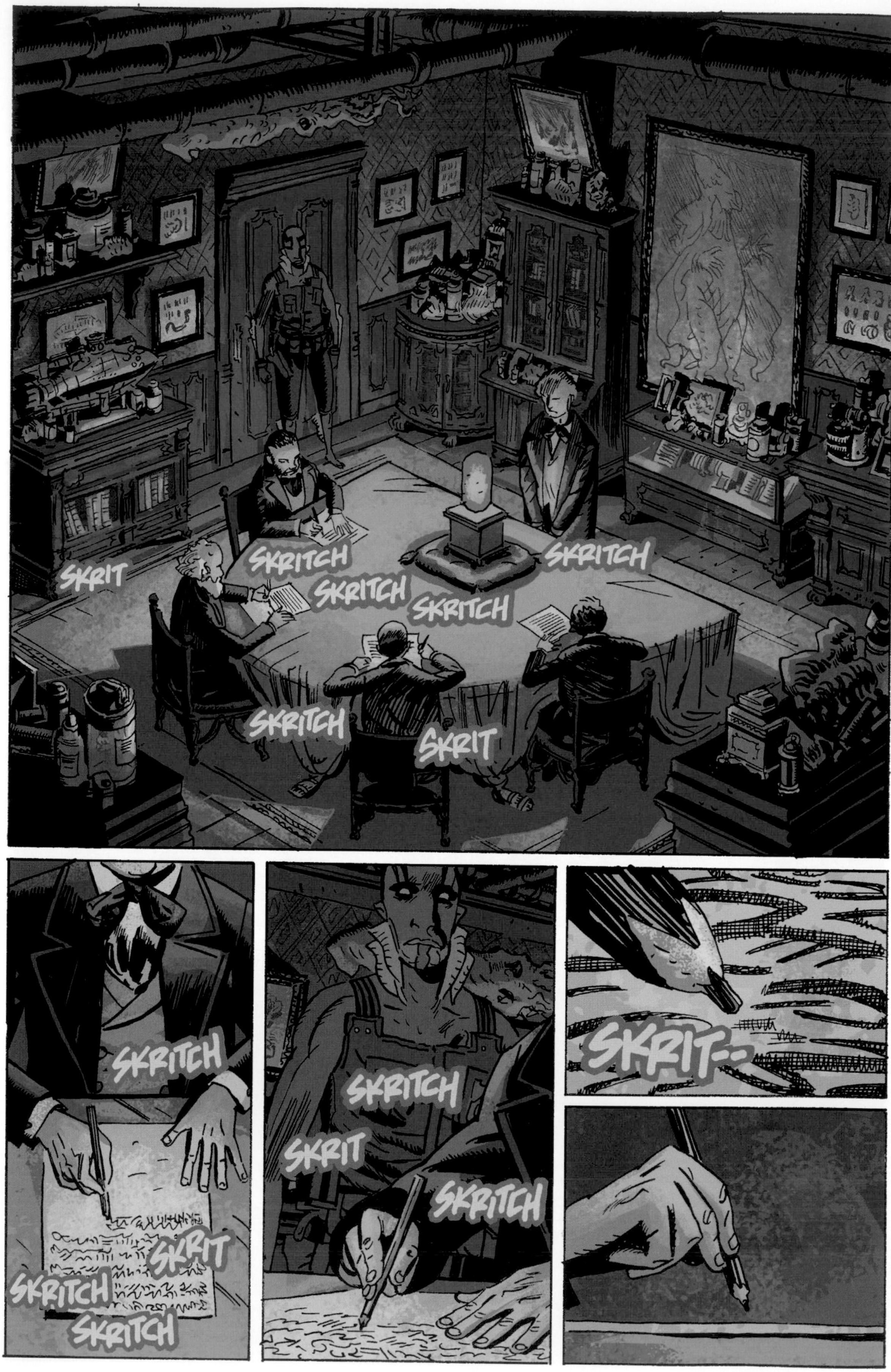
SKRITCH
SKRITCH
SKRIT
SKRITCH
SKRITCH
SKRITCH
SKRIT
SKRITCH
SKRIT
SKRITCH
SKRITCH
SKRITCH
SKRIT
SKRITCH
SKRIT-

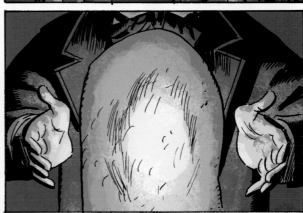

UGHURRAAGAGA UMAA UTHU GAA ATHEMM UGATHAAAR UGUGURATHAAAM UTH E MM UGG ATHAAA AGATHAA ETT URAAA...

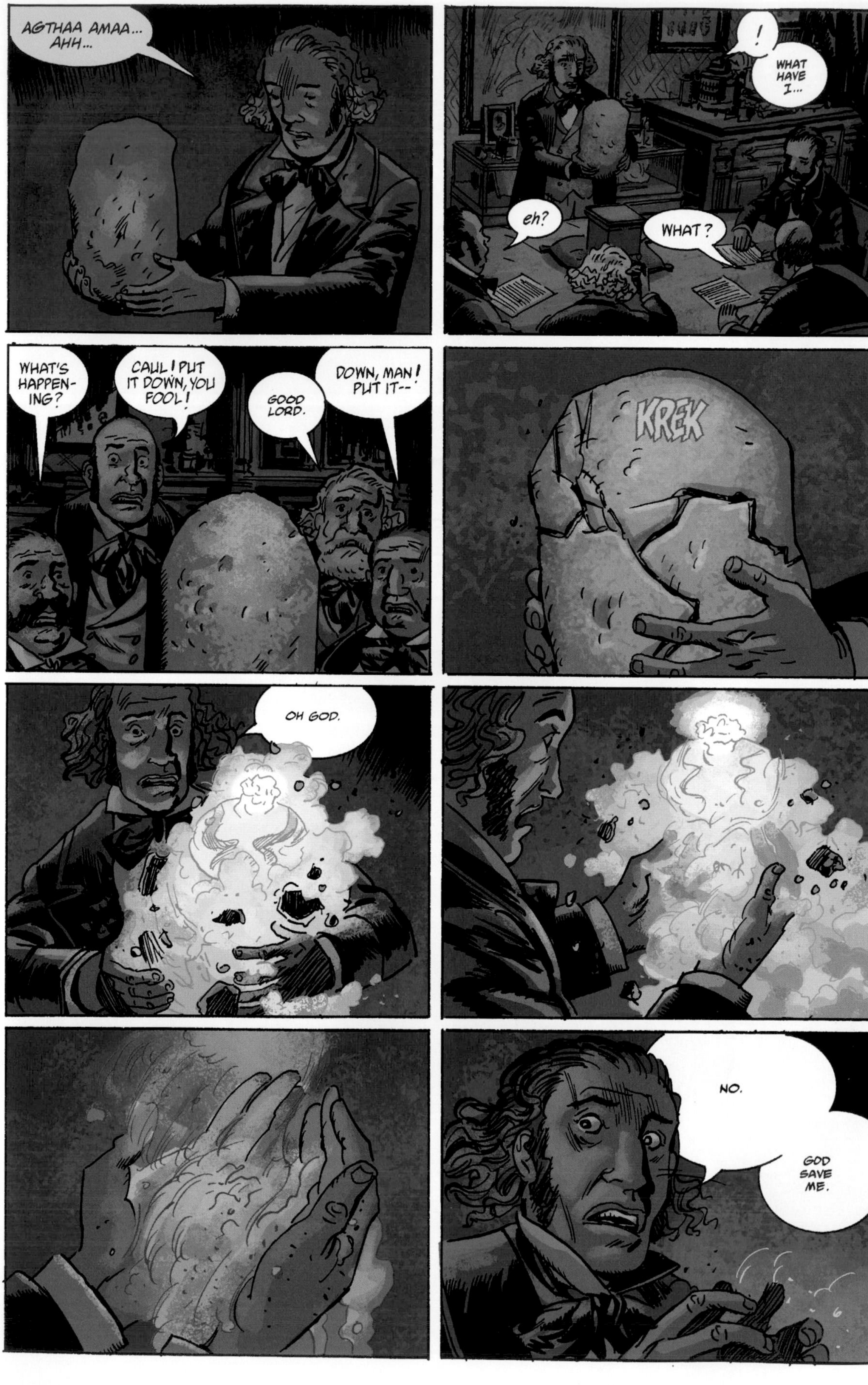
AGTHAA AMAA... AHH...
!
WHAT HAVE I...
eh?
WHAT?
WHAT'S HAPPENING?
CAUL! PUT IT DOWN, YOU FOOL!
GOOD LORD.
DOWN, MAN! PUT IT--
KREK
OH GOD.
NO.
GOD SAVE ME.

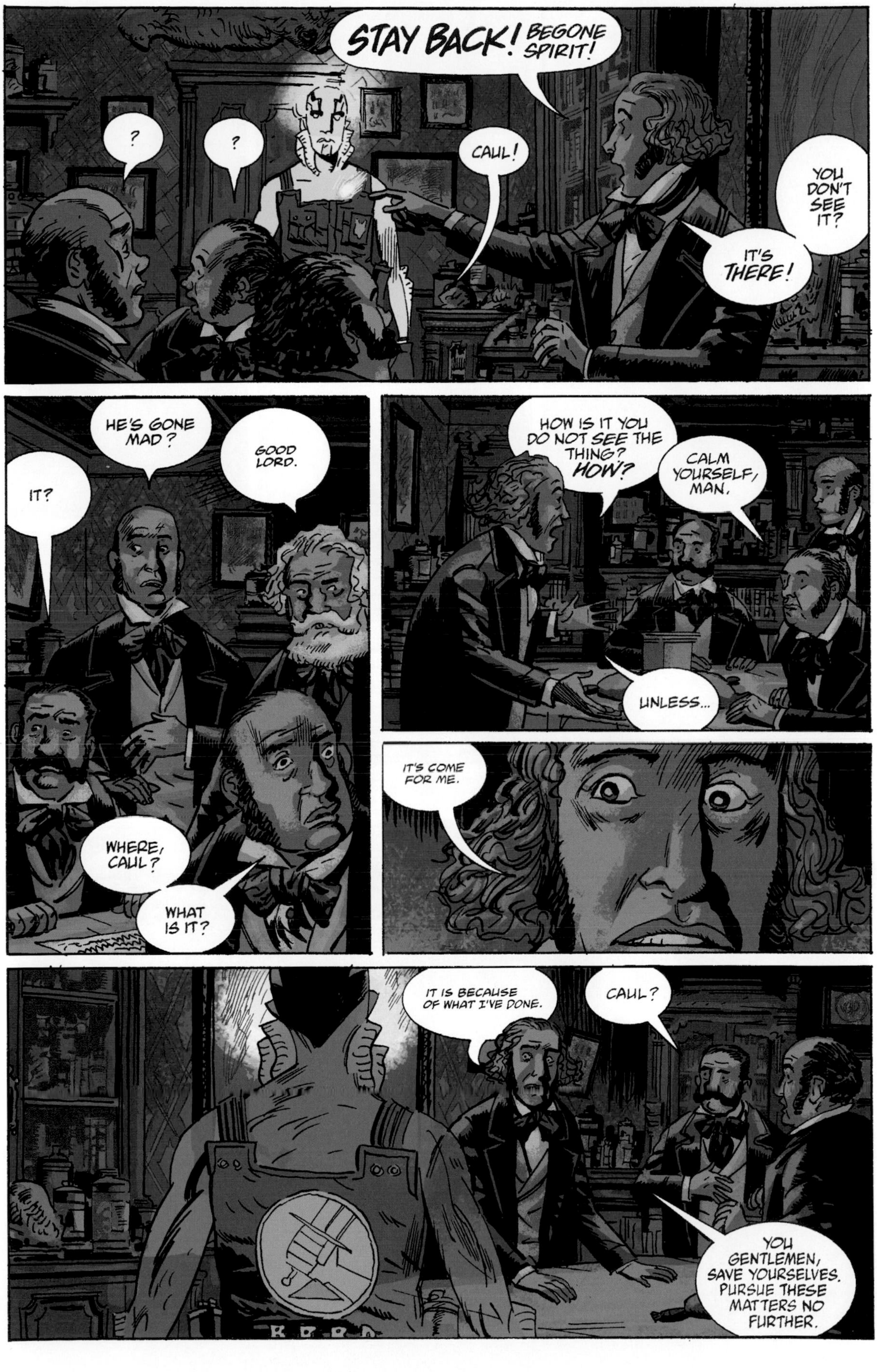
STAY BACK! BEGONE SPIRIT!
?
?
CAUL!
YOU DON'T SEE IT?
IT'S THERE!
HE'S GONE MAD?
GOOD LORD.
IT?
WHERE, CAUL?
WHAT IS IT?
HOW IS IT YOU DO NOT SEE THE THING? HOW?
CALM YOURSELF, MAN.
UNLESS...
IT'S COME FOR ME.
IT IS BECAUSE OF WHAT I'VE DONE.
CAUL?
YOU GENTLEMEN, SAVE YOURSELVES. PURSUE THESE MATTERS NO FURTHER.

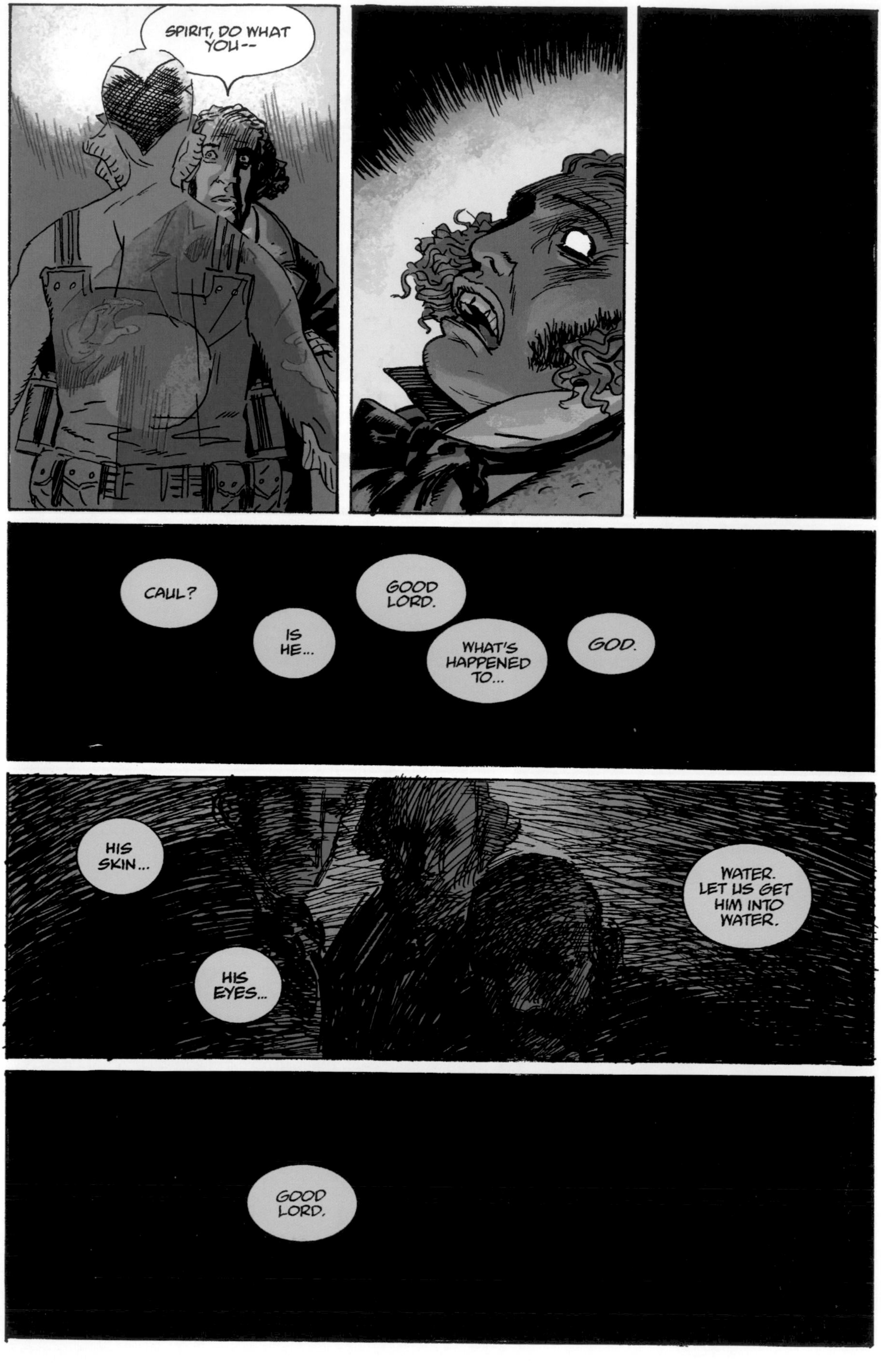
SPIRIT, DO WHAT YOU--
CAUL?
IS HE...
GOOD LORD.
WHAT'S HAPPENED TO...
GOD.
HIS SKIN...
HIS EYES...
WATER. LET US GET HIM INTO WATER.
GOOD LORD.

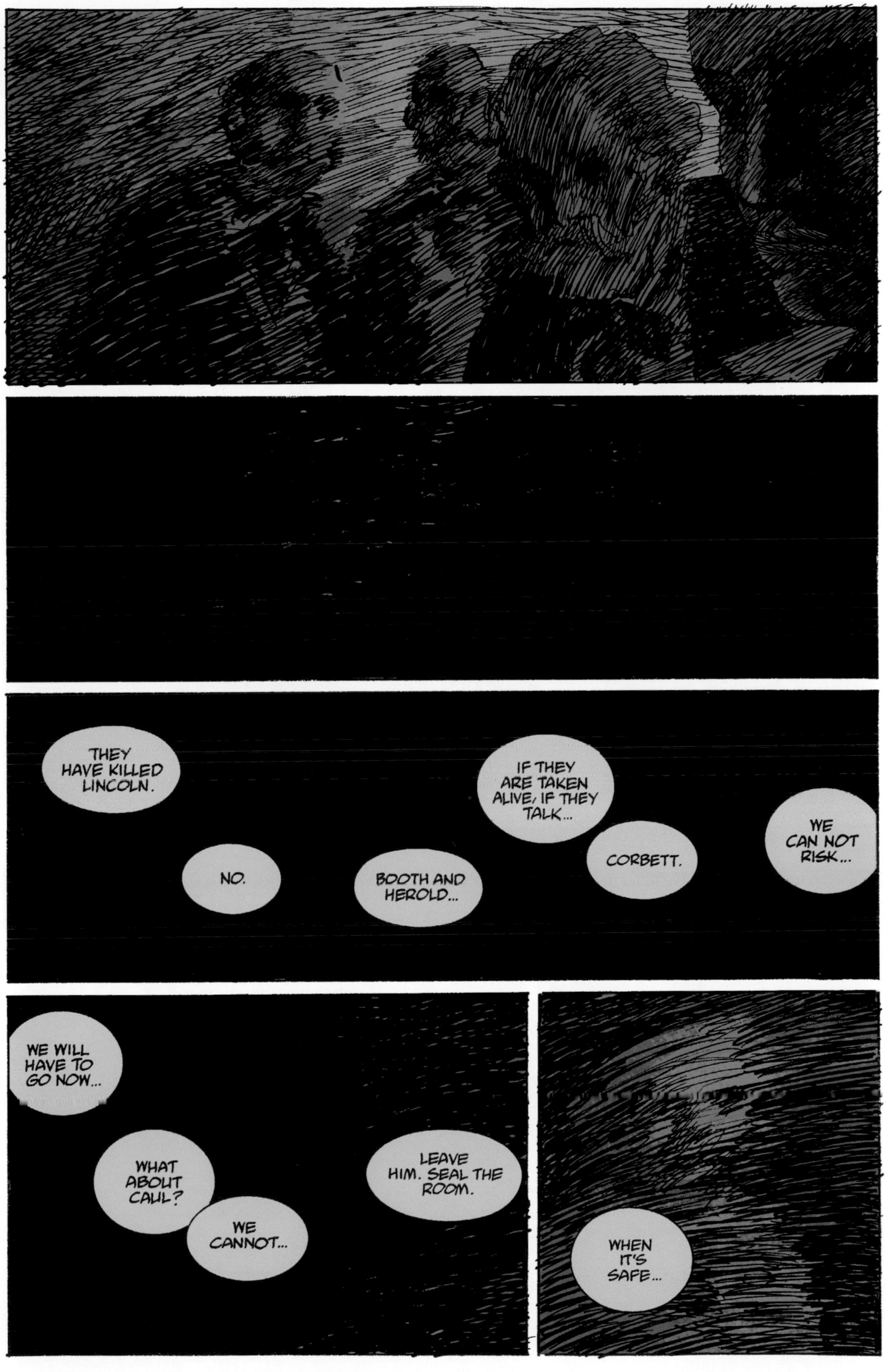
THEY HAVE KILLED LINCOLN.
NO.
BOOTH AND HEROLD...
IF THEY ARE TAKEN ALIVE, IF THEY TALK...
CORBETT.
WE CAN NOT RISK...
WE WILL HAVE TO GO NOW...
WHAT ABOUT CAUL?
WE CANNOT...
LEAVE HIM. SEAL THE ROOM.
WHEN IT'S SAFE...

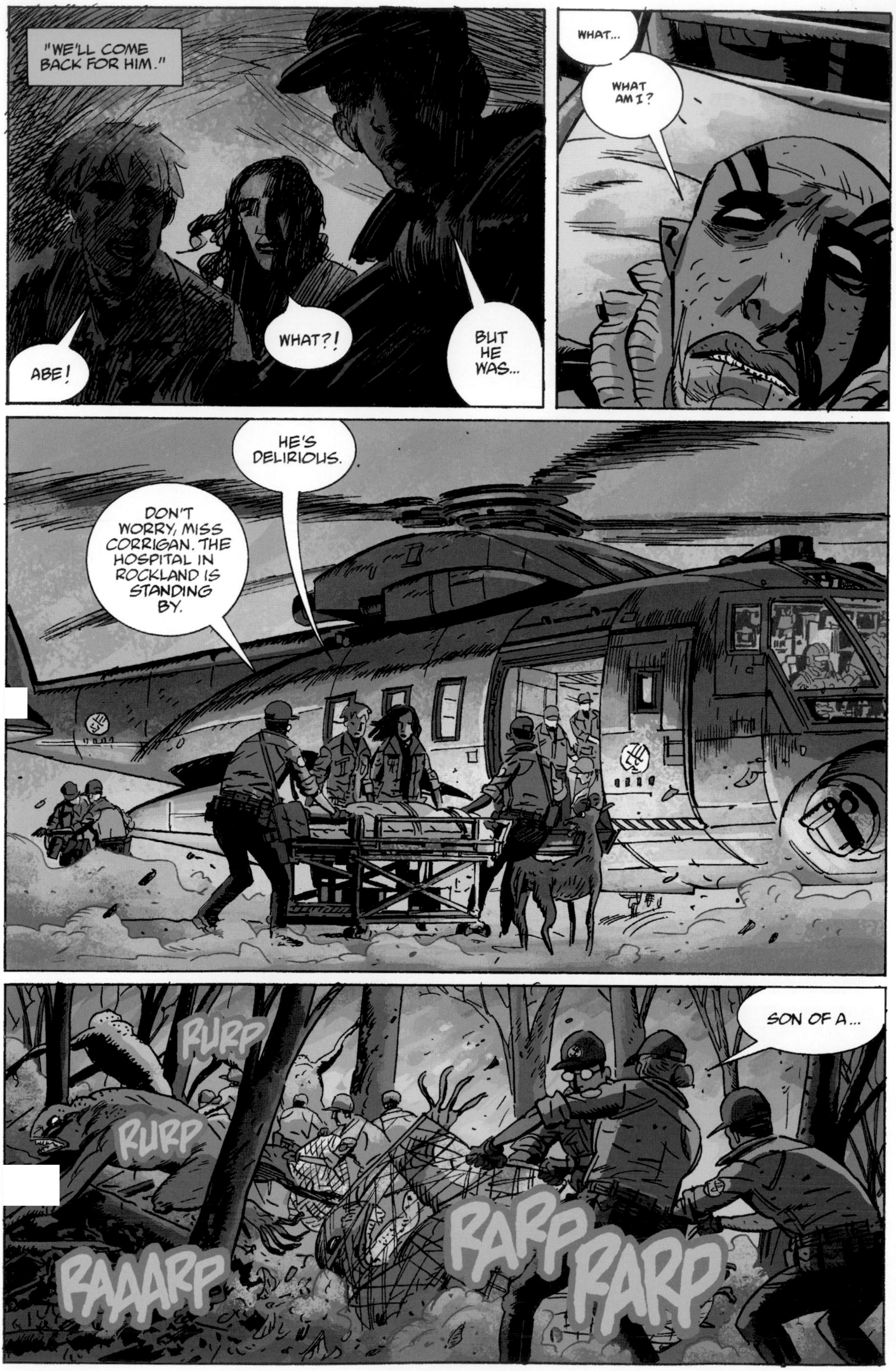
"WE'LL COME BACK FOR HIM."
ABE!
WHAT?!
BUT HE WAS...
WHAT...
WHAT AM I?
HE'S DELIRIOUS.
DON'T WORRY, MISS CORRIGAN. THE HOSPITAL IN ROCKLAND IS STANDING BY.
RURP
RURP
RAAARP
RARP
RARP
SON OF A...

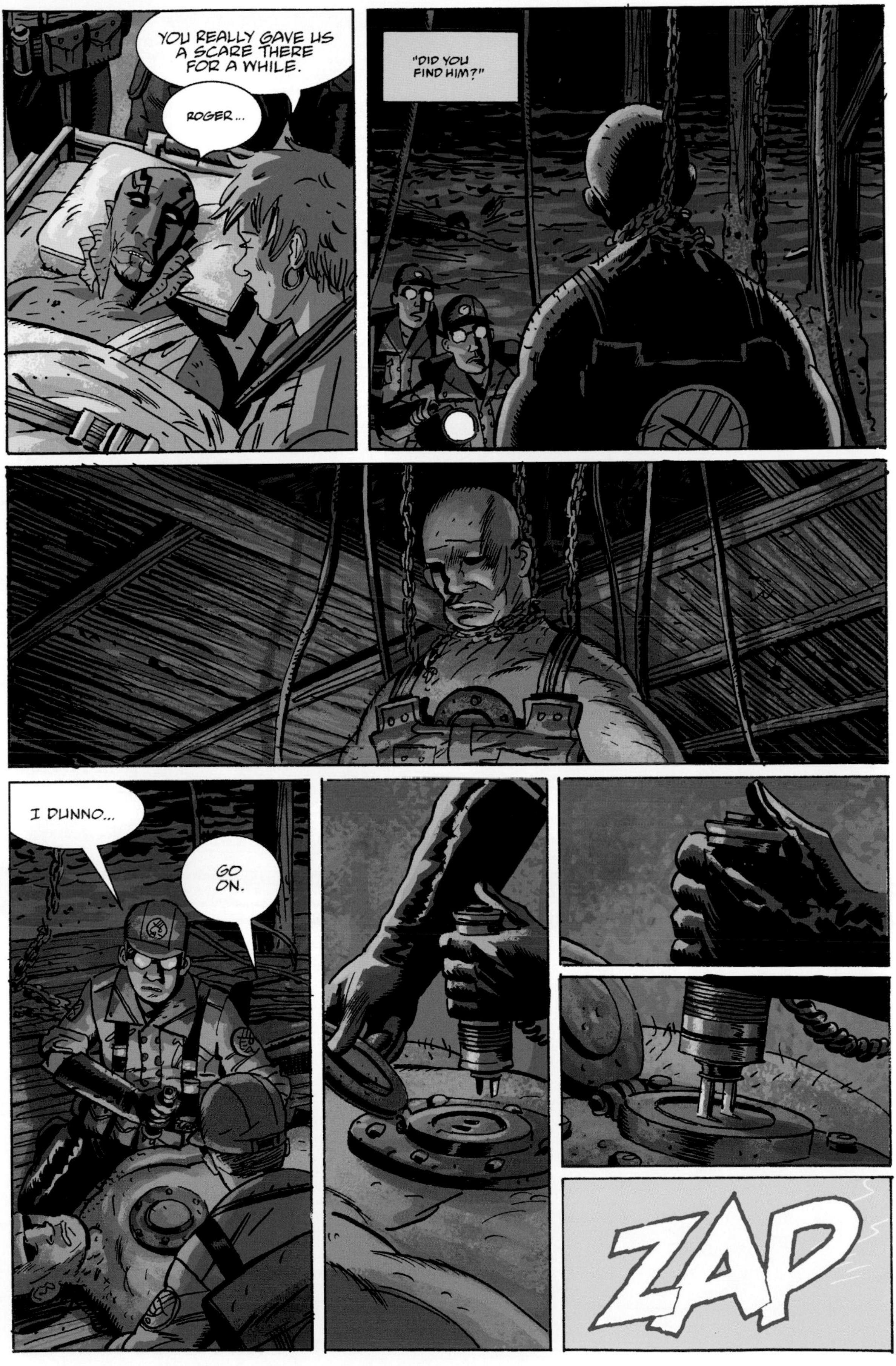
YOU REALLY GAVE US A SCARE THERE FOR A WHILE.
ROGER...
"DID YOU FIND HIM?"
I DUNNO...
GO ON.
ZAP

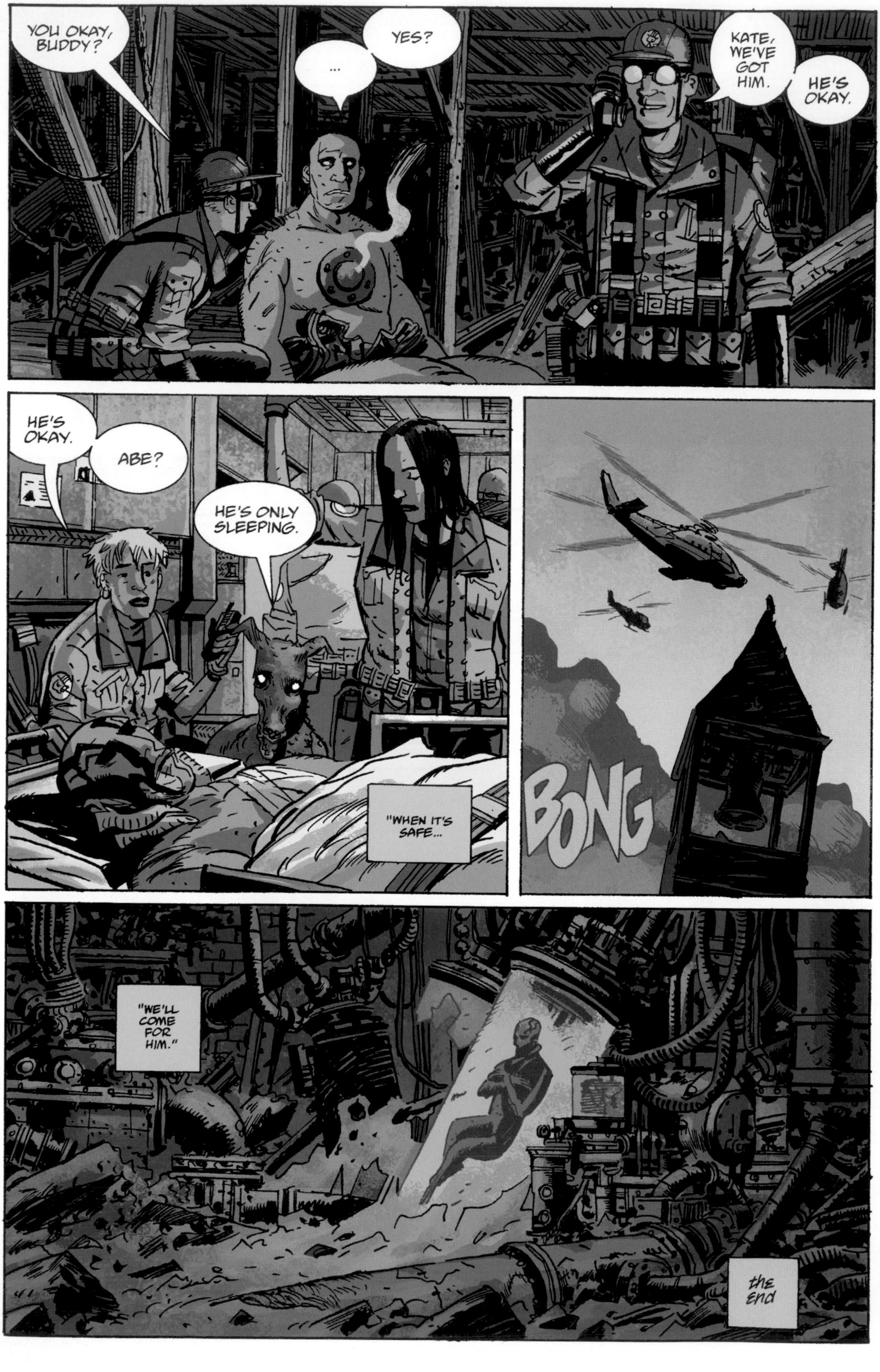
YOU OKAY, BUDDY?
...
YES?
KATE, WE'VE GOT HIM.
HE'S OKAY.
HE'S OKAY.
ABE?
HE'S ONLY SLEEPING.
"WHEN IT'S SAFE...
BONG
"WE'LL COME FOR HIM."
the end

AFTERWORD

The first B.P.R.D. book, *Hollow Earth*, was something of an experiment. We wanted to see if we could expand on the Hellboy world with a story that didn't have Hellboy in it. It worked, and we were all very happy. The next book, *The Soul of Venice & Other Stories*, was another successful experiment, allowing four different creative teams (five if you count the short story by Cameron Stewart and myself) to tell stand-alone B.P.R.D. adventures. But for this third book we—editor Scott Allie and I—wanted something different. We wanted to start a new, ongoing line of books, to treat the B.P.R.D. the same way I've been treating Hellboy all these years. So we needed something big to kick that off.

Back when I was drawing the first *Hellboy* series, even as I was destroying the pseudo-Lovecraftian god-monster Sadu-Hem, I was thinking he should come back some day—as a tiny fungus that works its way into a guy through a bullet hole causing him to swell up into something horrible that eventually escapes into a graveyard where it reanimates a bunch of rotting skeletons. Of course. Add to that the vampire-like man-frogs and Rasputin's promise that Abe Sapien would get speared to death, and this story started to take shape. But there was something missing. Fortunately, during filming of the *Hellboy* movie in Prague, I got hit with the flu (the scary-ass Eastern European kind) and was ordered to spend four days in my hotel room. Sweating and hallucinating, deprived of all human contact, I spent those ninety-six hours trying to come up with an ending for *Plague of Frogs*.

And I did.

The Secret Origin of Abe Sapien

Over the years I've toyed with the idea of working Abe's origin into a story. Trouble is, I sort of liked Abe not having an origin. I loved that he was just discovered in a jar in the basement. But I also loved the origin I'd come up with, and knew it added a new dimension to the character. And when I found a way for Abe to not only witness his origin, but actually participate in it—when I saw that by solving one mystery we were actually presenting an even bigger one—then I knew it was okay to finally tell the tale. But who do you get to draw something like that?

Guy Davis

What can I say? I've been following Guy's work for years—*Phantom Stranger*, *Sandman Mystery Theater*, *Nevermen*, and his own brilliant *Marquis* series. I am constantly amazed by his ability to draw anything and everything, apparently with little or no effort. He is a master of both clutter and understatement and is, in my humble opinion, the best "creature guy" in the business. So who better to draw the origin of Abe Sapien? Who better to kick off this whole new direction for the B.P.R.D.? I only hope that the promise of Victorian submarines and tenticular monsters will keep Guy around for a very long time.

There you go …

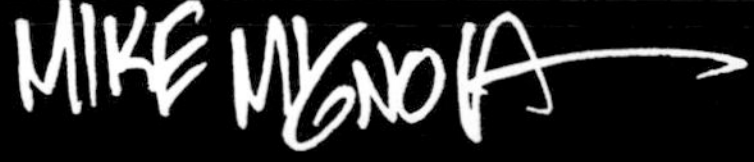

Mike Mignola
New York City

B.P.R.D.™

SKETCHBOOK

The following pages contain drawings and character designs by Guy Davis, with notes from the artist. The practice drawings on this page were done to get the feel of the characters.

Mike's description for a "fungus elephant-man" instantly put that connotation in my head and in early designs.

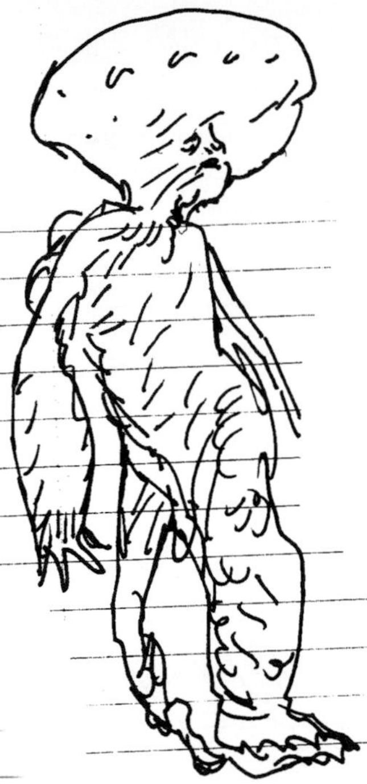

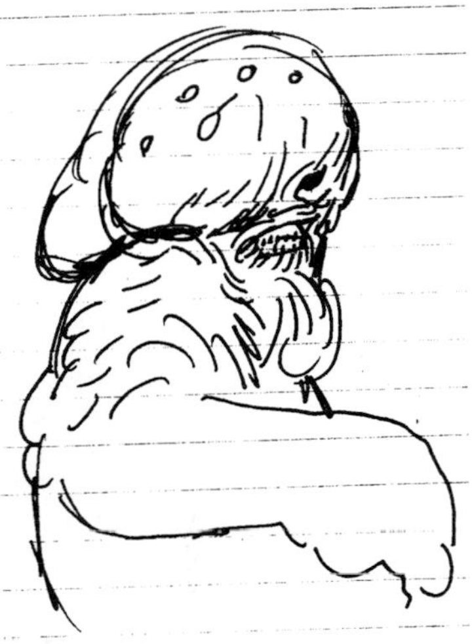

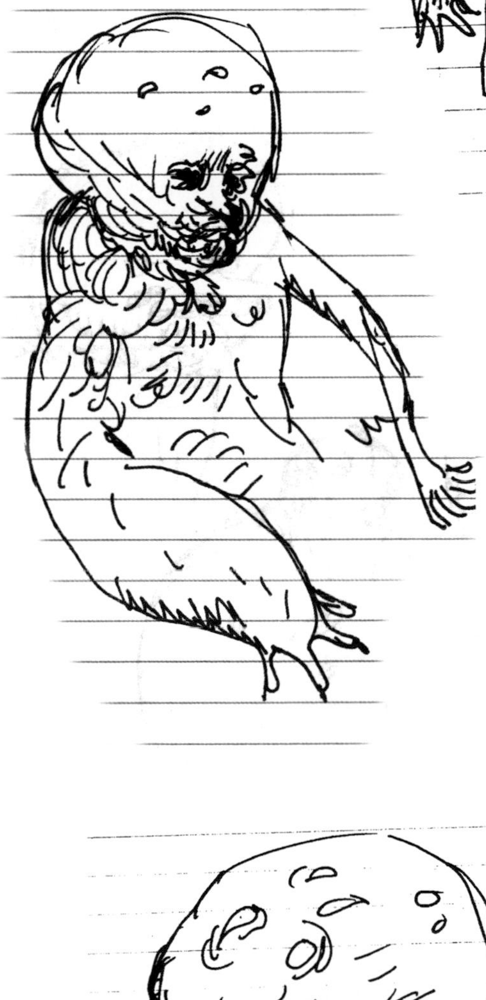

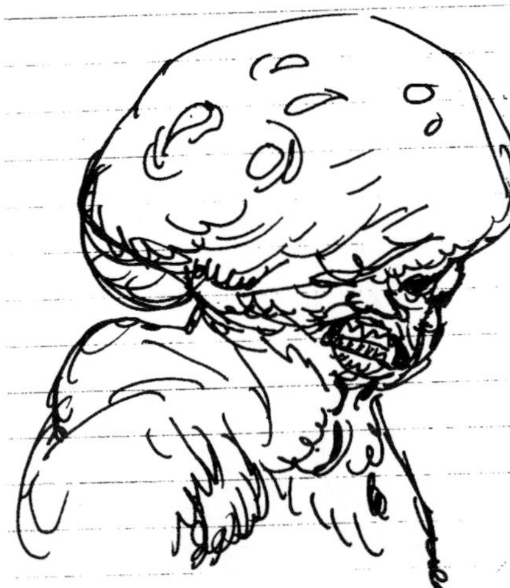

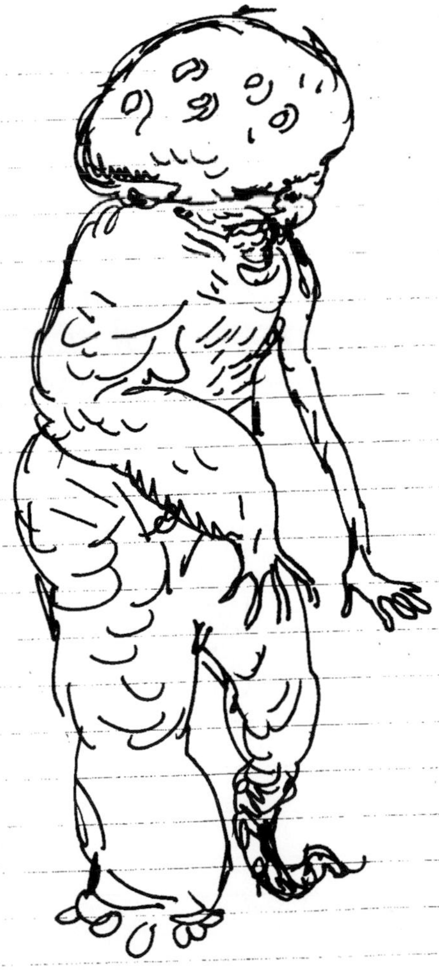

Early "jellyfish" designs for the entity from Chapter 5—the final version [opposite] incorporated some of Abe's design markings and gills.

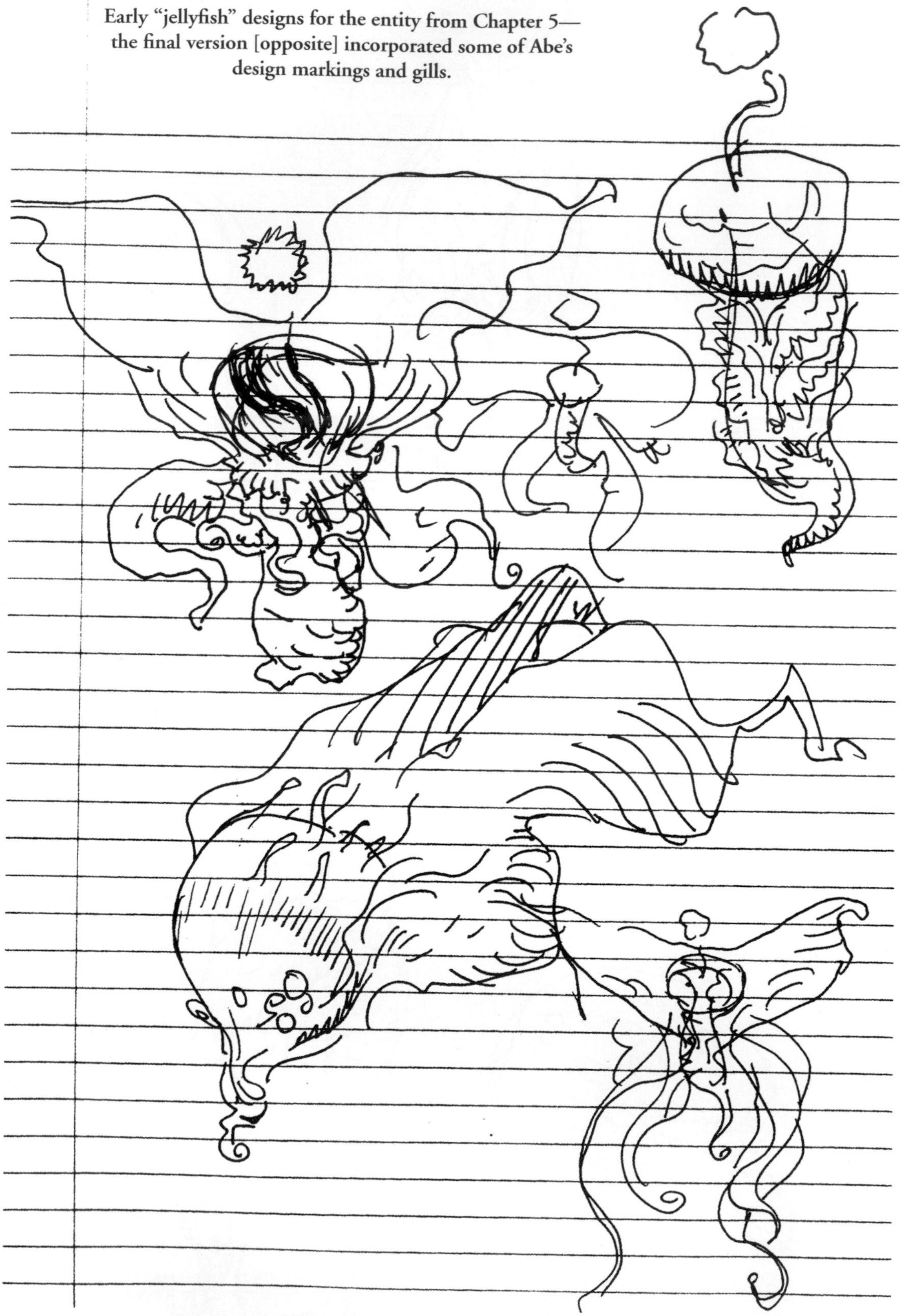

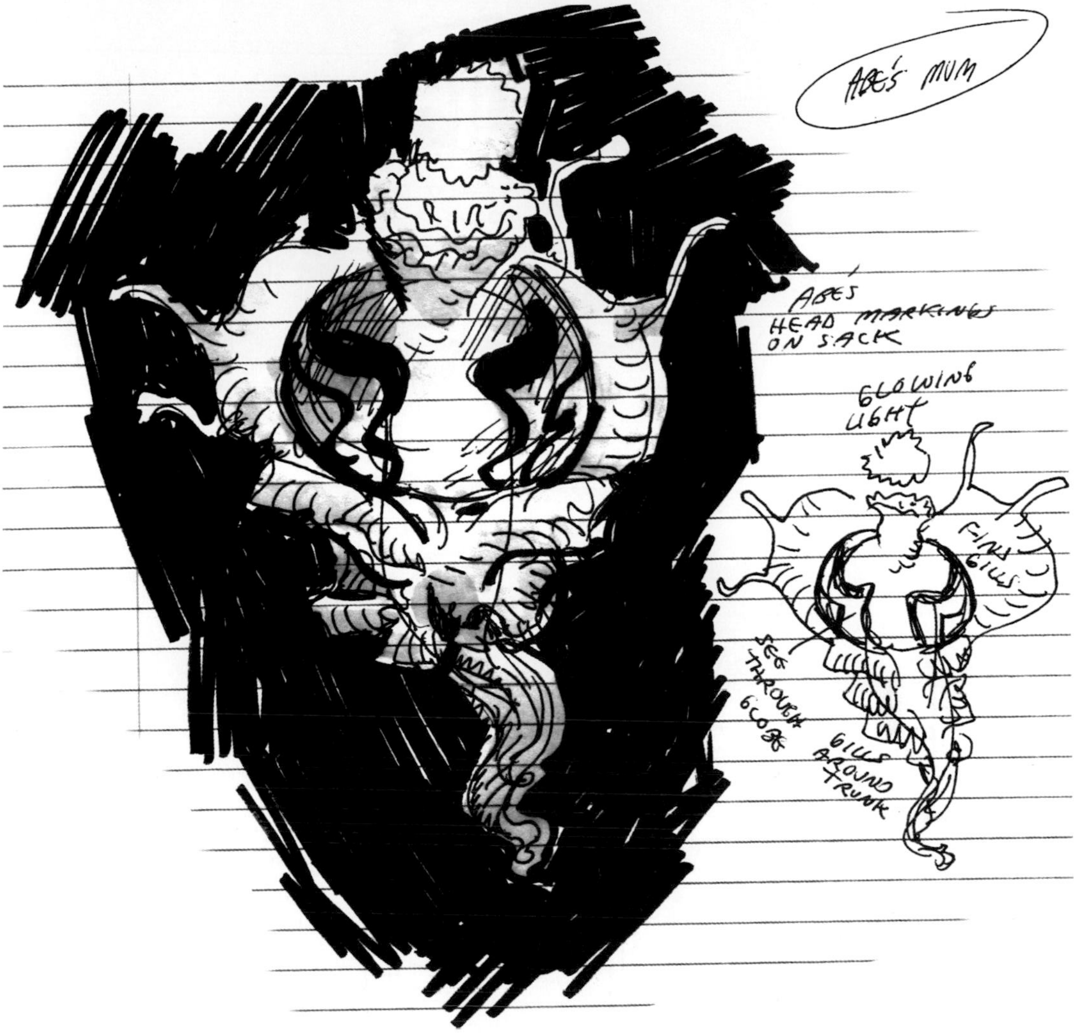
ABE'S MUM
ABE'S HEAD MARKINGS ON SACK
GLOWING LIGHT
FINS GILLS
SEE THROUGH GLOBE
GILLS AROUND TRUNK

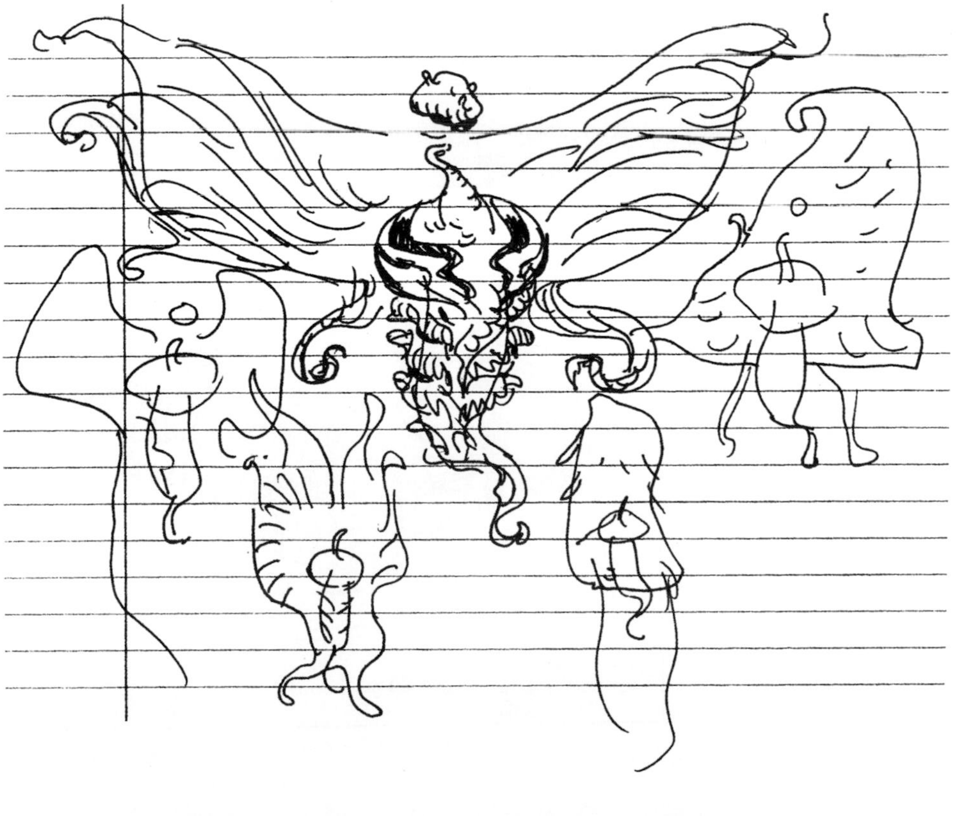

The Victorian submarine went through a number of different versions in both sketches and in the finished pencils with a lot of brilliant ideas from Mike [opposite] finally bringing it all together.

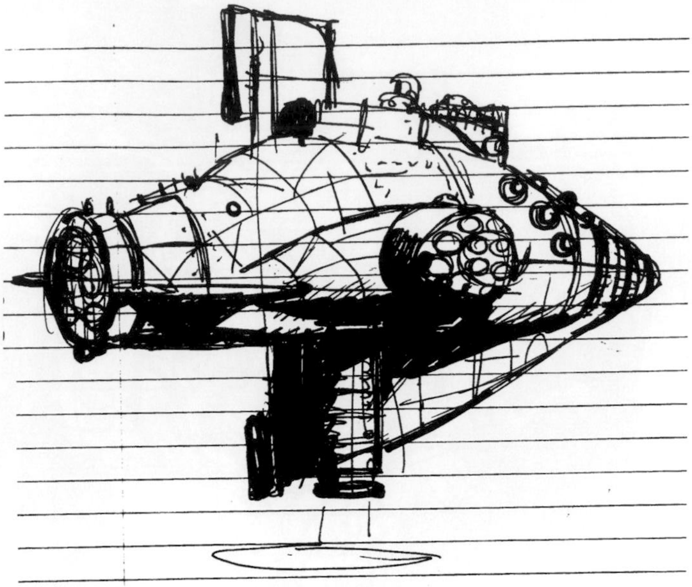

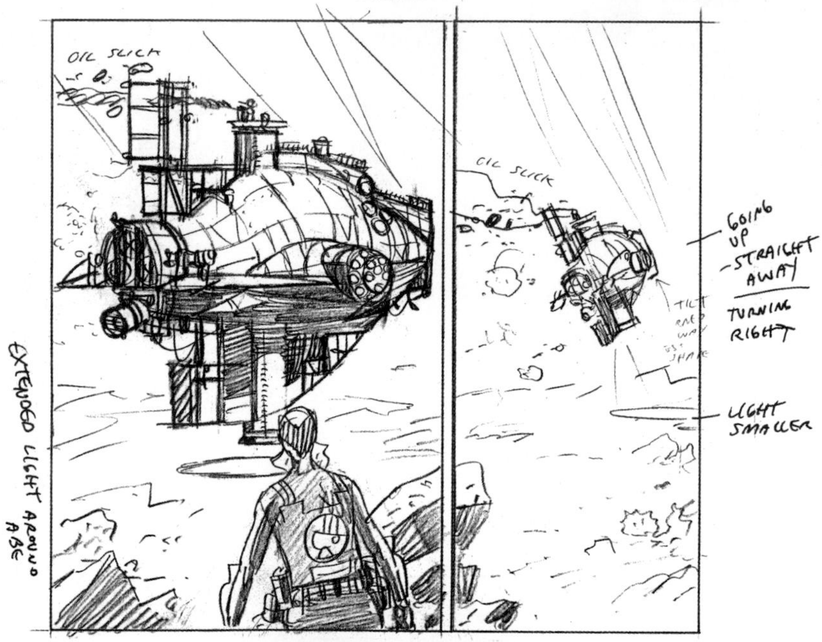
OIL SLICK
OIL SLICK
GOING UP
STRAIGHT AWAY
TURNING RIGHT
LIGHT SMALLER
EXTENDED LIGHT AROUND

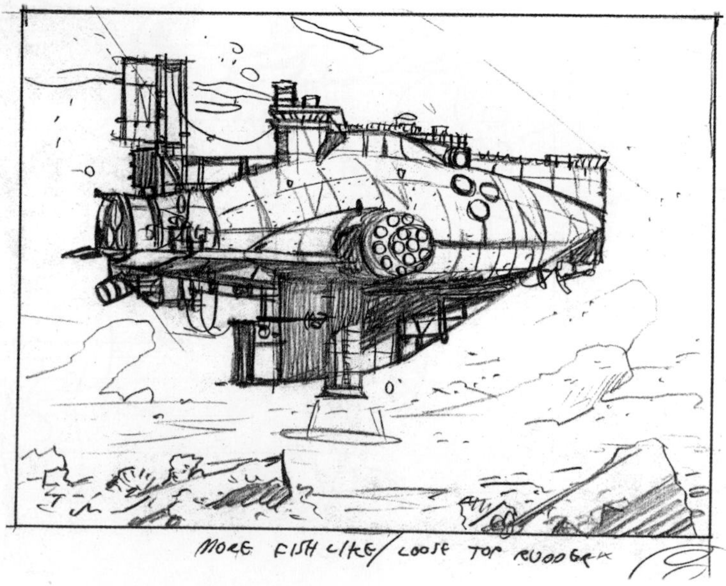
MORE FISH LIKE/ LOOSE TOP RUDDER

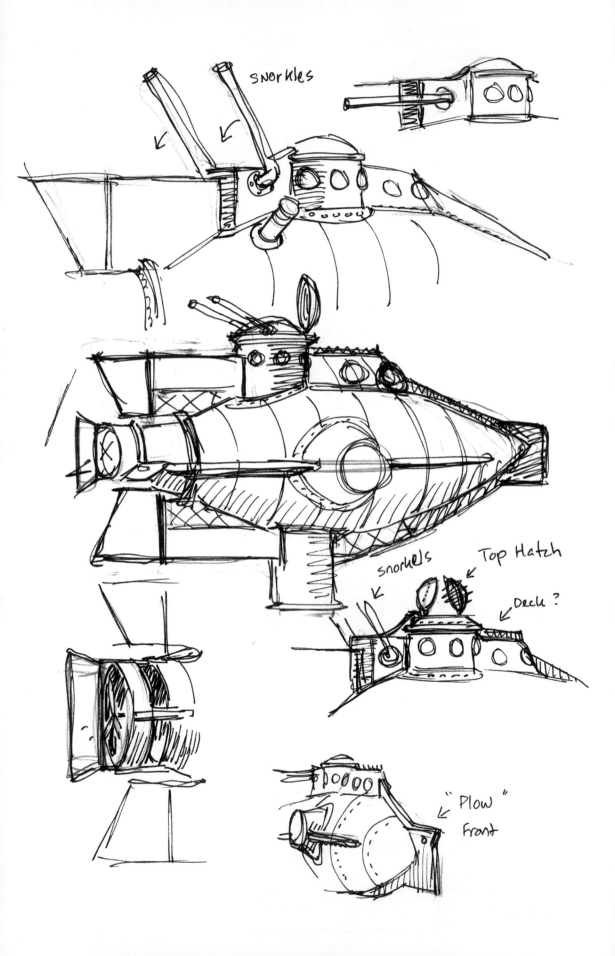

snorkles

snorkels

Top Hatch

Deck ?

"Plow" Front

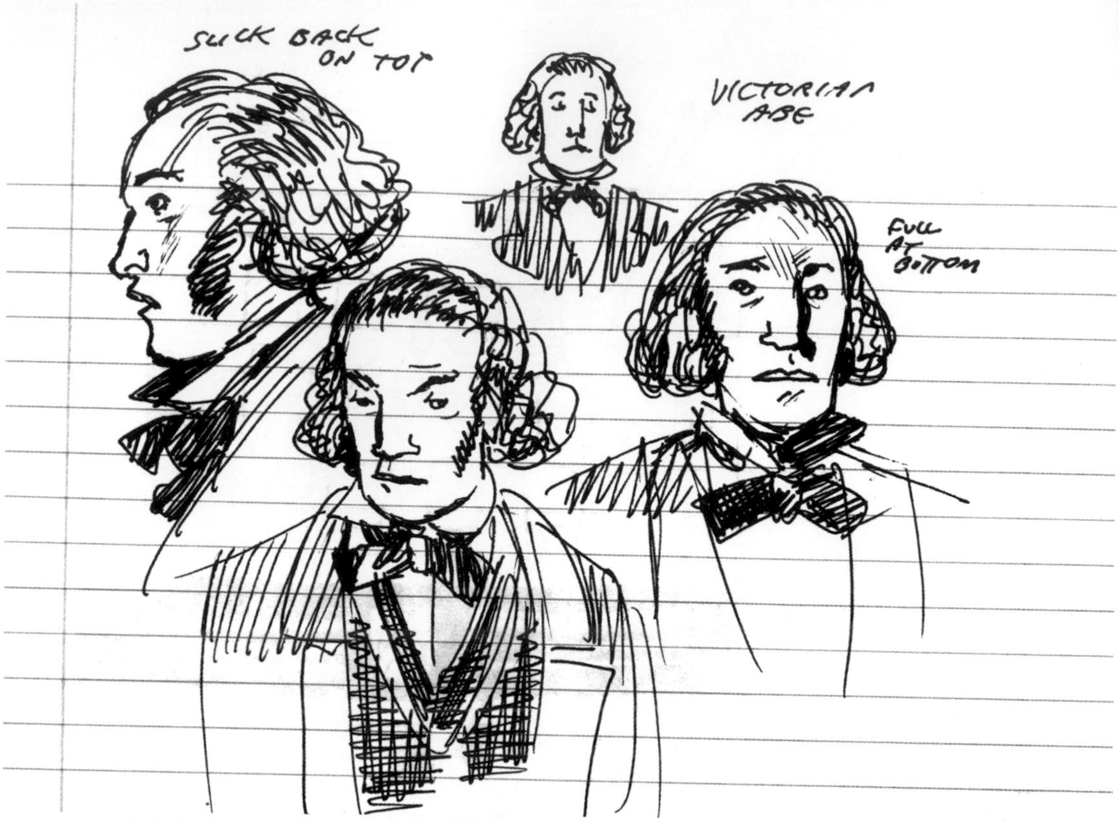
SLICK BACK ON TOP
VICTORIAN ABE
FULL AT BOTTOM

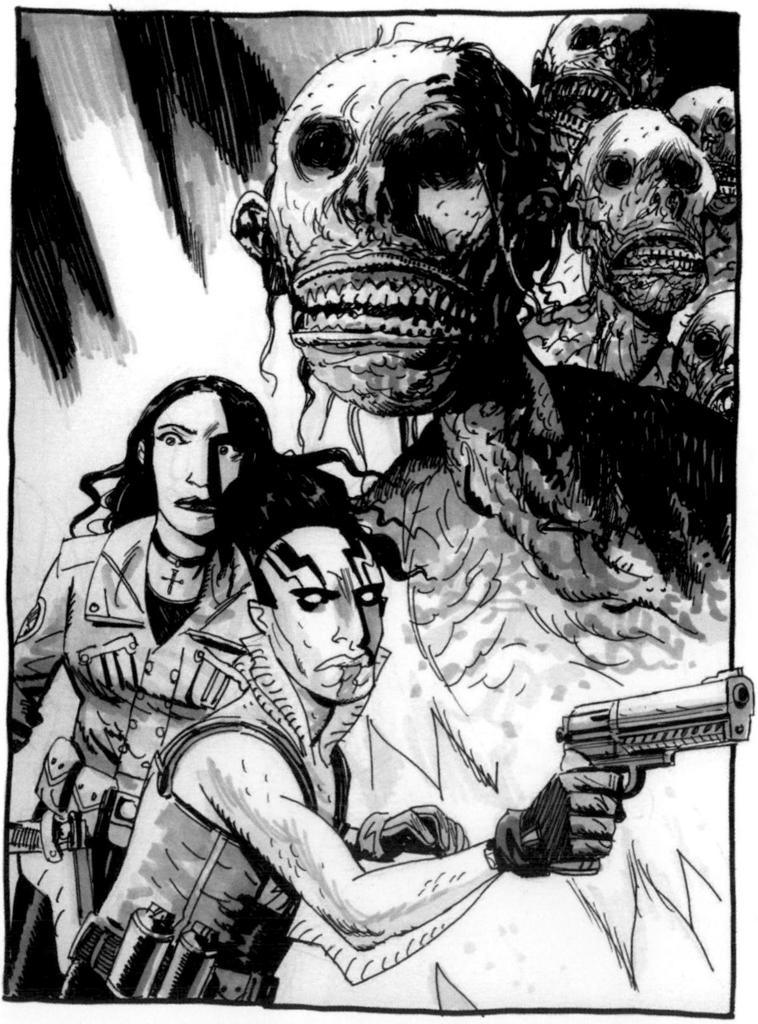

For "Victorian Abe," or Caul, I tried to keep the basic shape and facial features of Abe Sapien recognizable for his past human form. On the left, another commissioned drawing of Abe and Liz, pursued by zombies.

BPRD #5

Page 23

- Panel 1 - Abe on gurney looks up at Kate and asks about Roger. Kate Looks grim.
- Panel 2 - Cut to a couple agents entering the boat house where we last saw Roger.
- Panel 3 - Agents find Roger hanging. Looks dead.
- Panel 4 - They lower Dead Roger onto the floor.
- Panel 5 - Agent opens Roger's chest plate with one hand. It isn't a black hole but there's ~~sort of~~ an outlet in there. In ~~his~~ Agent's other hand he has some device with prongs.
- Panel 6 - Either close up of Prongs going into outlet or thumb pressing button on device (or both) -
- Final Panel is just sound effect "ZAP"

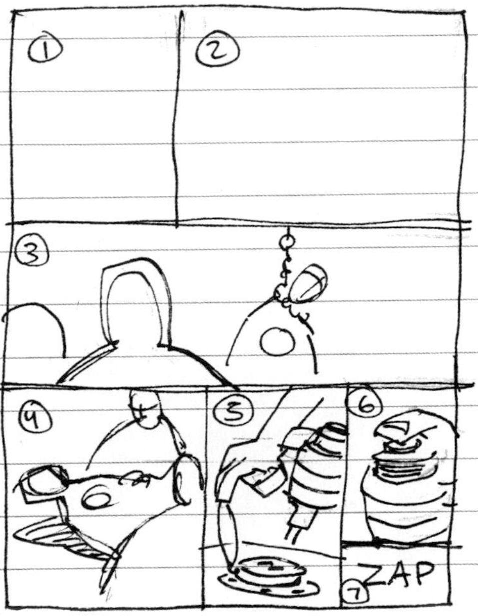

ZAP

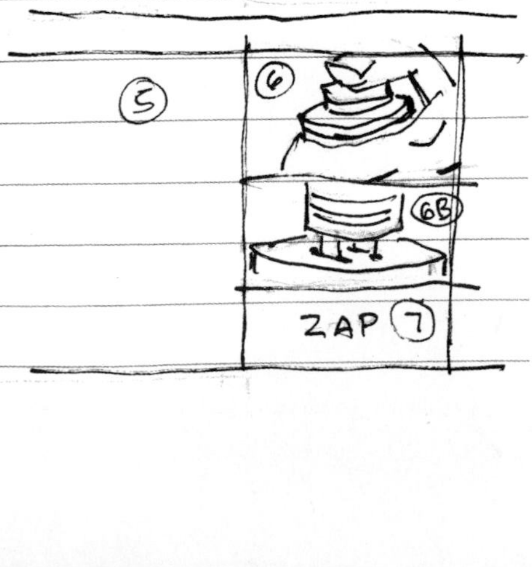

6B
ZAP

A sample of Mike's script and thumbnails, from the second-to-last page of the story. Often Mike would breakdown certain scenes that he had a specific pacing in mind for—to give it that Mignola flow—and then add the final dialogue after seeing the finished art.
—Guy Davis
Crab Point, Michigan

HELLBOY

by MIKE MIGNOLA

SEED OF DESTRUCTION
with John Byrne
ISBN: 1-59307-094-2 $17.95

WAKE THE DEVIL
ISBN: 1-59307-095-0 $17.95

**THE CHAINED COFFIN
AND OTHERS**
ISBN: 1-59307-091-8 $17.95

THE RIGHT HAND OF DOOM
ISBN: 1-59307-093-4 $17.95

CONQUEROR WORM
ISBN: 1-59307-092-6 $17.95

THE ART OF HELLBOY
ISBN: 1-59307-089-6 $29.95

HELLBOY WEIRD TALES
Volume 1
By John Cassaday, Jason Pearson,
Eric Powell, Alex Maleev,
Bob Fingerman and others
ISBN: 1-56971-622-6 $17.95

HELLBOY WEIRD TALES
Volume 2
By John Cassaday, JH Williams III,
P. Craig Russell, Jim Starlin,
Frank Cho, Evan Dorkin and others
ISBN: 1-56971-953-5 $17.95

**B.P.R.D. HOLLOW EARTH
AND OTHERS**
By Mike Mignola, Chris Golden,
Ryan Sook and others
ISBN: 1-56971-862-8 $17.95

**B.P.R.D. THE SOUL OF VENICE
AND OTHERS**
By Mike Oeming, Guy Davis,
Scott Kolins, Geoff Johns and others
ISBN: 1-59307-132-9 $17.95

ODD JOBS
Short stories by Mike Mignola,
Poppy Z. Brite, Chris Golden and others
Illustrations by Mike Mignola
ISBN: 1-56971-440-1 $14.95

ODDER JOBS
Short stories by Frank Darabont,
Guillermo del Toro and others
Illustrations by Mike Mignola
ISBN: 1-59307-226-0 $14.95

HELLBOY BASEBALL CAP
#17-106 $14.95

**HELLBOY LUNCHBOX
(& POSTCARD) 2**
Tin de-bossed full color
#11-836 $19.99

HELLBOY PVC SET
#10-666 $39.99

HELLBOY JOURNAL
#12-309 $9.99

HELLBOY TALKING BOARD
Pressed paper playing board with
wooden planchette
#10-248 $24.99

HELLBOY ZIPPO LIGHTER
#17-101 $29.95

To find a comics shop in your area, call 1-888-266-4226
For more information or to order direct:
•On the web: www.darkhorse.com
•E-mail: mailorder@darkhorse.com
•Phone: 1-800-862-0052 or (503) 652-9701
Mon.-Sat. 9 A.M. to 5 P.M. Pacific Time

Hellboy™ and © 2003 Mike Mignola. All rights reserved. Dark Horse
Comics® is a trademark of Dark Horse Comics, Inc., registered in various
categories and countries. All rights reserved.

 DARK HORSE COMICS™ *drawing on your nightmares*
darkhorse.com